ORGANIZATIONAL COMMUNICATION STRUCTURE

ORGANIZATIONAL
COMMUNICATION STRUCTURE

J. DAVID JOHNSON

Department of Communication
Michigan State University

Rn

ABLEX PUBLISHING CORPORATION
NORWOOD, NEW JERSEY

Printed in the United States of America

Library of Congress Cataloging-in-Publication Data

Johnson, J. David.
   Organizational communication structure / J. David Johnson.
      p.   cm. — (Communication and information science)
   Includes bibliographical references and index.
   ISBN 0-89391-721-4 (cl); 1-56750-069-2 (ppb)
   1. Communication in organizations.   2. Communication—Network analysis.   I. Title.   II. Series.
   HD30.3.J65   1992
   302.3'5—dc20   91-43116
                                    FTW   CIP
                             AFD 6690

Ablex Publishing Corporation
355 Chestnut Street
Norwood, New Jersey 07648

Contents

Preface

As I write this preface I am struck by Weick's maxim of rationality after the fact. I wrote this book initially for many reasons, but in the writing they crystallized, and, at times, they changed. Writing a book is a personally broadening experience, but the essential reason I wrote this book is to broaden the perspective of others concerning organizational communication structure. Structural research in many ways is the most narrowly based of all of the approaches to organizational communication. If it is to broaden its appeal, it needs to accomplish several things.

First, other people need to be let into the priesthood. Typically fundamental (and often elementary) ideas related to structural research are masked with jargon and mathematics that make them inaccessible to all but those few individuals who have a mathematical/statistical background and/or who were trained in a limited number of graduate programs which focus on network analysis. While much of what is said in this book could be (and has been) expressed in mathematical terms (often in my own writings), I purposively have avoided them in this book. My desire is to acquaint readers with the underlying substantive issues of structural research, not technical nor methodological ones.

Second, the number of approaches used in structural research needs to be expanded. While my first love is network analysis, network analysis is only one possible approach to organizational communication structure. In recent years network analysis has become overburdened. It has been used to pursue research questions that are more legitimately the domain of other approaches to organizational communication structure. This book is specifically designed to compare alternative approaches to structural research and to relate them to substantive problems.

Third, structural research needs to be used to address a range of substantive areas. This book is designed specifically to address issues related to what classes of variables determine structure and are the outcomes of it. It does this to demonstrate that structural research is applicable to a broad range of issues and problems, not just to self-reflexive inquiry, which essentially details how one aspect of structure relates to another aspect of structure. We learn more from relating structure to bodies of knowledge to which it is more weakly than strongly tied.

Fourth, structural research has suffered from a curious theoretical myopia in the last two decades within communication research. Most of its proponents have been more concerned with examining systems theory assumptions than they were necessarily with examining organizational communication structure. Structural research in the social sciences predates systems theory, and it addresses a set of issues fundamental to human social organization. It is, and it was, a mistake to consider structural research the servant of one theoretical perspective; rather, it is the domain in which a number of theoretical perspectives contend.

These then are the "hidden" agendas of this book. I sought to broaden the appeal of structural research along a number of dimensions, and, as such, the book is intended to reach an audience beyond the true believers. In doing this, it runs the risk of pleasing no one, since it is not a ritualized recitation of comfortable assumptions and stereotypes.

Regrettably, in broadening this book I also had to narrow it. It was beyond its scope to pursue specific 'how to do it' issues related to methodologies, to provide elementary introductions into specific approaches to structural research, to examine structure's role in various processes (e.g., decision making), or to examine interorganizational communication structure. The interested reader can consult the reference list for many excellent introductions into these topics.

Several people have helped me in the writing of this book. I would like to explicitly thank Dr. Sally Hartman Johnson and Dr. Rosanne L. Hartman for reviewing an earlier draft of the entire book. I would also like to thank Matthew Friedland for reviewing parts of an earlier draft. I would also like to thank my undergraduate organizational communication structure classes, and my graduate organizational communication structure seminars, for serving as the guinea pigs for a previous version of the first five chapters. I would also like to thank Karen Sager for her assistance in preparing the book. In advance, I would also like to thank my critics for what they will teach me when they react to this book

chapter 1

Introduction

It is well recognized that structures affect and constrain behavior and affect performance, coordination, and activities that go on in organizations. (Pfeffer, 1978, p. xiii)

Acts of communication can be described as the thread that holds any social organization together, if not the skeleton that determines its structure. (Pool, 1973, p. 3)

Nevertheless, I would say that Structure is a defining characteristic of an organization-*it* is what brings about or makes possible that quality of atmosphere, that sustained, routine purposiveness that distinguishes work in an organization from activities in a group, mob, a society, and so forth. (McPhee, 1985, p. 150)

Communication structure has traditionally been viewed as one of the central areas of organizational communication inquiry (e.g., Jablin, Putnam, Roberts, & Porter, 1987; Redding, 1979), and it has always been a traditional focus of communication courses and curricula (Downs & Larimer, 1974; Lewis, 1975; Pace & Ross, 1983; Rogers, 1979), yet few encompassing treatments of organizational communication structure have appeared in the literature. One of the reasons for this state of affairs is a misunderstanding of the breadth and depth of inquiry possible within the area of communication structure. Too often communication structure has become confused with one of the major approaches to examining it, network analysis (Monge, Edwards, & Kirste, 1978). As a result, the rich interplay of approaches, and the extent to which communication structure permeates the life of an organization, have been inadequately examined in the literature.

Of course, structural inquiry has always been fundamental to our thinking about human behavior in collectivities generally. Some of the most prominent thinkers in the social sciences, including Durkhiem, Parsons, and Levi-Strauss, have focused on structural research, and this line of research has constituted important schools of thought in anthropology, linguistics, social psychology, sociology, and general systems theory. In general, the focus of this work has been on systems and the enduring relationships between key elements that constitute a system. In particular this line of research has been concerned with the normative controls necessary for cooperative human relationships associated with the integration of members into collectivities (Parsons, 1969) and with the transformations by which deeper latent functions become transformed into particular manifest behaviors (Levi-Strauss, 1963). The themes established by these theorists will be elaborated on, with a focus on how they are played out in organizations, throughout the rest of this work.

Why is Structure Important?

The initial myriad of possible communication relationships presented to an individual by an organization becomes quickly constrained to a much more limited array of recurring communication relationships. This communication structure embeds the individual in a social system. It also has substantial consequences for him or her, and for the entire organization. Traditionally, the literature has focused on the following reasons why communication structure is important for organizations and for individuals within them.

Normative Behavior. On a more academic, intellectual level, the study of communication structure provides the researcher with a tapestry of such myriad texture, color, and form that it creates a delightful intellectual exercise—one which, not so coincidentally, is central to the life of any organization. Communication structure reveals what typically happens in an organization. Thus in a very real way it reveals the "world" of the organization and what is possible within it. If a formal linkage, such as that between a supervisor and subordinate, is not used, then, inevitably, communication breakdowns are going to occur. Thus, examining the communication structure may be the first step in diagnosing the communication problems of an organization.

Communication structure also reveals much of the unofficial world of the organization. If three of the seven top officers in an organization have a regular golf match, this may result in a natural coalition that binds them together in ways that go far beyond their formal organizational relationships. Informal relationships such as these reveal the needs of individuals, since these needs can be indirectly inferred from their communication patterns (Reynolds & Johnson, 1982). In short, structure an describe how things typically occur in an organization, the normative behavior of organizational members.

Enables Action. Communication structure determines what is possible in large organizations, since it enables action. "Networks make the achievement of output goals (such as production) possible" (Farace, Monge, & Russell, 1977, p. 179). The existing communication structure of an organization limits what is possible, if only by inertia, and at times quite formally. Geertz's spiderweb metaphor, which is often drawn in studies of organizational culture (e.g., Pacanowsky & O'Donnell-Trujilo, 1982), may also be quite appropriate here. At one in the same time a spider web constrains and enables action. A spider can make new strands in a web to meet new needs—but until it does, there are some things it won't be able to do, since the web constitutes a real boundary to action.

Without a predictable pattern of recurring relationships, coordinated activity within the organization would be impossible. The more constraints which exist, the more things occur in known, predictable patterns, the more information people have concerning the organization. Thus, when you increase constraints, you increase what is known and knowable about organizational operations. The sum total of these constraints determines the manifest communication structure of a system.

Without structure there would be chaos. Sometimes a little chaos is useful, but nothing can be achieved without some framework, just as not very much can be done in a totally constrained system, except what it is specifically designed to accomplish. "Structure is a fundamental vehicle by which organizations achieve bounded rationality" (Thompson, 1967, p. 54); structure provides organizational members with the limits within which efficiency may be a reasonable expectation.

Information Processing. Structure is often viewed as an information-processing tool, in part because of its role in promoting coordination between organizational entities (McPhee, 1985). One of the clearest implications of the dysfunctional aspects of a lack of structure comes in information load. Structure permits an organization to process more information. Since a lot of distinct information is processed by means of specialization, this information is then filtered before it is processed by other units. Thus, more information can be processed, since some responsibility is delegated to particular units, so that everyone does not have to handle the same information. As a result structure reduces information overload in organization (Rogers & Agarwala-Rogers, 1976) and thereby increases the efficiency of their operation.

Uncertainty reduction. Structure reduces uncertainty, thus lending predictability to organizational activities (Rogers & Agarwala-Rogers, 1976; Pfeffer, 1978). For organizations, this predictability is critical to the smooth functioning of day-to-day operations. Organizational members must feel confident that certain messages will flow to certain locations at certain times. It is often noted that management in particular abhors unpredictability; as a result, it often spends considerable time in designing organizational structures (e.g., formal organizational charts) which contribute to a subjective feeling of certainty. One of the reasons that informal structures remained hidden in management thought for so long is that awareness of their existence inevitably diminishes management's feeling of control over organizational operations. Indeed, structures are often designed to minimize, or at least regulate, individual variation in organizations (Dalton, Todor, Spendolini, Fielding, & Porter, 1980).

Social support. Communication structures can provide individuals with critical assistance which enables them to stay in an organization and allows them to grow within it. Communication networks can reduce stress experienced in jobs such as nursing (Albrecht & Ropp, 1982) and turnover within an organization. In addition, an individual's personal growth and career advancement within an organization can depend on his or her positioning within a communication structure. Mentoring networks can be critical to sponsoring an individual and leading him or her through the thicket of informal norms within an organization.

Integration. Not only do organizational communication structures integrate individual members into organizations, but they also integrate diverse parts of an organization together. As early as the work of Jacobson and Seashore (1951), and then Likert (1967), the key integrating function of communication structures was recognized. At least on an anecdotal level, it would appear that those graduate programs which offer some formal integrating mechanism (e.g., ritualized brown-bag lunches) have much stronger and cohesive programs than those that do not.

Dysfunctional consequences of structure. As McPhee (1985) points out, most treatments of structure in the organizational behavior literature tend to focus on the benefits of structure for organizations. However, especially in the context of radical humanist and cultural approaches to understanding organizations, structure can be viewed as having many negative consequences, especially in relation to its impact on organizational members. Structure and power, for example, are often intermingled, especially since those in power often control the more formal elements of structures. By controlling the flow of information and who has access to it, one controls the premises of discussion and the outcomes (Pfeffer, 1978). In addition, those in power can use structure to manipulate others, often against their own self-interest, and as a result structure (e.g., bureaucracy) can become the symbolic focal point for conflict and resistance in an organization (McPhee, 1985).

Structures can also bar innovativeness within the organization if they are too rigid and confining. Thus a balance must be reached between efficiency, which results from highly constrained systems, and effectiveness. While it is important to reduce information load, for example, it is also important to allow some leakage between units, so that new ideas and perspectives can be brought to problems. Total segmentation of an organization into isolated work groups may be just as harmful as no segmentation (Kanter, 1983).

The preceding partial enumeration of the reasons why structure is important to organizations demonstrates its pervasiveness and centrality to the study of organizations. Organizational communication structure has been viewed in many ways and used to examine different aspects of these issues in the past. Therefore, a clear, precise definition of structure is needed, along with an overview of the myriad approaches which are possible for examining it.

DEFINING COMMUNICATION STRUCTURE

Definitions of organizational communication structure are typically taken for granted in the literature. However, a closer examination of the key components of a definition of structure is central to examining the importance of the concept and the heuristic value of the various approaches available for exploring it. These approaches, such as network analysis, almost inevitably focus on one or another of the key dimensions of the construct. As such they inherently provide only a limited perspective on the concept of communication structure.

Table 1-1 systematically compares dimensions of the definition of *organizational structure* and *organizational communication structure* explicitly contained in definitions used by a purposive sampling of recognized authorities in the field. A glance at the table reveals that not every dimension of structure is contained in every definition, although they can often be implied on the basis of the author's discussion of structure. In addition, definitions of structure often confuse outcomes of structure (e.g., predictability) or antecedents of it with the concept itself. Traditionally, conceptualizations of structure have focused on the following dimensions, which will be discussed in more detail in the following sections: relationships, entities, contexts, configurations, and temporal stability.

Relationships

> The aggregate is merely the sum of the elements, but the structure depends on their relationships, in the broadest sense, including under relationships relative positions and indirect influences as well as direct connections. (Blau, 1981, p. 9)

Relationships have been the primary focus of most recent empirical investigations into communication structure within the field of organizational communication, since *structure* refers fundamentally to "a definable set of relationships which hold together a number of elements or

Table 1-1.   Explicit Dimensions of Structure in Prior Definitions

Author(s)	Dimensions				
	Relationships	Entities	Context	Configuration	Temporal Stability
Clayton (1974) p. 221	'relationships'	'elements or objects'		'juxtaposition one with the other'	
Conrath (1973) p. 95	'relations'	'people'	'perform their tasks'		
Dow (1988) p. 98	'resource and information flow'	'actors or subunits'	'social system generated by the decision rules'	'patterns'	'recurrent'
Farace, Monge, & Russell (1977), p. 60	'message exchange'	'members'	'organization'	'patterns'	'repetitive, recurring'
Goldhaber, Yates, Porter, & Lesniak (1978), p. 77	'interaction'		'communication network'	'pattern or arrangement'	'regularly occurring'
James & Jones (1976) p. 76	'systematic relationships'	'units and positions'	'organization'		'enduring characteristics'
March & Simon (1958) p. 170			'organization'	'pattern of behavior'	
Monge & Eisenberg (1987) p. 305	'relationships'	'collection of elements or parts'			'relatively stable and that change only slowly'
Rogers (1983) p. 24		'units'	'in a system'	'patterned arrangements'	
Thompson (1967) p. 51	'relationships'	'internal differentiation'		'patterning'	
White, Boorman, & Breiger, (1976)	'relations'	'concrete entities'		'patterns'	'regularities'

objects in juxtaposition one with another" (Clayton, 1974, p. 221). "The relations among *people* as they perform their *tasks* comprise organizational structures" (Conrath, 1973, p. 592). Thus, many definitions and discussions give an overwhelming priority to this particular dimension of structure, treating it as the primary ingredient of structure (e.g., Moch, Feather, & Fitzgibbons, 1983). In fact, often in the network analysis approach, which has become the premier approach for investigating structure, relationships become nearly synonymous with structure, slighting other dimensions of structure.

Perhaps even more troubling, traditionally, the approaches have tended to focus mostly on descriptive elements of relationships, such as task-related content. These surface communication relationships, however, are often manifestations of other more fundamental ways in which individuals relate (e.g., status, work dependencies, roles, power, authority, influence, norms, commitments, sentiments, kinship). These fundamental aspects of relationships form the deep structures of interaction, with acts of communication revealing their surface manifestations (Johnson, 1982, 1984, 1985; Richards, 1985). These deeper elements of relationships also move our thinking from the level of description to the level of explanation, just as the other dimensions of structure start to link structure to more explanatory factors.[1]

Entities

Organizations, in order to meet demands from their environment and in order to become more skilled, specialize their labor (Katz & Kahn, 1978). Thus, more and more entities (e.g., individuals and work units) emerge within the organization. In turn the increased number of units implies increasingly rich and diverse relationships among them. Following classic discussions of systems (Katz & Kahn, 1978) and contingency perspectives of differentiation and integration (Lawrence & Lorsch, 1967), entities and relationships between them have often been considered central issues in organizational theory (Blau, 1974a).

The nature of entities examined, as Table 1-1 reveals, are rather diverse in previous definitions, ranging from objects to units of a system. How entities are defined determines the level of analysis of communication structure research, an increasingly important issue in management (see

---

[1] An issue related to these deeper structures is the absence of relationships. Relationships which do not occur (e.g., no communication between two interrelated work units) may almost be as important as those that do (Knoke & Kuklinski, 1982). Especially in the context of constraints, the examination of missing relationships may lead to the identification of underlying factors which shape structures.

Dansereau & Markham, 1987, for an exhaustive discussion) and communication research (Berger & Chaffee, 1987). For example, most network analysis research is operationalized at the dyadic level, while most systems thinking seems to imply groups or units.

Context

> Context is the framework that embeds behavioral and structural aspects of organizations. (Jablin et al., 1987, p. 123)

Many of the definitions in Table 1-1 also explicitly state a context and/ or function, ranging from the relatively abstract social system (Dow, 1988) to the specific functions which structures enable, for example, "perform their tasks" (Conrath, 1973). Context provides meaning and direction to the activities embodied in a particular structure. Indeed, context is central to all explanations of communication (Hewes & Planalp, 1987). In this work the focus will be on the intraorganizational context. This does create problems with boundaries and the often difficult job of drawing lines around social systems.

Boundaries are notoriously permeable, especially at the edges of an organization, and it is often difficult to say where one system begins and another ends. It is also difficult to determine if relationships internal to the system are qualitatively different from relationships to similar entities outside of an organization's boundaries (Lincoln, 1982; Monge, 1987).

The relationship between context and structure is still one of the great unresolved, and often overlooked, areas of structure research. This issue is especially important, since contexts are often the determinants of the development of particular communication structures, and in this sense specifying antecedents to structure also implies a more complete definition of context.

Configuration

The preceding three dimensions, relationships, entities, and context, result in an overall configuration of the communication structure of an organization. The sum total of the relationships between entities in a given context results in an overall pattern which could be said to form a gestalt of the total structure of the organization. Thus structure moves beyond the inherent reductionism of individual relationships to the holistic patterning of an entire system (Blair, Roberts, & McKechnie, 1985):

> emergent properties are characteristics of social structure over which individuals have no control, even when these characteristics are the

aggregate results of their own actions, and these conditions of the social environment necessarily restrict what people's free will can realize. (Blau, 1981, p. 16)

The recognizable patterns formed by this gestalt can provide useful information about an organization, especially in the sense that recognizable patterns become one of the key ingredients necessary for information in general (Farace et al., 1977): "Structure communicates about the constraints organizational members face in the communication process" (Jablin, 1987, p. 390).

This notion of configuration, especially as it relates to patterning, is often contained in conventional definitions of structure: "We define *structure* as the patterned arrangements of the units in a system" (Rogers, 1983, p. 24). This focus on patterning has heavily influenced many of the modern analytic techniques focusing on communication structure, particularly the graphics components behind network analysis and communication gradients. These graphic pictures can provide powerful descriptive tools for people interested in determining what is happening in an organization. However, the patterns can only be suggestive of the forces that cause communication structure, which inherently seem to be represented in the other dimensions.

Preceding theorists have differed regarding the extent to which this overall configuration is planned or emerges from deeper forces operating within the organization (Dow, 1988). In general, this book will adopt the perspective that this overall pattern is the surface manifestation of the more determinative forces underlying these dimensions, which serve to constrain the activities of organizational members. *Constraint*, "the state, quality, or sense of being constricted to a given course of action or inaction" (*American Heritage Dictionary*, 2nd College ed., p. 314), refers fundamentally to the limits placed on human interaction. These limits determine the ultimate form that the interaction can take and regulate its course. But they should not be considered limitations; rather, constraints are also opportunities, since they provide the media for the enablement of action (Giddens, 1985, p. 270).

Temporal Stability

Structure also implies some degree of temporal stability or permanence, a relatively enduring set of linkages: "This structure gives regularity and stability to human behavior in a social system; it allows us to predict behavior with some degree of accuracy" (Rogers, 1983, p. 24). Indeed, "The dominant feature of organizational structure is its patterned regularity" (Ranson, Hinings, & Greenwood, 1980, p. 1). While this dimension of structure is often asserted definitionally, it is seldom examined empirically. For example, it is often assumed that networks generated from organizations reveal a stable pattern rather then one frame of a moving picture. However, "it is important to remember that structure is nothing more than the relationships among positions or roles in an organization, and since relationships change structures change also" (Pfeffer, 1978, p. 24).

The rate of change is especially problematic for communication networks, with Monge and Eisenberg (1987) arguing that this change is so rapid that it should be incorporated in the very definition of networks. However, this view seems to divorce structure from one of its primary conceptual roots. As March and Simon (1958, p. 170) point out in their definition, organizational structure is "relatively stable" and it "only change[s] slowly." And even though Pfeffer also views change as important, he also recognizes that change is not as frequent as one would expect (Pfeffer, 1978, p. 25), since there is also a certain inertia that is established, with direction of any gradual change heavily determined by already existing structures (March & Simon, 1958).

These views concerning temporal stability may also be contrasted in two of the metaphors cited earlier in this chapter. Most previous conceptions of structure have viewed it very much as a skeleton (Dalton et al., 1980; McPhee, 1985), a permanent embodiment of the organization, so permanent it is impossible to think of the body meaningfully without it. The Monge and Eisenberg (1987) view metaphorically places structure in the context of the spider web, which can be cast aside by the wind or other powerful environmental factors and then rebuilt. It would seem that a more appropriate view of structure may lie somewhere between these two extremes.

Structure needs to have some component at its core which is like a skeleton, which provides a framework and a psychological sense of permanence. But at the periphery it must also change to meet new circumstances. Perhaps structure can be thought of as embodying the characteristics of open office environments whose fixed features (e.g., outside walls, floors, ceiling) provide a framework with both physical and psychic boundaries. But within this relatively enduring framework, semifixed features (e.g., flexible barriers, desks, files, etc., can be moved to respond to changing organizational needs.

Definition of Organizational Communication Structure

The preceding dimensions of structure can be interwoven, then, in the following definition of *organizational communication structure,* which will be used in this book.

Organizational communication structure refers to the relatively stable configuration of communication relationships between entities within an organizational context.

PLAN OF THE BOOK

This book is divided into three major sections: approaches to, antecedents to, and outcomes of organizational communication structure. The approaches section focuses on a detailed conceptual discussion of the relationship of the four major approaches to structure to the basic conceptualization of structured outlined in this chapter. The discussion in each chapter will be organized around the five major elements of the definition of structure. Chapter 2 focuses on the most traditional approach, the formal approach, which concentrates on formal authority relationships. By and large, formal approaches view structure from the perspective of rational managerial design decisions intended to improve the efficiency and the effectiveness of the organization. This approach has real strengths in the areas of context and temporal stability, but some weaknesses in the areas of relationships, entities, and configurations. Chapter 3 focuses on network analysis, which excels in specifying configurations of relationships between entities in an organization. Networks try to capture emergent communication structure, the "actual" relationships engaged in by individuals as they go about their organizational lives. These communication relationships are not always planned, at least by the organization, and they deal with many things besides the accomplishment of formal organization goals. While network analysis has real strengths in these areas, it also has considerable weaknesses along the dimensions of context and temporal stability. Communication gradients represents a new approach to communication structure which is detailed in Chapter 4. Gradients try to capture the impacts of the physical and spatial contexts of organizations on the stable configurations of communication in an organization through the use of rich visual imagery. Gradients have substantial strengths in capturing context and temporal stability, but they also force us to think of relationships in considerably different ways than the other approaches entail. Chapter 5 examines the cultural approach to communication structure in organizations. Culture is at one in the same time constituted by structures, and the context within which structures are embedded. This chapter will focus especially on the way that culture determines the context of communicative relationships through rules and provides a major means of ensuring their temporal stability, partially through configurations at the group level. Antecedents to communication structure represent those factors which determine the ultimate shape and form of the configuration of communication relationships between entities in an organization. They represent underlying sources of constraint in the development of particular communication structures. Chapter 6 focuses on spatial factors, such as proximity, social density, access, and mobility, which determine in large part the basic preconditions for interaction in an organization. Chapter 7 focuses on the somewhat related issues of technologies. Technologies determine the imperative for the development of many relationships in organizations. In addition, technologies, especially the new electronic media, provide a means for organizational members to overcome the constraints of spatial factors. The human environment chapter, Chapter 8, focuses primarily on the impact of people on communication structures. It discusses the impacts of organizational demography and the nature of dyadic relationships on the development of particular organizational communication structures. The examination of antecedent factors in this section is not intended to be exhaustive; other factors such as stages in organizational life cycles, environments, and strategy could also be included. The intent in this section is to illustrate the impacts of antecedent factors on structure by focusing on what, arguably, have been the most important factors isolated in the literature.

The final section focuses on the outcomes, or consequences, of communication structure for organizations and for individuals within them. While structures can have many impacts on individuals, ranging from exploitation to stimulating motivation and growth, Chapter 9 focuses on the individual outcomes of support, satisfaction, and commitment. Communication structure provides individuals with both informational and emotional support which plays a crucial role in increasing the commitment of individuals to their organizations. In turn these processes affect the level of satisfaction workers have and their level of turnover. Organizational communication structure also has a number of impacts on organizational processes crucial to the effectiveness and efficiency of organizations, the focus of Chapter 10. The level of constraint revealed by structure often has paradoxical impacts, on which this chapter will focus. For example, the more segmented or differentiated an organization is, the more efficient individual units are likely to be, but the effectiveness of the overall organization can also be hampered, especially in terms of the organization's level of innovativeness.

The book concludes with a chapter which systematically brings all of these themes together. First, it discusses the heuristic value of each of the four major approaches for examining the larger concept of structure. Second, it details the relationship between the major approaches and antecedents to organizational communication structure, specifying the major benefits and shortcomings of the four approaches. Third, this chapter examines the strengths and weaknesses of each approach in specifying the outcomes of organizational communication structure.

Fourth, it identifies cognition as an area which may eventually grow into a new approach to structure. Fifth, it explores some of the metatheoretic problems which should be explored in future research on the concept of structure. Finally, it focuses on the relationship between structure and other major schools of thought in the organizational behavior and communication literature.

part I
Approaches to Organizational Communication Structure

chapter 2

Formal Approaches

The effective exercise of formal authority, in contrast, implies *limiting communication* to task relevant information and a systematic *exclusion of feelings* in the interest of efficiency. (Schein, 1965, p. 77)

Early approaches to studying formal communication structure in organizations concentrated on the organizational chart and the flow of messages vertically and horizontally within it. A typical research problem might concern itself with how the president in Baffle Manufacturing uses the organizational chart in Figure 2-1 to disseminate orders and instructions to control the operations of his or her organization using just the formal bureaucratic relationships specified in the chart. Thus, if the President wanted to order Worker 8 to accomplish some tasks, this message would need to be routed through 2 and 4, 8's superiors in the organizational hierarchy.

More recently researchers concerned with formal structure have tended to focus on more abstract variables associated with both formal relationships and the organizational chart, such as configuration, complexity, formalization, and centralization (Jablin, 1987). For several years, from the late 1970s to the early 1980s, research in this area was relatively moribund. However, in the last few years a number of reviews have appeared, related to formal communication structures in organizations, which indicate some rekindling of interest in this area (Dow, 1988; Jablin, 1987; McPhee, 1985, 1988). In general, these reviews suggest that formal approaches focus on the configurations resulting from the following characteristics of structure: formal authority relationships represented in the organization hierarchy (Dow, 1988; Jablin, 1987), differentiation of labor into specialized tasks (Dow, 1988; Jablin, 1987), and formal mechanisms for coordination of work among these tasks (Dow, 1988). These characteristics, along with the notion of goal or purpose, have been seen by some to represent the very essence of what organization is (Schein, 1965). In this chapter the focus will primarily be on the communicative elements of formal structure, especially in terms of their implications for controlling and coordinating the organization.

CONFIGURATIONS

Jablin (1987, p. 391), in discussing formal communication structure, defines *configuration* as the "shape of an organization resulting from the location and distribution of its formal roles and work units." While we have adopted a much broader view of configuration, including the overall pattern resulting from the structural dimensions of relationships, entities, and context, Jablin's definition captures the orientation of the formal approach, which has viewed formal structure both as empirical object of investigation and as an information-processing mechanism (Jablin, 1987). Thus, structure has certain properties which have almost a physical, objective character, at least as pictured on the organizational chart, which have become represented in terms of indices which capture these differing properties. This has been reflected in the persistent appeal of the conduit metaphor for formal approaches which tends to see structure as offering a series of pipelines for the flow of information in an organization (Axley, 1984). This flow of information through the structure, particularly in traditional perspective, reflects the information processing view of formal structure. In this section two primary approaches to the configuration of formal structures will be examined: *traditional perspectives,* which are clearly linked to the "objective" organizational chart, and *indices,* which attempt to identify underlying mathematical properties of formal positioning.

Traditional Views

Early research programs related to communication structure in organizations concentrated on the organizational chart (see Figure 2-1), which has also been referred to as the "organigram" (Rogers & Agarwala-Rogers, 1976). The formal organizational chart is embedded in the assumptions of the classical approach to rational management (Morgan, 1986). It specifies very clearly who reports to whom, and, in effect, constitutes a map for the routing of communication messages. It still is, as it was 20 years ago, the most popular method of describing organizational structures (Weinshall, 1966). Early approaches to formal structure primarily focused on the flow of messages within this organizational chart.

Downward communication originates from upper levels of organizational management and is targeted for lower-level personnel. This type of communication is meant to control the organization and the operations of

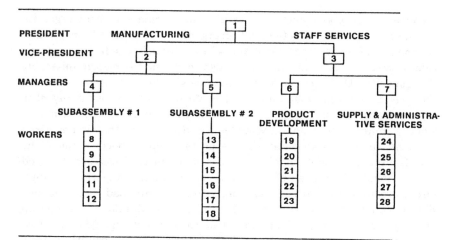

Figure 2-1. Baffle Manufacturing Organizational Chart

its personnel. Typically, downward communication messages, since they are official, are very formal and usually written.

Katz and Kahn (1978) describes five types of downward communication content. Job instructions account for the bulk of downward communication messages. These are usually very direct messages which instruct an employee to perform a specific operation at a particular place. Messages dealing with a job rationale attempt to put an employee's job in the context of others' work and tell an employee why it is important that they do particular things. Organizations typically do not answer the "Why am I doing this?" question of workers very well, leaving it up to the workers to decide what aspects of jobs are important and what they should concentrate on.

Somewhat related to job rationale is the indoctrination to the goals of the organization, which is intimately related to organizational socialization, a topic of growing concern to organizational communication scholars (see Jablin, 1984). These messages attempt to communicate to workers what the central values of the organization are, and, thereby, what it is the organization is trying to accomplish. For example, at McDonald's, QSCV stands for Quality, Service, Cleanliness, and Value. These are the central elements of this organization's culture, as well as the operational goals to which the organization attempts to indoctrinate its employees (Peters & Waterman, 1982). Most organizations do not pay enough attention to this particular type of downward communication, although recently its central important to excellent performance has been recognized (Peters & Waterman, 1982).

Probably the two biggest failures in downward communication content lie in feedback about performance and in information about organizational procedures and practices. Often organizations fail to adopt systematic means of providing members with feedback (such as appraisal interviews),and when they do adopt them they tend to perform miserably (Longenecker, Gioia, & Sims, 1987). Employees want to know how well they are doing and what they need to do to improve, but many elite organizations operate under the guideline that "no news is good news." That is, management operates under the assumption that it has hired excellent employees and, therefore, expects excellent performance. The very fact that someone is employed and is not being criticized is considered enough feedback. But employees also realize that, many times, supervisors are unwilling to confront them directly with bad news. So this silence could indicate approval or disapproval. Employees are often uncertain and anxious about how well they are doing. Manipulative managers will exploit this uncertainty, feeling that the resulting stress and tension will produce higher performance, but, as Peters and Waterman (1982) point out, excellent companies have the opposite philosophy. They believe that positive employee recognition is the best motivator.

Organizations often have powerful motivations to keep employees in the dark concerning procedures and practices as well. This area is one that raises many potential ethical questions concerning organizational behavior. For example, the cost of medical insurance is rising astronomically. In this situation, is it in the profit-making organization's best interest financially to send out complete and detailed information concerning health insurance? Or should its humane concern for workers offset any considerations of the cost involved?

There are a host of other problems with downward communication as well. Among them one of particular importance is the persistent problem of the distortion of downward communication messages.[1] These messages often do not arrive in a timely fashion, nor are they sufficiently well targeted to insure that they are distributed to the proper mix of individuals. In the last decade this persistent set of management problems has not received very much research attention, even though pragmatically it is one problem area which communication research is uniquely designed to address.

Like all vertical communication, *upward communication* (communication from workers to bosses) tends to be formal, in writing, and flows along the formal chain of command represented by the organizational chart. Upward communication is more important for control than for coordina-

---

[1] Unfortunately, space limitations prevent a comprehensive discussion of solutions to these problems; the interested reader may wish to consult such sources ad Downs (1967), Planty and Machaver (1952), Harriman (1974), and Wendlinger (1973) for comprehensive strategies for overcoming problems in downward communication.

tion of organizational activities. Without adequate upward communication from workers, management cannot react to change quickly enough to prevent major problems from developing for the organization. For example, if a salesman does not communicate to managers that customers are becoming dissatisfied with the organization's product line, then the organization will not have a new product line in place when the customer's dissatisfaction becomes a decision not to buy. Without feedback (workers providing management with their reaction to messages) the impact of downward communication is unknown, although many managers wrongly assume that, just because an order is given, workers will do what they are told.

Upward communication is also critical if an organization is interested in reacting to the problems and concerns of its workers. If workers have input into decision making through upward communication, they are more likely to react positively when decisions are implemented (Fidler & Johnson, 1984). Workers use a variety of techniques (see Schilit & Locke, 1982, for a review) to achieve upward influence, with the most common being logical presentation of ideas.

Horizontal communication is communication that occurs at the same level or sideways across the organizational chart. This type of communication is usually informal, face-to-face, and personal. Since it is much faster and more attuned to the personal needs of communicators, horizontal communication also tends to be used more to coordinate activities. For example, two workers may decide between them how they are going to tackle a particular project, who is gong to do what when, and may keep each other posted as to their problems and progress. This type of communication occurs outside of the formal organizational authority structure and thus lacks the formal rewards (and punishments) associated with vertical communication.

Perhaps the best known body of research relating to horizontal communication is Keith Davis's (1973) work on the grapevine (see Hellweg, 1987, for a recent review). The grapevine represents the informal flow of communication along primarily horizontal communication channels. Davis argues that the grapevine is a key indicator of the health of the organization, since it reflects the involvement of workers in the organization and their interest in its activities. Thus the grapevine can serve management's interest by making sure that workers have alternative means of getting the information they need. The grapevine is particularly active in times of high uncertainty, especially when critical problems are facing the organization and people tend to spread information they have a personal stake in. Surprisingly, despite the negative view people have of rumors, Davis has found that most information spread along the grapevine is accurate (estimates ranging from 75% to 95%).

Perhaps the primary reason why research related to formal views of structure has been neglected recently is that the world of organizations has become increasingly complex, which is reflected in the introduction of concepts like the grapevine, diagonal communication, and complex modes of integration. One of the first transitional attempts to deal with the complexity of communication in organizations was Katz and Kahn's (1966) notion of communication *circuits*. They argued that there are five major characteristics of communication circuits, or *networks*, in organizations. The first is the size of the loop which reflects the organizational coverage of a particular message. Does it reach the entire organization, or only one part? Another important characteristic is whether a message is repeated or modified as it passes through a circuit. Modification indicates that the message is altered in some ways as it goes through the organization. The third characteristic is the feedback or closure (no response is received) character of the circuit. Feedback implies that a response is received to a message, whereas in a closed circuit no response may be received. The final two characteristics, efficiency and fit with systemic functioning, will be addressed in more detail in Chapter 10, since they are the essence of organizational productivity. Katz and Kahn's (1966) description of communication circuits is important, because they recognized that more flexible approaches to communication structure were needed and that there were various relational elements of circuits which had crucial systemic impact.

Indices

More recently research related to formal approaches to organizational communication structure has focused on various indices of the overall configuration of formal structural relationships at the a macro level (Jablin, 1987). An *index* provides researchers with a systematic way of describing and organizational property in terms of a precise combination of other attributes. Many of these indices derive from the differentiation of the organization both vertically (e.g., number of hierarchical levels) and horizontally (e.g., number of separate work groups). This research has often been related to organization processes at the micro level, particularly psychological processes such as those involved in job satisfaction (see Chapter 9). Since there is no universal agreement concerning the dimensions of formal organizational structure (e.g., James & Jones, 1975; Porter & Lawler, 1965), here the focus will be on some of the elements that have been most clearly related to communication.

Size. Organizational size is not, strictly speaking, a property of structure. However, size has rather pronounced effects on other structural properties such as differentiation into work groups (Blau, 1981). Size has been found to influence such things as upward influence attempts among employees, with reliance on more informal methods, and merit, seen as being more important in smaller, private organizations (Schilit & Locke, 1982). In general, studies of the impact of organizational size provide only limited support for the notion that size is negatively related to the quality of communication (Jablin, 1987). A few studies have also examined the effect of subunit size, with the general conclusion that, as subunits increase in size, communication becomes more impersonal (Jablin, 1987).

Complexity. Complexity (or horizontal differentiation) is related to the number of different formal organizational groups. Results of research studies related to vertical complexity do not reveal a consistent set of relationships, suggesting the presence of various moderators, such as degree of professionalization of the work force (Jablin, 1987). On the other hand, there is fairly clear evidence that horizontal complexity relates positively to the frequency of communication (Jablin, 1987), especially with the need for coordinating diverse occupational specialties (Hage, Aiken, & Marrett, 1971).

Hierarchical level. Research in this area focuses on the vertical differentiation of the organization into various status levels. Studies have generally found that the time spent in communicating increases as one rises up the organizational ladder, but that the nature of the communication is heavily dependent on the nature of the organizational context (Jablin, 1987). For example, Bacharach and Aiken (1977) found that department heads engaged in more formal communication of all sorts than subordinates.

Centralization. Centralization refers to the degree to which authority is concentrated at higher levels of management (Jablin, 1987). Centralization also is a concept that has been used to refer to a person's positioning in a network of communication relationships. There are limits to how much organizational operations can be centralized. These limits are primarily determined by task factors and the capabilities, primarily information processing ones, of decision makers (Pfeffer, 1978).

Span of control. Span of control is defined in terms of the number of subordinates a supervisor has (Porter & Lawler, 1965). Greater vertical differentiation is usually associated with smaller spans of control, which concomitantly leads to greater supervision over individual workers. However,when professionals are the subordinates, there may be more consultation with subordinates by supervisors than close supervision (Brewer, 1971). While it could be assumed that this would lead to greater control by management over organizational functions, it paradoxically may lead to less control, since it increases the numbers of levels of the hierarchy and thus can lead to increased problems in vertical communication (Pfeffer, 1978). Span of control has other negative consequences as well. Not all jobs require close, personal direction by a supervisor; thus, low levels of span control result in unnecessarily increased administrative costs (Pfeffer, 1978). High levels of span of control may also encourage more individual initiative and growth (Porter & Lawler, 1965). In summarizing this literature, Jablin (1987) concludes that, while frequency of communication is affected by span of control, the mode and quality of communication is not necessarily affected.

Making sense of the wide array of indices used in formal approaches has sometimes been difficult, particularly since they cut across organizational levels and often have substantial conceptual overlaps. For example, while size has been primarily considered at the whole organizational level, it also has important impacts on group level processes. Complexity may also be considered at several levels, but it also is directly related to size. Centralization and span of control both conceptually relate to issues related to control by management of organizational functions. Some attempts have been made to impose a more clear cut set of overarching distinctions on these indices.[2] For example, Dalton et al. (1980) suggest a distinction can be made between structural indices and structuring indices. *Structural* qualities refer to more objective, physical characteristics primarily associated with the formal organizational chart, while *structuring* refers to policies and activities which constrain the activities of organizational members such as the degree of centralization. While interesting, this distinction does not address completely the problems of substantive overlap and differing levels of analysis.

FORMAL RELATIONSHIPS BETWEEN ENTITIES

Since the formal approach almost exclusively conceives of the organization in terms of authority relationships between formally defined positions, it has been heavily influenced by Weber's work on bureaucracy (Moch et al., 1983; Monge & Eisenberg, 1987; Ranson et al., 1980; Rogers & Agarwala-Rogers, 1976). Even when nonauthority relationships are considered, they are defined in terms of their association with ones of authority, such as the traditional breakdown between formal and informal structures. This focus on formal relationships centers this approach on managerial concern and also tilts its direction to more rational views of communication structure.

This view of relationships substantially limits the breadth of coverage of formal approaches. As subsequent chapters will make clear, much

---

[2] Jablin (1987), while recognizing that the literature offers no clear consensus on dimensions of formal structure, argues that there are four key dimensions which predominate in formal approaches: configuration, complexity, formalization (the degree to which rules govern relationships), and centralization.

broader perspectives of communication structure are possible. But this limitation may be a strength to managers whose primary pragmatic concern is how they can consciously, rationally plan to improve the operations of organizations. As a result, organizational design efforts are essentially related to the formal approach, and they are concerned with controlling behavior so as to produce a more efficient/effective organization (Pfeffer, 1978).

The formal approach has operated at all levels of analysis, from message distortion processes at the individual level to the overall configurations of relationships throughout the whole organization. Primarily it has been concerned with relationships between the formally defined entities of supervisors–subordinates (which we will return to in much more detail in the human environment chapter) and of differentiated work units. The focus of concern theoretically is on how these relationships can be controlled and coordinated to achieve higher levels of organizational performance. Indeed, some would argue that the central impetus underlying the development of structures is the formal differentiation of entities into specialized groups defined by tasks which are dependent on each other and thus require communication to coordinate their activities (Dow, 1988; O'Neill, 1984; Pfeffer, 1978; Thompson, 1967). The relationships between these differentiated entities becomes a natural and crucial area of concern for communication research from a formal perspective, and some have considered differentiation to the very foundation of a collectivities social structure (Blau, 1974a).

Managing interdependence between units by coordinating and controlling their activities is critical to organizational design (Pfeffer, 1978). The greater the interdependence among work units the greater their need for coordination (Cheng, 1983). In turn, the higher the levels of coordination required, especially by more personal mechanisms, the greater the volume of communication (Hage et al., 1971). These processes are also crucial because of the many communication problems associated with hierarchies, such as blockage of information and slowing of message flow, as well as the natural tendency for rivalries to develop between functionally separated units (Lee, 1970).

A variety of means (e.g., matrix, human relations, and formal integrating mechanisms) have been used to encourage interaction between entities of the formal organization, which the organizational chart in effect serves to isolate (O'Neill, 1984). There is a relatively rich literature on various levels of coordination, reflected in such notions as loose coupling and the strength of weak ties, which will be covered in more detail in later chapters. Perhaps the most comprehensive, systematic discussion of this issue, especially in the context of formal structural approaches to design related to information processing, is found in the work of Galbraith (1973, 1974).

Galbraith's central assumption is that the greater the uncertainty faced by the organization, the more it must concentrate its efforts on communication, particularly integrating mechanisms designed to increase the levels of coordination between work units (Galbraith, 1973, 1974). These integrating mechanisms, especially the more personal ones (e.g., liaisons), also overcome some of the inherent communication problems (e.g., failures to report critical information) of the hierarchy (Lee, 1970). The organization's capacity for handling communication related to coordination will determine how much interdependence, and relatedly differentiation, it can handle (March & Simon, 1958). One way to increase the efficiency of communication is to minimize the need for it by such strategies as coordination by plan, where units concentrate on fulfilling formally assigned tasks which fit into the larger whole (March & Simon, 1958).

At relatively low levels of uncertainty, an organization can rely on rules and programs, the hierarchy, and goal setting to accomplish integration. These strategies constitute the traditional formal managerial structure of an organization, and they will be used in sequence as uncertainty increases within an organization. Rules and programs refer to procedures established in advance for relatively predictable organizational behaviors. Each unit contributes its part of the larger project without much need for communication between units. For example, a plan may be in place which specifies in great detail the contribution of each unit to a production process. However, even the most detailed plan often runs into difficulties in implementation. Exceptional circumstances may arise which require coordination by management to insure that proper levels of relationships are maintained between units. This intervention by the hierarchy insures completion of the project. As uncertainty increases, management may decide that it is more efficient to coordinate units by establishing targets for them. Management lets the units themselves decide how the targets will by achieved. Coordination is achieved by each unit reaching the goal set by management.

However, as uncertainty reaches even higher levels, the traditional hierarchical approach runs into difficulty, and the organization is confronted with strategies which involve a departure from traditional perspectives of coordination. Essentially, the major choice an organization faces is whether to reduce the need for information processing or increase its capacity to process information. Reduction in need depends primarily on the strategies of creating slack resources and self-contained tasks, which are both aimed at reducing the need for communication between units. Increasing the capacity requires investments in vertical information systems, such as computer-based management information systems, and the creation of lateral relations, which require a heavy investment in human resources. The creation of lateral resources involve much more personalized integrating mechanisms such as liaisons, task forces, and teams. These latter two strategies are so important that they will be treated much more comprehensively in later chapters.

Recently work on expert systems has created an exciting hybrid of many of these integrating mechanisms which considerably enhances the ability of an organization to coordinate and control its operations. In expert systems, rules derived from knowledge workers and/or experts (e.g., engineers, systems designers) are incorporated into computerized vertical information systems. Thus, "expert systems are computer programs that couple a collection of knowledge with a procedure that can reason using that knowledge" (Feigenbaum, McCorduck, & Nii, 1988, p. 6). These systems embody many characteristics of artificial intelligence systems. They can result in more thorough and consistent decision making. Expert systems are used primarily in diagnosing problems such as those associated with, for example, automobiles, steam turbines, or steel blast furnaces. They have also been used successfully on a wide array of additional tasks, including processing medical claims, selecting the appropriate chemical formulation for a particular application, and filling sales order for complex minicomputer configurations. Expert systems can be used in conjunction with other systems to automatically inform another part of the organization if something goes wrong, thus improving the speed of horizontal communication (Feigenbaum et al., 1988). These systems offer a whole host of new possibilities in formal communication systems. They also point to how far formal approaches have come since the traditional work focusing on problems in vertical communication.

CONTEXT AND TEMPORAL STABILITY

The context of formal structure lies in the "official world" of the organization. Most often it can be conceived of as embedded in the formal authority structure of the organization, usually associated with bureaucracy. In this context communication is conceived as flowing along the proscribed pathways of the organizational chart, and the content of communication is limited to those production-related matters that concern the organization. While this formal approach constitutes a limited view of the role of communication in organizations, it still may be, especially operationally, the most important role of communication, and certainly one that management must at least try to control. Indeed, "the contest over organizational structures represent a contest for control of the organization" (Pfeffer, 1978, p. 18).

Because formal communication is firmly embedded in the official world of the organization, there are a number of forces that act to make it one of the most stable of the various approaches to structure that will be examined in this book. "Organizational structures, then, are the resolution, at a given time, of the contending claims for control, subject to the constraint that structures permit the organization to survive" (Pfeffer, 1978, pp. 223-224). Thus they represent a state of equilibrium among contending forces to power in the organization (Dow, 1988).

Indeed, Pfeffer (1978) argues that changes in the formal structure should be thought of as quasirevolutions, because of the powerful constraining forces that protect its stability. One of these, of course, is risk of newness. Nobody knows with absolute certainty that a change will make the organization or his or her position within it better. Any change, of course, increases uncertainty, with the associated discomforts that most in the organization would just as soon avoid. Individuals also desire to preserve existing structures to retain their power, which emanates from these formal structures (Morgan, 1986).

PLANNED VS. EMERGENT VIEWS OF STRUCTURE

We have ample data to show that the formal structure (the official allocation of positions) does not *determine* the pattern of human relations in an organization. Nevertheless, it does set certain limits upon the shape of that pattern. (Whyte, 1949, p. 308)

In part, the communication network is planned; in part, it grows up in response to the need for specific kinds of communication; in part, it develops in response to the social functions of communication. At any given stage in its development, its gradual change is much influenced by the pattern that has already become established. Hence, although the structure of the network will be considerably influenced by the structure of the organization's task, it will not be completely determined by the latter. (March & Simon, 1958, p. 168)

Formal approaches were the earliest to examine organizational communication structure, but increasingly the power of informal forces came to be recognized in organizational thought. The entire communication structure of an organization is composed of elements of both, with other ingredients as well, as future chapters will reveal, and is not reducible to either (March & Simon, 1958). Blau has argued that communication in organizational hierarchies is a function of (a) structurally induced communication needs, and (b) the opportunities structure provides for interaction (Brewer, 1971). Allen (1977), in reviewing his own research stream, has found that, while formal communication may be marginally more important than informal, the two are functionally independent of each other. The interaction between formal and informal approaches has always been problematic for structural theorists, since in many ways they represent diametrically opposed positions on what structure is (Dow, 1988), with both perspectives also appealing to different underlying metaphors, mechanistic and organismic, respectively (Morgan, 1986).

Indeed, two very different types of communication activities have come to be represented in these two views of structure (Contractor, Monge, & Eisenberg, 1987). The question may not be which view is correct—both may be, for different organizational phenomena—but what each view contributes to our understanding of organizational communication structure (Monge & Eisenberg, 1987). Dow (1988) has recently contrasted these two views of organizational structure using different labels: *configurational* (formal) and *coactivational* (informal, network analysis).[3]

The configurational view emphasizes the authoritative coordination of work in the service of stated organizational objectives, while the coactivational view focuses on recurrent patterns of interaction. According to Dow, the configurational view's emphasis on formal authority leads to theoretical omissions, particularly concerning the forces of the "market" underlying many informal relationships in organizations. Thus the configurational view focuses on the intentional design of the organization by management and has difficulty conceiving of any other basis for structures (McPhee, 1985; Dow, 1988).

However, "in the coactivational view, an organization is a communication network in which actors or subunits recurrently process resources and information" (Dow, 1988, p. 56). These informal structures function to facilitate communication, maintain cohesiveness in the organization as a whole, and maintain a sense of personal integrity or autonomy (Smelser, 1963). In the coactivational view it is the joint activity of organizational actors over time which reveal structures. The emergent properties of interactions between entities, which constitute something of a different nature than just their individual contribution, represents the underlying thrust of all structural approaches to some (Blau, 1981). The relative importance of these two views may depend on what stage in its life cycle the organization is in. Relatively new organizations may be more coactive, while more mature organizations may be relatively configured (Monge & Eisenberg, 1987).

Administrative rationality in the Weberian sense has always been a central concern of the formal approach (e.g., Thompson, 1967), and with it has come the assumption that structures are designed to control behavior in such a way as to produce efficient/effective operations (Pfeffer, 1978). Thus, structures are conceived as fitting into a preconceived, rational plan, rather than viewed as representing rationality after the fact (Weick,

---

[3] Somewhat similarly, Ranson et al. (1980) distinguished between the frameworks of organizations constituted by the formal configuration of roles and procedures, and by interaction represented by patterned regularities and process.

1969). But structure can also be conceived of as a result of the contention of various entities for power and influence (Pfeffer, 1978). "The idea of rationality is as much a resource to be used in organizational politics as a descriptive term describing the aims of organizations" (Morgan, 1986, p. 195). Intentionality and rationality become much more complex issues in the coactivational view, with deeper forces and the "invisible hand of the market" governing the formation of structures.

While there had been considerable empirical work within the separate camps, very few attempts have been made to examine the relationships between the two empirically. Conceptual attempts often offer only superficial analysis of their differences, such as Monge and Eisenberg's (1987) positional approach. This approach examines the communication relationships between formal positions in a network analysis framework. As a result it is essentially a means of coopting the formal approaches into network analysis frames of reference, and it thus ignores central elements of a formal approach such as authority relationships and formalization. A recent attempt to systematically compare formal and informal groupings and their impact on the levels of role ambiguity essentially found more similarities than differences between the two types of groupings and suggested a complex set of contingencies in which one or the other would have the most impact on role ambiguity (Hartman & Johnson, 1990). Much work remains to be done to determine the nature of overlaps and differences between emergent and planned views of structure; with some arguing that the views are so divergent it is impractical to simultaneously consider both (Blau, 1974a).

STRENGTHS AND WEAKNESSES

Substantive Weaknesses

There are a number of weaknesses inherent in the formal approach.[4] First, it offers only an incomplete view of organizational communication struc-

---

[4] The literature in this area is confused and confusing, with a host of methodological problems: limited samples, focusing on different types of organizations, different variables, different operationalizations of the same variables, differing cross sections (James & Jones, 1976), lack of clearly formulated concepts, limited methodological designs, and inappropriate analyses (Berger & Cummings, 1979). Perhaps the gravest methodological problem confronting work related to formal structure is the validity of its measures. Operationalizations such as group, department, or hierarchical level may have meaning only in one particular organization (Berger & Cummings, 1979). In addition, some operationalizations in effect combine apples and oranges when they, for example, treat all formal relationships as if they are equivalent (McPhee, 1988). The formal relationships between the highest levels of management may be qualitatively different from the relationships between first-line

supervisors and workers. Indices themselves can become merely labels, which, while convenient to the researcher, have no real significance to the individuals involved (Rice & Mitchell, 1973).

Weinshall (1966, p. 619) identifies the heart of these problems in describing the meaning of the organizational chart for management: "It is a mixture of what they believe to be the formal relationships and what, in their opinion, such relationships should preferably be." This is especially troublesome, since the "proscribed frameworks stand in rather superficial relationship to the day-to-day work of the organization" (Ranson et al., 1980, p. 2). Communication can flow along prescribed pathways, but it need not. In addition, some of the pathways may be very well traveled, while others are not traveled at all. Most indices treat all linkages as equally important, but the formal structure may be very much like a highway system, with vast differences in load and cyclical peaks of communication.

All of this raises the question of what the measures of formal structure really mean, especially in communication terms. For example, Jablin (1987) notes that it is rather ironic that very little of the span of control literature directly examines communication variables, even though most explanations for the impacts of span of control are couched in communication terms. Indeed, the express purposes of the design of certain formal structures is to minimize the costs of coordination and communication (Thompson, 1967), and, in general, hierarchical systems require much less communication than other systems (Simon, 1960). Picturing formal structures as communication structures may be illusory. Some have argued that, implicitly, most formal approaches focus on entities rather than on the relationships between them (Moch et al., 1983). Thus, the emphasis on communication is weakened, since communication is inherently a relational phenomenon (Rogers & Agarwala-Rogers, 1979b). Some separate out formal structure from communication behavior completely, suggesting we should examine the impact of factors like span of control on communication variables such as quantity, quality, and form (Jablin, 1987). However, Jablin (1987) also recognized that formal properties such as formalization, centralization, and complexity are fairly directed linked to communication behaviors. In fact, their operationalizations often contain communicative elements, which may account in part for the mixed empirical findings Jablin (1987) notes in this area. If one operationalization of a conceptual variable contains a communication measure and another does not, then, when these variables are related to other communication properties, naturally the strength of the association for the noncommunication operationalization is going to be reduced.

But this raises the larger conceptual issue: what is the relationship between formal structure and communication structure? They are clearly not one and the same thing, but their overlaps, such as in the case of centralization, can be substantial. One strategy, as Monge and Eisenberg (1987) suggest, is to reduce formal structure to what they call the *positional approach,* which captures formal communication relationships between positions. However, this approach ignores important elements of the formal approach, especially the level of formalization associated with rules.

For the moment, the best that can probably be hoped for is an explicit treatment, in empirical studies when formal structure is related to communication properties, of how the operationalizations clearly relate to both underlying conceptual variables. Otherwise our measures may contain elements of both, masking true relationships between variables. This problem is exacerbated by the traditionally univariate focus of most formal studies, which do not capture the complex interaction between variables (Berger & Cummings, 1979; Jablin, 1987; Porter & Lawler, 1965). However, this complex set of interactions may, at its heart, be attributable to a failure to systematically conceptualize the nature of the relationships between variables (Berger & Cummings, 1979; Porter & Lawler, 1965). As was noted earlier, formal structural indices are highly interrelated with each other, which suggest they may reflect more general underlying conceptual dimensions (Kim, 1980).

ture, since it captures only a limited subset of possible relationships (Brewer, 1971; Rogers & Agarwala-Rogers, 1976). Second, the formal approach ignores the active roles that individuals play in shaping their focal communication networks and in seeking information (Monge & Eisenberg, 1987). Third, it also offers only a somewhat awkward and heuristically limited portrayal of the configuration of communication patterns, compared to the network analysis and gradient approaches. Fourth, the reification of formal structures reduces the adaptability of the organization to change, since, once structures become official, they become more difficult to change. Finally, and perhaps most importantly, the traditional view of communication structure reinforces some dangerous assumptions that managers often hold—that messages flow along the conduits represented by the organizational chart without blockage or interruption, that management is in charge, and that messages actually reach their destinations (Axley, 1984).

Substantive Strengths

There are several key strengths to the formal approach. First, it deals directly with the issue of predictability as it relates to control, especially in vertical communication. The organizational chart was originally intended to map out patterns of control across the whole organization, thus making relationships between interactants clear, at least in terms of who was in charge. Thus the manipulation of formal structures gives management a useful tool for designing organizational structures. It is somewhat of a paradox, though, that management's prime means of control is so ineffective. Second, the organizational chart is often a reflection of temporal stability. That is, it reflects rationality after the fact (Weick, 1969). This means that, after people in the organization have been behaving in a particular way long enough, these relationships tend to be formalized on the organizational chart (Connolly, 1977). Once they appear there, they take on a permanence that they might not have otherwise had. Third, the organizational chart also reveals a guide to action, suggesting how things should occur in the organization. Members of the organization should realize, however, that this guide is only a practical starting point, a framework, which they may need to flesh out and deviate from to meet new problems and concerns. Finally, this approach's focus on authority relationships might be quite appropriate, since arguably these relationships form the foundation for any organization.

chapter 3

Network Analysis

Network analysis represents a very systematic means of examining the overall configuration of communication relationships, both formal and informal, within an organization. The most common form of graphic portrayal of networks contains nodes, which represent social units, and relationships of various sorts between them (see Figure 3-1). These elements of graphic representations are essential to most network analysis definitions: "In general, the term 'network' is taken to mean a set of *units* (or *nodes*) of some kind and the *relations* of specific types that occur among them" (Alba, 1982, p. 42).

Because of its generality, network analysis has been used by almost every social science to study specific problems (e.g., Alba, 1982; Barnes, 1972; Foster, 1979; Mitchell, 1969; Monge, 1987; Smith, 1980; Tichy,

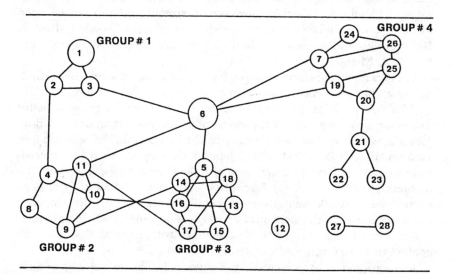

Figure 3-1. Baffle Manufacturing Production Communication Network

1981; Tichy, Tushman, & Fombrun, 1979; Wigand, 1977, 1988), and it has been the primary means of studying communication structure in organizations over the last decade (Johnson, 1988a; Monge & Contractor, 1987; Monge & Eisenberg, 1987). In fact, so much attention has been paid to network analysis that a comprehensive review, particularly related to computer programs (see Farace & Mabee, 1980; Rice & Richards, 1985; Johnson, 1987e, 1988b), data gathering methods (see Richards, 1985; Monge & Contractor, 1987), and interorganizational networks (Eisenberg et al., 1985), of all material related to it is beyond the scope of this chapter. This chapter will focus on the relationship between network analysis and the more encompassing concept of communication structure. In particular it will focus on the real strength of the network analysis approach to communication structure, its analysis of configurations of relationships.

LINKS AS RELATIONSHIPS

What really determines the analytical power and breadth of any network analysis is how the relationships between nodes, referred to as *links,* are defined. Links are the basic datum of network analysis (Rogers & Kincaid, 1981; Wigand, 1977); they are its fundamental property. Unfortunately, in most network analyses, linkages are defined very crudely, revealing relatively simplistic understandings of the communication process (Richards, 1985). For example, a typical network study might focus on a count of the number of production-related messages between two organizational members. Recently, however, interesting attempts have been made to define linkages from the perspective of the respondent (Bach & Bullis, 1989) and in terms of their cultural properties (Eisenberg, Contractor, & Monge, 1988).

   Links can be conceptualized in a variety of ways. It is very important, however, that any conceptualization be systematic and that it full capture various relational properties (Richards, 1985). A useful framework for discussing link properties is the model of social interaction developed by Johnson, which has been empirically tested in a program of research (see Johnson, 1980, 1982, 1984, 1985). Johnson developed this model specifically to provide a richer description of linkage properties; to address the problem of the incomplete, descriptive definitions of link properties in traditional network analysis research (Richards, 1985). His model is intended to specify the elemental structure of ongoing, stable interactions, and it is couched at a rather higher level of abstraction, so that it can be applied to a large range of situations.

   Johnson's model is presented in Figure 3-2. The model contains six elements which constitute the domain of social interaction and, for our

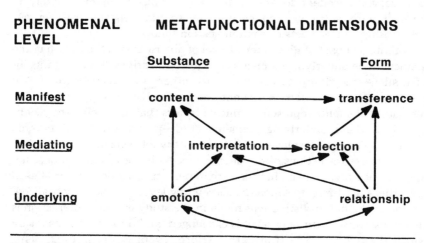

PHENOMENAL   **METAFUNCTIONAL DIMENSIONS**
LEVEL

Figure 3-2.   Johnson's Model of Social Interaction

purposes, represent the major dimensions of communication linkages: content, interpretation, transference, selection, emotion, and relationships. Two distinctions, metafunctional role and phenomenal level, can be used to classify each of these elements and to identify the unique portion of the domain of social interaction each of these elements occupies. In Figure 3-2 these two major distinctions are denoted by all capital letters, and their subcomponents are the underscored terms. These distinctions entail natural causal orderings of the variables in any continuing interaction. In general, the model posits that elements at deeper phenomenal levels, especially emotion and relationships, determine those elements are more surface levels, a view which has also been associated with cultural approaches to networks (Monge & Eisenberg, 1987).

A fundamental premise of the model is that social interaction is characterized, not only by the manifest acts usually observed during the course of an interaction, the typical focus of most network analysis research, but also by the elements that underlie and determine these acts. Thus, three phenomenal levels are distinguished in the model: *manifest, mediating,* and *underlying.* Two factors determine whether an element can be placed at each phenomenal level. The first is the temporal nature of the element: is it relatively fleeting and hence one of the manifest elements, or is it relatively enduring and therefore one of the underlying elements? The second factor is an element's level of abstraction. Here the concern is the extent to which another element is subsumed or determined by other elements. For example, relationships subsume selection by determining whether someone will be selected. In turn, selection is a necessary antecedent to any transference. Thus I am more likely to interact with a friend, and once I choose him, on the basis of our relationship, surface acts of communication follow.

An integral part of an element's level of abstraction is the nature of the element. The underlying elements describe basic drives of interactants for affiliation—the desire to associate with others to accomplish or fulfill needs, goals, or instincts that cannot be accomplished individually. The mediating elements represent cognitive factors that determine the means by which these underlying elements or deep structures will become manifest. The manifest level constitutes observable acts in an interaction; these acts are reflections of the deeper process in social interaction, and, as such, they reveal them, but they are imperfect reflections, since at each level there are limits to which the succeeding levels can be fully realized.

One of the oldest distinctions made in the study of social interaction is that between *substance,* or what is exchanged, and *form,* or the means by which the substance is transmitted (Hare, 1960; Simmel, 1902). This metafunctional distinction is also made in network research (Alba, 1982; Knoke & Kuklinski, 1982). Of the six elements in the domain of social interaction, three can be clearly identified as the substance of the interaction: content, interpretation, and emotions. The other elements— transference, selection, and relationships—govern the form of manner in which these substances are transmitted or expressed. For the metafunctional distinctions, the substance exchanged during the interaction is generally posited to determine its form of expression at the same phenomenal level.

The Underlying Elements

Relationships and emotions are the two underlying elements in Johnson's model of social interaction. *Emotions* reflect the affective states that exist between interactants. Of primary importance here are those emotions that bond individuals together, such as a need for affiliation, rather than those that exclusively deal with the individual, such as depression. The role of emotions has long been recognized in group interaction research (e.g., Bales, 1950; Hare, 1960), but it has generally been slighted in both communication and management research. The role of emotion in organizational communication structure will be developed in more detail in later chapters, which focus on the human environment of organizations and social support.

Relationships in the model reflect the nature of the bonding between interactants.[1] Thus, while a link represents all of the factors in the model and is more characteristic of the global definition of relationships used elsewhere in this book, relationships are more narrowly defined in the model to represent the deep structure of the interaction. In addition, "A relation is not an intrinsic characteristic of either party taken in isolation, but is an emergent property of the connection or linkage between units of observation" (Knoke & Kuklinski, 1982, p. 10). Relationship is an underlying element, because "interaction grows out of the roles we play, the defined relationships we have in various groups" (Ittelson, Rivlin, & Proshansky, 1970, p. 127).

There are two primary types of relationships. Contextually determined relationships are associated with situationally or culturally determined roles. For example, Katz and Kahn (1966) view organizations as "fish nets" of interrelated offices. Contextual properties are intimately associated with asymmetry. Essentially, *asymmetry* means that a relationship is not the same for both parties. This is an important property of organizational networks, since there are a multitude of differences between organizational members, especially in term of status and the direction of communication. Thus, power/dependence relationships are an especially important class of asymmetric relationships (Lincoln & McBride, 1985).

Actor-determined relationships reflect the idiosyncratic bondings which characterize relationships between particular interactants. For example, importance, a variable that has traditionally been examined in network studies (e.g., Richards, 1985), provides a direct assessment of the tie between an informal communication relationship and work performance. It can be associated with the more abstract concept of work dependency which relates fundamentally to the degree of access individuals have to needed task-related information (Johnson & Smith, 1985). Often individuals in networks come to rely on their peers for work-related

---

[1] Relationships can represent a variety of things, and the literature identifies numerous relational factors which underly network linkages. For example, Eisenberg et al. (1985), in reviewing the literature on interorganizational linkages, make a distinction between perspectives operating on the flow of information and those operating from a flow of resources. Smith (1980) discusses the following factors which could serve as a basis for interactional factors in a network: resources, norms, exchange, and support. Tichy et al. (1979) view organizational networks as systems of four types of exchange: expressions of affect, influence attempts, information, and exchanges of goods and services. Lincoln and Miller (1985) have argued that exchange and homophily theories are two alternative perspectives which could explain linkages between human service organizations, with homophily explaining many of their empirically derived relationships. Many of these perspectives implicitly or explicitly operate from an exchange theory perspective (see Cook, 1982, for a review).

advice. These peers are not formally assigned by the organization, but rather these relationships develop more informally, often as a result of friendships. Thompson (1967) asserts that these work-dependent relationships determine communication channels in an organization to a greater degree than such factors as affiliation, influence, and status.

The Mediating Elements

Elements of social interaction at the mediating level, *interpretation* and *selection,* act to translate, or transform, the underlying elements into manifest acts. These elements constitute the psychological processes in interactions that transform emotions into particular interpretations (e.g., affiliation needs result in a label of friendship) and relationships into particular levels of selection (e.g., status differences result in greater attention), which, in turn, determine the nature of the manifest acts of an ongoing social interaction. In general, elements at this level have been slighted in organizational communication structure research and in network analysis research in particular, although increasing attention is being paid to them in the context of relational and cultural approaches to networks (Monge & Eisenberg, 1987; Eisenberg et al., 1988).

Norton and Pettigrew (1979) implicitly recognize this level when they suggest that manifest acts in an interaction must be translated through the cognitive processes at the mediating level through attention. Attention is only one element of what is called *selection* in the model. The second process of selection is a major determinant of network structure. Actors choose to attend to someone from among a variety of interactants; the pattern of these selections determines the structure of a network. Once someone is selected, then the level of attention will vary, depending on the influence of the other elements of social interaction specified in the model.

The manifestation of these selection processes at work is most clearly revealed in the link property of reciprocity. *Reciprocity* refers to whether or not both parties to a relationship characterize it in the same way. Reciprocity has been considered primarily a measurement property of linkages (Richards, 1985), but it can be directly related to substantive processes as well, such as selective perception and selection attention (Alba, 1982; Jablin 1980a) or the total volume of communication in an organization (Monge & Contractor, 1987). For example, often a supervisor will not be as aware of relationships with workers as they are of the relationships with his or her bosses. So, when asked with whom they communicate, they will forget about a worker, but the worker will remember his or her relationship with the boss. This linkage is therefore unreciprocated; the worker believes it exists, but the manager does not. Unreciprocated linkages, linkages where one party does not agree that a relationship exists, are quite frequent in organizations. Monge et al. (1978), for example, report percentages of reciprocation ranging from 37% to 100% across a number of empirical studies. The implications of this problem and its impact on network analyses is currently an under-developed area of network research (Rice & Richards. 1985).

Perhaps the most frequently made distinction between elements of social interaction is that between *interpretation* and *content* (e.g., Bales, 1950). Interpretation, in Johnson's model, represents the connotative meaning associated with expressed symbols. Cicourel (1972) and Pearce and Conklin (1979) have maintained there is a need to distinguish between the manifest acts represented by content and their underlying meanings for interactants. In network analysis research this distinction has been clouded, with an especially high degree of commingling between function and content (Stohl & Redding, 1987), with most discussions implicitly putting function at the level of interpretation in Johnson's model, with functions revealed in particular manifest contents.

However, many network theorists confuse interpretation and content. treating both as synonymous with function and also with other forms of relationships (e.g., Mitchel, 1969). "The content or function of the relation crates some of the messiest problems for network analysis" (Richards. 1985, p. 112), especially so because most category schemes are incomplete. and some behaviors can represent multiple functions. While there are a wealth of potential schemes developed for describing the content of functional networks, there is not a terribly high degree of consonance between them (see Farace et al., 1977; Monge & Eisenberg. 1987: Stohl & Redding, 1987). For example, Berlo (1969) identifies three organizational communication functions, production, innovation. or maintenance. which only partially overlap with Redding's (1972) task. maintenance. and human functions. Indeed, Farace et al. (1977) suggest that different functional schemes may be necessary for different organizations and that functions may even differ at different levels of the same organization.

The Manifest Elements

if the concept of structure is to have any scientific meaning. it cannot be located at the manifest level. and it is not therefore another way of saying 'pattern.' (Gregory. 1978. p. 45)

The manifest level of social interaction contains the content and transference elements. In essence these elements constitute the "stream of behavior" (Pearce & Conklin, 1979). *Content* is the denotative meaning of symbols expressed during an interaction. This is the literal meaning of what is said, the meaning of the interaction to a third party who is unaware of the background of the actors and other factors that may influence the true meaning of symbols for interactants. Content is perhaps the most direct manifestation of the functions of a relationship; but some content can reveal multiple functions. For example, in sending a number of production-related messages to a worker, a supervisor accomplishes a production function, but he or she may also be accomplishing a social support function for the worker.

Transference refers to the overt acts of symbol exchange; the means (for example, physical method/channel) by which symbols are transmitted between parties in an interaction. These channels might include written, face-to-face, telephone, or telecommunication networks. Properties of channels will be discussed in much more detail in Chapter 7. The behavioral acts represented in this element are not in and of themselves relationships, although certain types of behavior, such as high levels of communication contacts, may be indicative of particular types of relationships such as friendships (Richards, 1985).

An important general property of a link which is reflected in transference is *strength*. Typically the frequency of communication is used to indicate the strength of a link (Richards, 1985); however, there are many different indicants of the strength of transference, each of which has different implication for communication studies. For example, wide-ranging contacts of short duration may indicate individuals have yet to find satisfying relationships, while a few focused contacts of long duration may indicate high levels of response satisfaction (Johnson & Smith, 1985; Johnson, 1987a).

Combining Link Properties

The manner in which these various properties of links are combined can determine the analytical power and depth of any one network analysis, since a network is defined by the nature of the linkages it examines. Thus, if we wanted to look at a network that paralleled the organizational chart, we would specify that only linkages involving production content, which are in writing, asymmetrical, and unreciprocated, should be included. Alternatively, an informal network could be defined by production and maintenance contents, face-to-face channels, symmetricality, and reciprocated linkages. It might be also very interesting to look at multivariate networks. These are networks where strength is determined by more than one factor—by weight, frequency, and duration of a link, for example (see Johnson, 1987c). These multivariate networks allow us to combine a number of factors for a much more sophisticated conceptualization of communication linkages. One could also look at more than one network, say the formal and informal, and see how they overlap. This examination of multiplex networks can give us a more in depth view of any one individual's overall participation in an organization (Minor, 1983). For example, the president of a corporation might be at the center of the production network but relatively isolated from a social network. This would paint a picture of a relatively cold and aloof management.

Multivariate networks. The central problem for multivariate network studies is the identification of critical dimensions upon which linkages are based and the specification of the interactions between them. Both of these issues have only recently received research attention, and this area is ripe for ground-breaking research. In contrast to multiplex network studies, which generally focus on the differences in linkages across functional networks (Minor, 1983; Albrecht & Ropp, 1984), multivariate network studies focus on different properties of linkages within the same functional network.

Johnson (1987c) has conducted the only systematic investigation into the nature of multivariate communication networks. This study investigated the nature of multivariate networks formed from various mathematical combinations of three major variables, *importance, frequency,* and *response satisfaction,* which have been previously identified in the literature as central to our understanding of organizational communication (Johnson & Smith, 1985; Richards, 1985). Importance is a structural variable which influences individual information-processing needs and system performance, while response satisfaction is a key indicator of relational factors and more generally of the communication climate of an organization. Frequency is one of the fundamental indicators of the strength of communication linkages in organizations.

The examination to multivariate networks based on these theoretically rooted variables could enhance our understanding of communication networks more than the typical focus on the mere frequency of certain types of functional content (Richards, 1985). In concrete organizational circumstances it is the unique weighting of variables such as these which should determine the actual functioning of the network. Naturally, links which are strong on all of these dimensions might have different characteristics than links which are strong on one and weak on another. Thus focusing on importance, or the salience of a communication linkage for the accomplishment of assigned tasks, should enable us to more specifically tap into linkages crucial to systemic performance. Relating importance to response satisfaction, which reflects an interactant's subjective perceptions of a positive affective tone associated with an information source, and to frequency,would assess the unique weighting of these particular variables on group formation and individual role occupancy. Indeed, the literature suggests that these substantively distinct variables also should produce different behavioral manifestations.

Johnson's (1987c) study examined binary, univariate, additive, multiplicative, and exponentiated combinations of these linkage properties. The most striking thing about the results of this study, which was conducted in a large retail store over three points in time, was the general similarity of the various multivariate networks, especially at times 2 and 3. Particularly noteworthy was the formation of one large group in every network. Further the few existing discrepancies were probably attributable to methodological artifacts[2] or the instability of the initial network at time 1, which was relatively early in the life of this organization. Thus it would appear that the various multivariate methods used for calculating the strength of linkages between actors was not as important as the mere presence or absence of a linkage, as revealed in the binary network.[3]

Thus, at least for NEGOPY, the particular computer program used in this research (see Richards & Rice, 1981), Johnson's (1987c) study revealed that role classification and group formation were not substantially affected by widely different methods of determining the strength of dyadic linkages. However, further development of multivariate network-related techniques can lead to theoretical and methodological advances in network analysis, since it provides researchers with new means of thinking

---

[2] Most of the differences between networks were probably attributable to the sensitivity of network analysis generally to missing data, rather than to substantive reasons. Respondents in this study were much more likely to complete the frequency indicators for all linkages, while a subset of the linkages (approximately 5%) had missing data for either the importance or response satisfaction measures.

[3] The results point to a number of general problems with network computer algorithms, particularly the version of NEGOPY (Richards & Rice, 1981) used in this study, at least in connection with this research application. First, the existence or nonexistence of a linkage was much more important that subtle gradations in the degree of relationship. Thus, the difference between 0 and 1 was much more important than subsequent differences in numerical scores, as revealed in the general similarities found in comparing the binary networks to the scaled multivariate ones. Thus, in effect, a wealth of potential information on the relative intensity of relationships was "wasted." Second, this was exacerbated by the apparent insensitivity of the parameter settings of the version of NEGOPY used in this study to subtle differences in group formation—thus, the tendency to form very large groups that has been evident in other research (see Farace & Johnson, 1974). Third, the link weighting formula used to calculate strength had a number of limitations. Most importantly in this form it could only manipulate two linkage properties with linear or multiplicative relationships. Given the large number of dimensions possible for human relations, this was a critical deficiency. While NEGOPY did have its problems in this application, it still constituted a considerable improvement over other available programs, which do not even permit this sort of analysis and thus allow only primitive definitions of linkage properties (see Farace & Mabee, 1980; Rogers & Kincaid, 1981; Rice & Richards, 1985).

about, describing, and studying the linkages which form the basis for communication networks (Farace & Mabee, 1980). These new techniques could capture the more "rich" descriptions of communication relationships inherent in the work of interpersonal, intercultural, and group communication scholars. This in itself would represent a quantum leap in sophistication for organizationally based network analysis, which has typically examined only one dimension of communication linkages (Richards, 1985).

Multiplex networks. While network analysis holds much promise, a number of problem areas hinder its development. One of the most pressing of these is the nature of overlap, or correspondence, between differing networks (e.g., friendship as opposed to work) (Farace & Mabee, 1980; Rogers & Kincaid, 1981). The nature of these overlaps is of great pragmatic concern, since it can suggest the inherent capabilities of individual actors within systems, and it also has rich implications for the understanding of social systems generally (Reynolds & Johnson, 1982; Roberts & O'Reilly, 1979). Organizations are actually composed of a variety of overlapping and interrelated networks of differing functions (Jablin, 1980a); however, functional dimensions are but one of the many dimensions along which network linkages can be multiplexed (see Eisenberg et al., 1985; Minor, 1983; Tichy et al., 1979). Multiplexity is a network concept that has received increasing attention in recent years (Monge & Eisenberg, 1987). At its heart it refers to the extent to which different types of network relationships overlap: "The relation of one person to another is multiplex to the extent that there is more than one type of relation between the first person and the second" (Burt, 1983, p. 37).

The degree of multiplexity has been related to such issues as the intimacy of relationships (Minor, 1983), temporal stability of relationships (Minor, 1983; Mitchell, 1969; Rogers & Kincaid, 1981), reduction of uncertainty (Albrecht & Ropp, 1984), status (Albrecht & Ropp, 1984), the degree of control of a clique over its members (Rogers & Agarwala-Rogers, 1976), performance (Roberts & O'Reilly, 1979), redundancy of channels (Mitchell, 1969), and the diffusion of information within networks (Minor, 1983). Multiplexity is also crucial to processes of social contagion, since it can be expected that individuals with a high degree of participation across different types of networks might be more affected by contagion processes than those individuals involved in only one type of network (Hartman & Johnson, 1989). Thus, the breadth of someone's linkages might serve to provide an individual with a variety of information sources, as well as repetition of certain effects, which determine such contagion-related processes as attitude change.

Perhaps the key, and often overlooked issue, in multiplexity studies is the association between different types of networks and the conceptual phenomenon of interest. Thus, if someone is primarily interested in innovation studies, innovation networks are of primary importance. However, other networks may have great importance as well, particularly social ones (Albrecht & Ropp, 1984). In addition, too high a level of aggregation of network contents (e.g., all work-related content) can create problems in intepreting data. For example, Krackhardt and Porter (1985) speculated that workers were more likely to talk about job duties than general organizational goals. Therefore, they argued it was less likely that cohesion-related social contagion would impact on commitment. Unfortunately, because of the operationalization of network function, this post hoc explanation could not be tested; however, when separate content networks were examined by Hartman and Johnson (1989), this assertion was called into question. So the first issue that confronts a researcher interested in multiplexity is, What different types of networks will be examined? As we have seen, this is a question whose answer may provide the researcher, at one and the same time, with too much and too little information, given the large array of functional category schemes which have been proposed.

On the other hand, there is neither much theoretical guidance nor specific empirical work that describes the linkage between particular functional networks and nonnetwork theoretical variables (Rogers & Kincaid, 1981). Hartman and Johnson (1989) examined the relationship between multiplexity and role ambiguity and commitment. They found direct associations between functional networks and these concepts. Role ambiguity was most directly linked to conflicting information or perceptions of roles; thus, it is most closely linked to the uniplex network relating to job duties. On the other hand, commitment was most directly tied to organizational goals. In addition, the other functional networks of satisfaction and nonwork impacted on commitment. As a result the multiplex combination of these network properties had more of an impact on commitment than they had for role ambiguity. The results bear out the importance of specifying appropriate functional/content networks in the framework of multiplexity. Thus, the overall pattern of results stresses the importance of carefully considering the nature of multiplex networks. As Rogers and Kineaid (1981) point out, prior network analysis results must be viewed with skepticism, because of their lack of concern with multiplexity and specific network contents.

CONFIGURATIONS OF RELATIONSHIPS AMONG ENTITIES

Inherent in the concept of networks is a recognition of the complexity of communication structure; however, network analysis is also concerned with the isolation of particular configurations which reduce to a small number of specific network patterns (Farace & Mabee, 1980). As a result, another great strength of network analysis lies in the variety of means available for examining configurations of communication relationships. In this section the focus will be on three primary means of depicting network configurations: communigrams, individual patterns of relationships, and network indices.

Communigrams

Network analysis can be a very systematic and complete means of looking at the overall pattern of communication linkages within an organization. One way this can be accomplished is through graphic representations. Figure 3-1 contains a communigram reflecting the network of relationships found in a sample organization, Baffle Manufacturing. The circles in the figure represent nodes, in this case individuals, and the lines indicate communication linkages. This form of graphic portrayal is very flexible, since the nodes can be any type of entity and the linkages represented by the lines can be of any kind (Farace & Mabee, 1980).

Visual imagery has always been one of the most important ingredients of network studies, but unfortunately, the nature of these images has not advanced very far in the last 40 years (Klovdahl, 1981; Knoke & Kuklinski, 1982; Weinshall, 1966; Wigand, 1977). There are also inherent limitations in the ability of graphic displays to capture multiplex relations and differences in strength (Wigand, 1988). Another problem with communigrams is that, if the n gets too large, the graph becomes uninterpretable. For example, Johnson (1986) reported a network for a retail store which had an n of 178. NEGOPY, the particular network analysis program used to analyze the data, detected one large group of individuals within this store. The resulting communigram in Figure 3-3 is nearly uninterpretable, which is a general problem as well with computer-drawn linkages of dense cliques (Rice & Richards, 1985). However, other means of capturing configuration of relationships can somewhat ameliorate this problem.

Individual Patterns of Relationships

Network roles. An individual's communication role is determined by the overall pattern of his or her communication linkages with others. Some individuals, labeled *nonparticipants* (e.g., isolates), have relatively few communication contacts with others (e.g., 12, 27, and 28 in Figure 3-1). *Participants,* on the other hand, form intense patterns which represent communication groups and linkages between these groups (e.g., 3, 5, and 15). Several research studies have found key differences between these two kinds of individuals, with participants being more outgoing,

Figure 3-3.   Communigram for the Retail Store

influential, satisfied (Goldhaber et al., 1978), and having more coherent cognitive structures (Albrecht, 1979) and nonparticipants deliberately withholding information, having lower satisfaction with communication (Roberts & O'Reilly, 1979), and reporting less identification, variety, feedback, and required interaction (Moch, 1980).

The most important communication role is that of a liaison (6 in Figure 3-1). Reynolds and Johnson (1982) have conducted the most systematic review of research related to liaisons, a summary of which is provided in this section (see also Table 3-1). The liaison links two or more communication groups, while not being a member of any one group. This strategic positioning of liaisons has earned them the label of *linking pins,* who, through their promotion of more positive climates and successful coordination of organizational functions, serve to hold an organization together (Likert, 1967). The role of the liaison in the coordination and control of organizational activities is closely tied to the concepts of integration and differentiation. That is, as the organization divides into more and more groups, greater efforts have to be made at pulling these groups together through integrating mechanisms (Galbraith, 1973; Lawrence & Lorsch, 1967). These integrating mechanisms are crucial to organizational survival, since without them the organization would be a collection of groups each going off in its own direction. Typically, liaisons are the most efficient personal integrating mechanism because of their strategic positioning. Due to their centrality and their direct linkages with others, liaisons reduce the probability of message distortion, reduce information load, and increase the timeliness of communication.

Unfortunately, however, liaisons are relatively rare occurrences in organizations, which is reflected in the generally low level of communication between diverse groups in organizations (Farace & Johnson, 1974). Given their central role in organizational operations, it is important to understand the factors that make it more likely that an individual will come to assume this role. These factors are summarized in Figure 3-4. Liaison emergence also is central to increasing the level of information which flows between diverse groups in organizations; and as a result coordination and control. Thus, our discussion of liaisons provides a

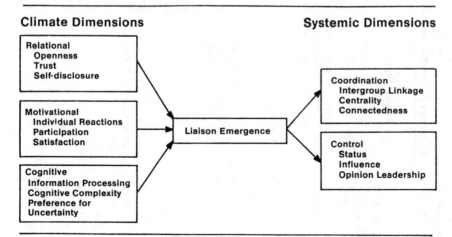

Figure 3-4.   A Model of Factors Relation to Liaison Emergence*

* Reynolds and Johnson (1982, p. 558)

Table 3-1.* Empirical Findings Differentiating Liaisons from nonliaisons^a

Dimensions	Study			
	Amend (1971)	MacDonald (1976)	Schwartz & Jacobson (1977)	Albrecht (1979)
I. Systemic				
A. Coordination				
1. Intergroup linkage	Liaisons had greater peer communication diversity;* information output diversity.*	Liaisons perceive themselves as having more contacts.	Liaisons perceived as having more contacts;* liaisons had more university level committee memberships.*	
2. Centrality	Network centrality.*		Perceived as having more structurally diverse contacts.*	
B. Control				
1. Influence	Liaisons have greater control over flow of information;* peers perceive them as effective.*	Nonliaisons perceive liaisons as having more influence, liaisons did not perceive selves as having more influence.	Liaisons perceived to have more influence in power structure;* more general persuasiveness;* first source information.	
2. Status		Liaisons tended to be in supervisory positions, higher civil service grade.*	Liaisons tended to be administrators, devoted more time to administrative duties.*	
3. Opinion leadership	Liaisons found to be opinion leaders.*		Liaisons perceived as dyadic opinion leaders.*	
II. Climate				
A. Relational		Liaisons perceive work related system as more open.	Nonsignificant differences between liaisons and nonliaisons in: who initiates contact, trustworthiness, confidence in source credibility.	Non-key communicators perceive foreman as being more distant in an MDS space, perceive self as exerting more influence in determining rules of interaction.*

B. Motivational	Liaisons more satisfied with jobs and organizational communication system.*	Key communicators identified more with their jobs, perceived themselves as closer to management. Key communicators more often perceived downward directed communication as timely, accurate, believable, useful, and adequate.*
C. Cognitive	Liaisons had more information input diversity.	Nonkeys had smaller cognitive spaces, less variability and magnitude in their judgments.
III. Demographics	Liaisons have longer tenure.	Liaisons devoted less time to teaching duties,* more likely to be full professors. Nonsignificant differences for age, time devoted to research, consulting, highest degree held, length of employment, and publication rate.

ᵃFour recent studies concerning the differences between liaisons and nonliasions are reviewed in this table: Amend (1971) used sociometric techniques to study 50 members of 7 academic departments at Michigan State University; MacDonald (1976) used matrix manipulation to study 185 individuals in a federal bureaucracy; Schwartz and Jacobson (1977) used matrix manipulation to examine 142 professionals in a college faculty; and Albrecht (1979) used the Negopy computer program to compare bridges and liaisons (termed key communicators) ($n = 36$) with other communication roles ($n = 29$) in a manufacturing plant. Bernard and Killworth (1977) and Jablin (1980a) discuss the various methodological difficulties associated with these procedures. Table taken from Reynolds and Johnson, 1982, p. 553.

*$p < .05$

preview of our discussion of antecedents to communication structure and outcomes of communication structure which will be more comprehensively examined in later chapters.

The first set of factors which cause liaison emergence are relational factors. Since network analysis is essentially a means of representing patterns of linkages, the quality of these relationships become important determinants of the patterns of linkages for individuals. So the overall satisfaction of an individual with his or her linkages with others can affect his or her frequency and duration. For a liaison one such relational factor which is of critical importance is openness, which is generally conceived of as a willingness to impart or accept information. If information is to flow freely in an organization, then it is critical that network participants maintain open communication relationships. The research results summarized in Reynolds and Johnson (1982) suggest that liaisons are indeed more open in their communication with other organizational members, with liaisons being more receptive to differing types of communication encounters, and often sought out by others in their communication networks. Indeed, liaisons may emerge because others initiate contact with them, partly because they perceive liaisons as being more open. As a result liaisons become sources of scarce and valuable information, which results from the wide diversity of their contacts.

Another set of factors relating to a liaison's emergence is his or her cognitive abilities. Because the liaison stands at the center of organizational groups, this role has unique information processing demands. Liaisons must process information from diverse sources whose messages are often couched in different technical languages. In organizational contexts the liaison's information-processing abilities have been associated with cognitive complexity. The highly cognitively complex individual is able to recognize important differences among bits of information (differentiation), perceive the relative significance of these bits (discrimination), and, finally, assimilate a great variety of information into coherent and/or novel perspectives (integration) (Schroder, Driver, & Streufert, 1967). Indeed, several empirical studies have found a relationship between cognitive complexity and positions in communication networks (Albrecht, 1979; Schreiman & Johnson, 1975; Zajonc & Wolfe, 1966).

While relational and cognitive factors are essential to a liaison's role performance and are necessary for liaison emergence, motivational factors determine whether or not an individual will aspire to such a role and perform effectively within it. The emergent nature of network linkages is in part a picture of the more voluntary and spontaneous choices that organizational members make in their communication relationships. Thus they may describe, in part, the need-fulfillment strategies of organizational members. Typically, liaisons in production-communication networks can be said to fit into the classification of upwardly mobile individuals in organizations (Presthus, 1962). The needs of upwardly mobiles individuals are fulfilled within the organization. They are active seekers of information who constantly survey the organization for information useful to their own advancement.

Traditionally, control in organizations has been viewed as occurring within the formal communication structure. Roberts and O'Reilly (1979) have argued that effective control in an organization corresponds to the extent to which networks link critical task groups. Increasingly, management functions can be viewed as similar to those of a liaison, a factor reflected in the finding that liaisons tend to be managers. An effective manager must also be able to perceive coherent patterns from diverse information inputs and to form clear judgments which can serve as the basis for organizational action. However, only a minority of all managers occupy liaison positions in informal communication networks. Those who are liaisons appear to use persuasion to accomplish their objectives. In fact, many of the characteristics of a liaison—openness, trust, sensitivity to others, and getting a wide array of input—have also been used to specify the characteristics of democratic managers and, more generally, of open communication climates. While there has been much research attention paid to communication roles, especially in relation to other organizational factors, some rather central issues related to them have not received enough critical attention in the literature. First, there are multiplicity of role-related concepts, especially for the crucial linking roles, with little consensus across researchers on a definitive set of roles and/or operationalizations of them (e.g., Rogers & Agarwala-Rogers, 1976; Tichy, 1981). Second, forcing individuals into crude categories which have not received appropriate attention concerning their validity and reliability may serve to mask crucial relationships between individual configurations and other organizational variables. Third, curiously, many individuals who have argued for the value of networks for studying emergent communication patterns seem to be content with a priori designations of roles which might not reflect emergent network properties (e.g., Reynolds & Johnson, 1982).

Network Indices

> The goal of network analysis is to obtain from low-level or raw relational data higher level descriptions of the structure of a system. (Rice & Richards, 1985, p. 106).

This goal is achieved primarily through the use of various mathematical formulae or indices reflecting particular patterns of organizational communication relationships (Edwards & Monge, 1977; Wigand,

1988). These indices can inherently be linked to an issue of growing importance in communication, management, and social science research-levels of analysis (Berger & Chaffee, 1987; Dansereau & Markham, 1987; Granovetter, 1979; Monge, 1987) and, in part, account for the popularity of network analysis, since they are very sophisticated means of attacking levels of analysis problems associated with network research (Knoke & Kuklinsi, 1982; Farace & Mabee, 1980).

If researchers are to avoid pure reductionism, they must systemically account for the impact of higher order processes in organizations. For example, supervisor–subordinate dyadic relationships cannot be understood without reference to higher order organizational processes, such as authority systems (Dansereau & Markham, 1987). Similarly the aggregate of all supervisor–subordinate relationships may have important implications for groups processes, particularly those associated with decision making and team building. Thus, network analysis can be used as a systematic means of linking micro- and macroperspectives of organizations (Alba, 1982; Tichy et al., 1979). Central to these arguments concerning levels of analysis is the notion that higher level social phenomenon (e.g., group and whole organizational) cannot be explained just by combining the attributes of individuals who make up a system (Monge, 1987). This section will focus on the inherent flexibility of network analysis indices in portraying configurations of relationships centered on an individual's positioning, pathways of relationships, and the group and/ or systems level of aggregation, a rather common breakdown of the levels of analysis in network research (Farace & Mabee, 1980).

Individual positioning indices. Individual positioning indices, such as anchorage (see Barnes, 1972) and integrativeness (see Farace & Mabee, 1980; Wigand, 1977), try to mathematically capture an individual's location within the configuration of communication relationships of a network. As with most network indices there are a variety of ways of calculating indices for individual positioning which can have important implications for relationships to nonnetwork variables. For example, Brass (1981) reports a study in which three different individual-positioning measures were used in a study of a newspaper to examine their impact on job characteristics and such organizational outcome variables as satisfaction. *Centrality* referred to the extent to which a worker could reach others in the network through a minimum number of links. *Criticality* revealed the degree to which an individual's position was crucial to the flow of materials in a work flow network. *Transaction alternatives* referred to whether or not redundancy was built into the system in terms of inputs to particular individuals and their outputs to others.

While centrality and criticality were strongly related to job characteristics, they had a different pattern of associations, and transaction alternatives did not relate strongly to job characteristics. On the other hand transaction alternatives and criticality had significant relationships to satisfaction, while centrality had nonsignificant relationships. Brass's findings point to the importance of measures of individual positioning in explaining nonnetwork variables and also to the importance of carefully considering the wide array of the different possible indicators in this category and carefully conceptualizing their relationships to other variables.

Pathways indices. Indices associated with pathways primarily deal with how easily a message can flow from one node to another node in a network and are intimately related to matrix manipulation (see Knoke & Kuklinski, 1982). For example, *reachability* focuses on how many links a message must flow through to get from one node to another, usually expressed in terms of the shortest possible path, an issue which has profound implications for an individual's ultimate influence in a social system (Barnes, 1972; Mitchell, 1969).

Another way of conceptualizing this problem is in terms of the small world studies done by Milgram. These studies focuses on the paths people actually used in getting a message to a relative stranger in another geographic location, with the usual finding that relatively few linkages (7.3 to reach a stranger across the continental U.S.) were needed to reach someone (see Monge, 1987, for a brief review). Studies in this area have a number of implications for the productivity of organizations, especially in terms of efficiency and effectiveness.

Connectiveness indices. Perhaps the greatest level of development in network indices comes in the area of the relative connectiveness of larger social aggregates, either groups/cliques or the larger social system (see Edwards & Monge, 1977, for a systematic review of the different properties of a wide variety of connectiveness indicators). Essentially, the issue of connectiveness refers to whether or not all of the possible linkages in an aggregate are being utilized. This has important implications for processes like attitude formation in groups (Danowski, 1980) and a group's relative cohesiveness. At the whole-system level this issue relates to the extent to which the organization is divided into separate groups, differentiation, and the level of integration between the groups, usually represented by bridges and liaison linkages. As Lawrence and Lorsch (1967) have established in their ground-breaking research, this area has important implications for the ultimate productivity of organizations in contingency theory perspectives and also for conflict resolution, issues which will be discussed in more detail in later chapters.

CONTEXTUAL FACTORS

it is the ongoing context, which provides meaning and allows overt behavior to be interpreted and understood. (Richards, 1985, p. 110)

As the empirical tests of Johnson's model of social interaction suggest, contextual factors, such as the presence of intrusive environmental stimuli, have substantial impacts on interactions. In organizations the context for individual linkages is in part composed of the configuration of the larger network, a topic which will be discussed in more detail in the human environment chapter. In addition, a variety of factors which will be examined in the antecedent chapters, such as space and technology, act directly on the formation of particular network structures (Monge & Eisenberg, 1987).

Perhaps the most well-known, and at times most difficult, issue associated with the context of networks is where to draw the boundaries around networks. The nature of the specific entities which will be examined in a network analysis is determined by what boundaries are established (Alba, 1982). This is especially problematic, since boundaries suggest some discontinuity in relationships (Barnes, 1972), implying that relationships across boundaries are in some cases qualitatively different than those within the network's boundary (Monge & Eisenberg, 1987). In one of the more extended discussions of this issue Lauman, Marsden, and Prensky (1983) distinguish between nominalist and realist views of this problem. In the *realist* approach, the researcher adopts the vantage point of the actors in defining boundaries, while the *nominalist* imposes a conceptual framework which serves his or her own analytical purposes.

There are difficulties with each of these approaches. For example, an individual faculty member's realist network may be composed of graduate students and professionals at other institutions. These individuals may be more important for the individual faculty member than are his or her department colleagues (Mullins, 1968), which would most likely be the entities contained within the boundaries of a nominalist study. On the other hand, trying to define the boundaries of one set of nodes that encompasses all of a department's individual faculty members' relevant contacts would be a nearly impossible task, with grave methodological problems, especially those associated with sampling procedures (Alba, 1982).

TEMPORAL STABILITY

It is often assumed that networks are relatively temporally stable (Monge et al., 1978; Rogers, 1983; Tichy et al., 1979). However, the few empirical studies which have been done over time often reveal considerable variance in networks across time, although such studies typically have been done in the early stages of an evolving organization (e.g., Johnson,

1987c). Perhaps communication networks should be viewed as representing stability in the presence of flux, with periods of stability punctuated by change (Monge et al., 1978). Of course, change can also be temporarily stable, at least in the sense of cycles of activities which, over a long period of time, are stable but which, at particular times, may produce vastly different patterns of relationships among organizational members.

Problems with the temporal stability of networks are perhaps best reflected in Rice's (Rice, 1982; Barnett & Rice, 1985) study of change in a network of computer conferencing groups over a period of 25 months:

> the rate of change in the communication patterns in the network increased. There was an initial slow rate of change which then accelerated, oscillated, accelerated and showed a period of stability before accelerating again. (Barnett & Rice, 1985, p. 315)

There are several general factors which determine the relative temporal stability of networks. First, for linkage properties, there is some suggestive evidence that multiplexity and instrumental content (e.g., getting financial rewards) are positively related to stability (Rogers & Kincaid, 1981). Second, seasonality (Danowski & Edison-Swift, 1985), stages in an organization's lifecycle (Monge & Eisenberg, 1987), and sequences of work-related activities (Monge, 1987) can result in dramatic changes in network configurations across time. Third, context can affect the stability of networks, since communication linkages are going to be affected by the social structure's stability (Monge et al., 1978; Monge & Eisenberg, 1987). In Barnett and Rice's (1985) study, part of the observed change of the network was attributed to the introduction of new groups into the network, which naturally changed the network's boundaries. In Danowski and Edison-Swift's (1985) study, change in network computer patterns were linked to a merger which resulted in funding and staff changes, although the researchers suggested that the network returned to a stable baseline after these changes were assimilated.

Increasingly, organizations are viewed as constantly changing, which leads Monge and Eisenberg (1987) to argue for recasting them as emergent networks, reflecting an organization's constant reorganizing:

> The perspective we have been describing is characterized by constant change. Organizations continuously add and delete people. And those people constantly forge and dissolve their linkages to one another and to the outside world. (Monge & Eisenberg, 1987, p. 311)

All of this raises the question of how appropriate network analysis is as an indicator of communication structure, the larger conceptual framework within which network analysis is embedded (Monge & Eisenberg, 1987).[4] Rogers and Kincaid (1981, pp. 312-313) sum up this issue quite nicely:

> If there were complete instability, with each link representing only a will-o'-the-wisp, here-today-gone-tomorrow quality, no communication structure would exist, other than a fleeting slice in time. If this complete instability were characteristic of most network links, network analysis would be futile as a scientific means of understanding and predicting human behavior.

The severity of the problem of the temporal instability of networks depends in part on how important it is for our conceptualization of communication structure. Some have gone so far as to argue that only temporally stable, recurring relationships should constitute linkages, that temporally unstable relationships fail to meet the criteria for a network linkage (Aldrich, 1982). If some temporal stability is necessary for a phenomenon to be considered part of structure, then there is a real question of how appropriate network analysis is for revealing communication structure. This issue is especially problematic in the light of the emphasis placed on network approaches for the examination of communication structure (Monge et al., 1978); since they are far and away the most prevalent approach (Monge & Contractor, 1987).

STRENGTHS AND WEAKNESSES

Substantive Weaknesses

Network analysis has various substantive problems.[5] First, networks tend to be temporally unstable, which raises the issue of how much of structure they actually reveal. Second, while many view networks as the most

---

[4] There are also a number of methodological problems associated with the temporal stability of networks. For example, clique configurations can differ dramatically across time (see Johnson, 1987c); however, a systematic means of evaluating their differential properties is not available (Farace & Mabee, 1980). This is perhaps the greatest problem for comparing networks over time, partially because it interacts with the problems of missing data. In any over-time study of a social phenomenon there are two sources of change; one is change due to measurement error, and the other is true, substantive change. Because networks are so sensitive to missing data, the intermingling of these two sources of change is quite dramatic, particularly if just reciprocated linkages are used. This might be one reason that the studies which have been conducted over time typically use procedures, such as computer monitoring, which minimize the change due to measurement error (e.g., Barnett & Rice, 1985; Danowski & Edison-Swift, 1985).

[5] The major weaknesses of network analysis lie at the level of methods, particularly measurement (Rogers & Kincaid, 1981). Methodologically, network analysis is perhaps the least robust of the commonly used social science techniques: "it should be observed that most

viable route to a unified theory of social structure, others see them as best suited for describing existing patterns of communication relationships, especially since there has been a noticeable lack of theoretical work relating to network analysis (Alba, 1982; Blau, 1982; Granovetter, 1979; Smith, 1980), particularly concerning organizational processes (Blair et al., 1985; Fennell, Ross, & Warnecke, 1987; Monge & Eisenberg, 1987; Schrader, Lincoln, & Hoffman, 1986). Indeed, one of the reasons for the popularity of network analysis is that it is relatively value- and content-free, since the network metaphor contains few hidden assumptions about human nature that can act to cloud inquiry (Smith, 1980). On the other hand, this means that network studies are often too descriptive, since there is no explicit theoretical guidance for them (Alba, 1982).

---

network analysis procedures assume perfect measurement..." (Farace & Mabee, 1980, p. 384). A number of more specific problems are associated with this general difficulty.

First, there are several problems with the selection of the appropriate number of nodes to be includes in a network analysis. A combination of data-gathering and computer analysis problems sharply limit the size of networks which can be examined. In practice there are also a variety of methodological difficulties associated with the collection of the data (Jablin, 1980a), which in effect place ceilings on the use of particular methods for particular networks (e.g., observational techniques can be only used with very small n's) These problems are exacerbated by the difficulties associated with sampling from populations to obtain network data (Alba, 1982; Knoke & Kuklinski, 1982). So, in practice, network analysis has been done on a census of the members of relatively small social systems.

Second, network analysis is very sensitive to methodological difficulties in data collection. For example, the problems with missing data and reciprocity which we discussed earlier interact to create grave problems in determining how relationships should be analyzed. There is also considerable divergence of views about what is the most important, subjective or objective measurement of networks, which is related to the problem of whether people can accurately self-report their communication linkages (Jablin, 1980a; Richards, 1985; Monge & Contractor, 1987). Indeed some argue that it may be impossible to gather accurate network analysis data from individuals' self-reports of their communication activities (Bernard & Killworth, 1977; Bernard, Killworth, & Sailer, 1980, 1982; Killworth & Bernard, 1976, 1979). While these conclusions have been questioned on a number of grounds (Burt & Bittner, 1981; Farace & Mabee, 1980; Romney & Faust, 1982; Richards, 1985; Tutzhauer, 1989), this line of research still identifies measurement as one of the major problems which network analysis research today must grapple with (Alba, 1982; Knoke & Kuklinski, 1982; Richards, 1985). Fortunately, especially in terms of the automated auditing of network data, there have been a number of systematic recent attempts to come to grips with measurement issues (Danowski, 1988).

Third, there is some uncertainty about the robustness of network computer programs and their algorithms, especially for clique detection (Alba, 1982), and no real consensus concerning appropriate parameter settings (Jablin, 1980a; Rice, 1979; Stohl & Kakarigi, 1985). Somewhat relatedly, there are substantial limits to the size of networks that can be analyzed by particular algorithms. In addition, by design or in practice, most network computer algorithms permit only primitive scaling, usually binary; really complete, rich descriptions of linkages are difficult to accomplish.

Substantive Strengths

On the other hand, network analysis offers many compelling advantages in the investigation of organizational communication structure. First, it is a very practicable method for examining the overall configurations of communication contacts in a large social system, which can also provide an elegant description of them (Farace et al., 1977; Rogers & Agarwala-Rogers, 1976). Second, it provides very specific and direct information on the pattern of an individual's linkages, since networks are based fundamentally on the notion of dyadic linkages (Mitchell, 1969). Thus it moves us away from an exclusive focus on the individual to a more conceptually correct focus on the relationship as the unit of analysis (Moch et al., 1983; Monge & Contractor, 1987; Rogers & Agarwala-Rogers, 1976). Third, it permits the derivation of a host of other measures from the aggregation of these individual linkages, including clique identification, roles, metric (e.g., connectedness), and this data can be aggregated at various levels of analysis, including interpersonal, group, and whole organization. In this regard it can be used as a systematic means of linking micro- and macroperspectives of organizations (Tichy et al., 1979). In sum, network analysis offers the most complete picture of the overall configuration of communication relationships, both formal and informal, yet developed, and certainly a much more complete view than offered by formal approaches alone (Monge & Eisenberg, 1987).

chapter 4

Communication Gradients

Communication gradients portray communication intensity in a physically bounded plane through the use of rich visual imagery. In general, gradients detail the rate of increase or decrease of variables in magnitude through topological or graphical representations. For communication research, gradients represent communication levels of varying intensity within some physically bounded plane, such as the floor of an assembly plant. Thus they provide a picture of where communication is occurring within an organization. They also provide information on the linkage of communication levels with other organizational factors. For example, a gradient might reveal that communication is highest at the intersection of two hallways, and lowest at the dead-ends of hallways. Gradients have long been used to describe phenomena in other disciplines, such as geology and meteorology (Monkhouse & Wilkonson, 1971). Gradients can make a significant contribution to our understanding of organizational communication structure by detailing the communication configurations which result from spatial and technological contexts.

New Approaches to Configuration

One of the essential factors association with the growth of any discipline is the availability of a number of techniques by which the researcher or theorist can conceptualize and/or analyze with the phenomenon of interest. The need for new methodologies in organizational research has generated much interest and concern in the last several years (e.g., Hackman, 1982). Communication gradients represent a new methodology for investigating the communication structures associated with the physical setting of an organization.

Development of gradient-related techniques can lead to conceptual advances, since it provides researchers with new means of thinking about and analyzing the relationship between organizational communication structure and antecedent factors. One of the primary ways that it does this is through its inherent visual representation. These visual representation have the potential for becoming metaphors of powerful heuristic value.

> The highest art, both in itself and in graphical display, is finding the unexpected. Done properly pictures...offer us the greatest hope of doing just this. (Tukey, 1980, p. 492)

These visual images may describe more concretely complex communication relationships in a manner which makes them more comprehensible and which can stimulate analytical thinking and investigation (Schmid & Schmid, 1979).

In fact, cartographers have increasingly come to see their maps as a communication instrument (Taylor, 1983). They delineate three uses for maps, which nicely parallel the range of potential applications of communication gradients.

> A *communicative* use for the storage and dissemination of spatial information; an *operative* use involving the direction solution on maps...of various practical problems,...and a *cognitive* use, for spatial and even spatial-temporal investigations of natural and social phenomenon, and the acquisition of new knowledge about them. (Salichtechev, 1983, p. 12-13)

In general, it has been argued that some of the most useful discoveries in the history of science have been associated with visual imagery and visual representations (Klovdahl, 1981). Today's advances in computer graphics offer us a host of opportunities for the development of new tools for examining communication structure. The advances in computer graphics are particularly important, since they provide the link between raw information and the visual images necessary to perceive it.

Graphic Representations

Gradients can be generated from a number of different computer graphics procedures. In this section various plots of data drawn from two illustrative data sets will be compared to demonstrate the utility of gradients for examining organizational communication structure. Three different procedures of SAS/GRAPH, which is a component of the more general Statistical Analysis System (SAS) (SAS Institute, 1982), will be used here to represent communication intensity within a plane of coordinates: GCONTOUR, a contour plotting program; G3D, which produces three

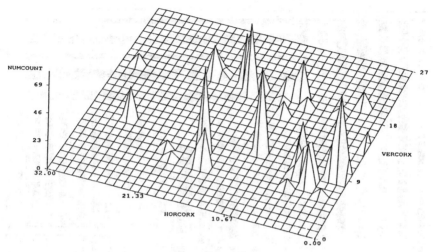

Figure 4-1.   Communication Gradient for Warehouse

dimensional grids of data points: and G3GRID, which interpolates data into a regular grid given particular functions (SAS Institute, 1981).[1]

The sample computer graph found in Figure 4-1 provides us with representations of communication intensity within the bounded plane represented by the map of a warehouse/distribution center found in Figure 4-2. The warehouse is dominated by very tall bins, well about eye level (represented by the solid black lines in Figures 4-2), and a conveyor belt (which is represented by the enclosed white space which meanders through the middle-right of the figure). The graph generated from G3D, found in Figure 4-1, provides a dramatic pictures of intense communica-

---

[1] One cannot overlook the fact that these graphic tools have been developed in other disciplines for other problems. However, examining their applicability to communication structure problems could lead to the development of more precise tools for examining structural phenomenon. For example, several key modifications to this technique would be helpful in making it an even more valuable addition to our set of tools for analyzing the communication structures of large information systems. First, it would be more heuristically valuable to have the actual map, instead of the grid drawn on the plane of the coordinates. Second, techniques for picturing communication in organizations which have more than one floor or which are physically separated are needed, since the current representations are limited to one contiguous, flat plane. Finally, the comparative advantages of different graphical representations need to be more fully assessed. For example, while G3D produces dramatic visual images, it can also distort the data. In Figure 4-1 it is difficult to tell with certainty that the warehouse manager (coordinates 10, 10) has the highest peak number of contacts. In addition, this dramatic peak overshadows an area of lower intensity almost directly behind it.

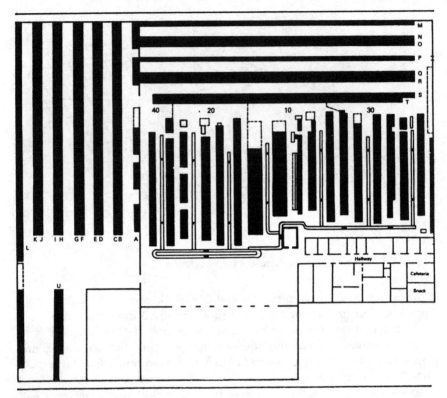

Figure 4-2. Warehouse Map

tion areas within the warehouse in three dimensions. The grid which forms the plane plots out the location within the warehouse of communication activities with the horizontal coordinates (HCORDWX) for work stations arrayed along the bottom and the vertical work coordinates (VCORDWX) arrayed along the right side of the figure. These coordinates, then, represented locations of individuals at work stations in the plane of the warehouse, with dimensions drawn to the scale of 32 horizontal units and 27 vertical units of eight feet. The elevated areas represent peak communication activities along the z axis (labeled for the variable NUMCONT for number of contracts). The higher the elevation, the greater the frequency of communication. For example, the highest peak is represented by the warehouse managers cubicle at coordinates 10, 10.[2]

The GCONTOURS program of SAS/GRAPH is also useful for isolating peak communication areas. In Figure 4-3 GCONTOURS provides a two-

---

[2] More detailed reports of the methods, procedures, and comprehensive reports of the results can be found in Johnson (1987b).

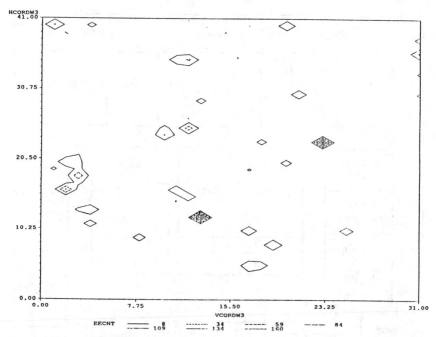

Figure 4-3.   GCONTOUR Representation of Communication Activities Within the Retail Store

dimentional, top-down perspective of communication within a rather typical discount retail store (see Figure 4-4 for layout). The grid which forms the plane plots out locations within the store with horizontal (arrayed along the left side of the figure) and vertical coordinates (arrayed along the bottom). The solid lines surround areas of communication activities. The more lines within the solid lines, the greater the intensity of the communication activity. Thus this figure is somewhat akin to a topographical map of communication activity. The larger the area covered by VCORW3 1-3 and horizontal coordinates 14-21 represents the overlaps of communication which occur at the check-out area.[3]

Graphic Indices

Communication gradients can potentially be directly linked to mathematical expressions, especially in relation to the topological representations of planes, as well as statistical analysis, as demonstrated by SAS/GRAPH's linkage to a sophisticated statistical analysis system. For

---

[3] For more detail on the store and the methods of collecting the data the interested reader can consult Johnson and Smith (1985).

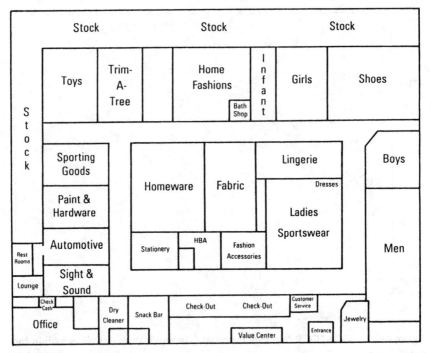

Figure 4-4.   Store Map

example, Figure 4-5, drawn from the retail store data, presents the results for the G3GRID procedure. The surfaces generated by this program interpolates a function of two variables onto a rectangular grid. In effect, the surface generated is similar to what could be formed if a stiff, thin metal plate were forced through the data points (SAS Institute, 1982). This figure demonstrates the inherent potential of gradients to be "fitted" to mathematical expressions.

RELATIONSHIPS

The gradient approach requires new ways of thinking about relationships. While for network analysis relationships could be cast in terms of linkage, for gradients relationships might be better thought of in terms of relative intensities of communication which occur at particular locations. Location becomes an entity with its own unique properties and characteristics. Thus, while the previous approaches focused on individuals, roles, or groups as the entities, gradients broadens our thinking to include communication events primarily characterized by nonhuman organizational properties.

The elements of Johnson's model of social interaction, however, still have a great deal of relevance for gradients. The gradients examined so far have reflected transference elements, since they focus on frequency (see Figures 4-1, 4-3, 4-5). Figure 4-6, drawn from the retail store data, demonstrates the interesting differences which can occur in gradients when different functional contents are examined. Coordinates were generated for both a respondent's work station and also for the place where he or she normally took breaks. This is somewhat akin to separating both production and maintenance contacts in network analysis and it permits us to focus specifically on particular types of communicative functions associated with specific spatial locations. As this figure reveals, the rest areas in this store centered around two locations; the snack bar (28,3) and

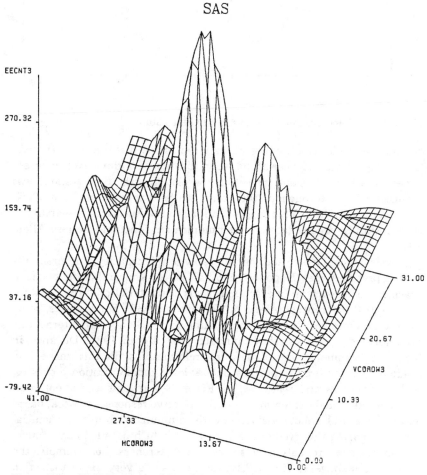

Figure 4-5. G3GRID Graph of Retail Store

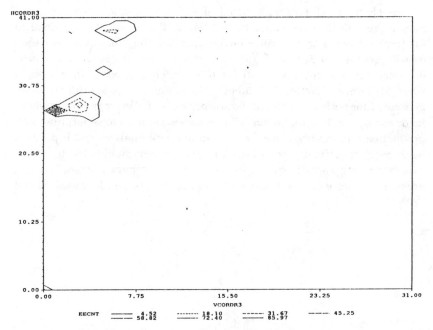

Figure 4-6. Communication in Rest Areas in Retail Store

the lounge (39,5). Contrasting Figures 4-3 and 4-6 is quite instructive. There was almost no overlap between locations for these two different types of activities. Communication associated with work stations was diffused widely throughout the store, while that with rest areas was narrowly constricted. This suggests a fecud area for future research, the relationship between place and communication function (see also Allen, 1977).

Physical location also adds considerably to the capacity of interactants to interpret messages (Rapoport, 1982). It is well known that the personal space characterizing an interaction reveals characteristics of relationships (e.g., status differences) (Aiello & Thompson, 1980). For example, some interactions may be viewed as threatening primarily because interactants are impinged on in a way they cannot control (Brower, 1980). Distance, in fact, can become a way of defining relationships. In this connection gradients can be used to portray deeper-level communication processes, such as emotions and relationships. Figure 4-7 reveals a gradient composed of individual perceptions of their affective responses to work, based on their overall level of satisfaction with communication in this organization. Comparing this gradient to Figure 4-1, which detailed communication frequencies, reveals some important differences. For example, the warehouse manager's office (10,10) did not have a very high satisfaction score, perhaps reflecting the communication demands placed on this

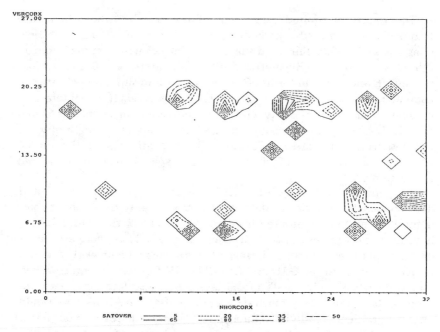

Figure 4-7. GCONTOUR Representation of Warehouse

position, which had the highest peak for communication frequency. In contrast, coordinates (3, horizontal coordinates arrayed along bottom, 20) far removed from the rest of the people in the organization revealed a very high satisfaction score. This might be associated with the correlational finding that workers become more satisfied with their relationships with their supervisors with increasing distance (Johnson, 1987b).

Gradients have particularly important implications for the selection element of Johnson's model, especially in terms of the key differences in conceptualizing relationships between gradients and network analysis. Gradients are inherently more usefully thought of in terms of intensities and probabilities, and as such can give us important insights into why certain relationships do not materialize. Thus gradients are inherently more capable of picturing the world of forces, probabilities, and fields associated with the physical environment's relationships to communication structure. Selection can be conceived of in terms of the probabilities of communicating with others at various distances from an individual's physical location.[4]

_____

[4] The examples used in this chapter have been based on actor-based approaches, in part because of their familiarity and the relative ease of gathering this type of data. Locationally based approaches, which measure all communication, regardless of the actors involved, occurring within a location, may have more potential for generating high-quality gradients.

The relatively limited assortment of others with whom there are frequently reciprocated contacts constitutes a person's information field (Hagarstrand, 1953). This field sharply diminishes with distance from an interactant's position (Hagarstrand, 1953). Hagarstrand (1953) describes this information field in terms of a cone with diminishing probabilities of communication with increasing distance. This assertion has an interesting corollary, that is, the closer two interactants are, the more their information fields overlap, which could also have a bearing on strength of weak ties notions (Grano vetter, 1973). Thus the strength of weak ties can be conceived of in terms of shared physical spaces as well as shared interactants.

In organizational settings Allen (1977) describes access in research and development laboratories as determined by gradually diminishing communication up to 50 feet away from an interactant, with communication beyond that characterized by a dramatic drop-off. Thus there are direct parallels between Allen's and Hagerstrand's work. Their work also has direct analogues to the G3D and GCONTOUR figures presented earlier, especially where individual's are isolated. At these locations there are cones, although they have much sharper drop-offs then Allen's work would imply. A gradient of individual information fields could reveal much about the probabilities of an individual receiving information from others in the organization and whom they will select to communicate with.

Combining Relational Properties

Gradients can be generated from combining linkage properties. In many ways, gradients have even more potential in this regard than network analysis, because of the sophistication of the graphic images that are becoming possible with advanced computer applications. In terms of multivariate attributes, the association of gradients with advanced statistical packages, like SAS, permits an incredible range of statistical and computational transformations on intensity measures. So the development of sophisticated conceptions of relationships in connection to gradients is not as limited by computer algorithms. In addition, multiplexity can be examined in a variety of interesting ways. For example, color coding could be used to portray the different locations of various functional communi-

---

In particular, locationally based approaches are likely to reduce the problems of large proportions of the space having no communication and the exaggerated peaks associated with individual work stations. Thus they are likely to smooth out the contours of gradients. They could therefore make gradients more fine-grained and continuous. In turn, this would reduce the 'strain' on computer algorithms, especially in terms of interpolation problems between data points. On a conceptual level locationally based approaches may also be more capable of representing the forces and fields linking communication structure to various contextual factors, particularly when entities are conceived in terms of location.

cation contents. Another approach could involve overlaying the rest areas and work stations on the same map, using different colors which highlight the functional linkage of particular communication behaviors to particular locations. Alternatively, in three dimensions, differing grids could be placed one on top of the other, with appropriate spacing between, to highlight the different intensity levels of particular locations associated with particular functions.

CONTEXTS

Gradients can make a significant contribution to our understanding of organizational communication structure by detailing the communication configurations which result from spatial and technological contacts. Elsewhere, even more detailed arguments have been made concerning the role of embedding features of technology and space on communication structure (see Chapters 6 and 7); here, a brief empirical example will illustrate some of the potential of gradients for graphically capturing the impact of these contextual factors.

The warehouse data generated from the G3D contour plotting program, found in Figure 4-1, demonstrated clearly that communication intensity in this warehouse was associated with the flow of work and the constraining influence of fixed and semifixed features. One area of communication was clustered within the office area with very little leakage outside, because of the constraints of fixed walls; relatedly, the highest peak was represented by the warehouse managers cubicle at coordinates 10, 10. The areas in the warehouse associated with shipping were in the lower middle of Figure 4-2, and this was the location of another cluster of communication activity. The other clusters toward the rear of the store were associated with departments (10, 20, 30, 40) where the goods were initially left by forklifts to be stocked in bins. Thus, as expected, technological and spatial factors shaped the communication structure of this organization.

Somewhat similarly, in the retail store, the relatively separated tasks shaped the communication structure. In fact, most of the store was characterized by a rather diffuse, isolated pattern of activities of relatively low frequency, characteristic of the sort of pattern one would expect of jobs which are not highly interdependent. The impact of fixed and semifixed features can be noted in the dearth of communication activities associated with such physical features as aisleways.

Thus, gradients are especially useful for examining spatial factors which constrain the development of communication structures. Particularly important here are such features as the presence of intrusive fixed barriers (e.g., the aisleways in the retail store), presence of semifixed features (e.g., bins in the warehouse), and ownership/territoriality, all

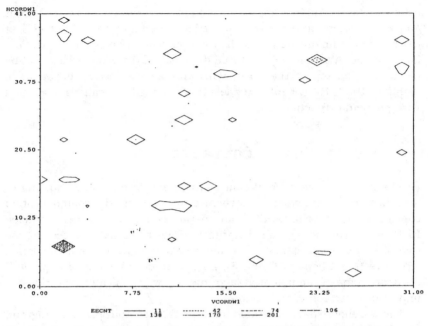

Figure 4-8.   Time 1 Sample Gradient for Number of Work Station Contacts

factors which may impede and regulate the flow of interaction in an organization (Allen, 1977; Davis, 1984; Sommer, 1967).[5]

Regrettably, some of the very contextual elements of the gradients approach which enhance its heuristic promise also limit the range of its applicability. First, gradients are most appropriate for organizational situations occurring in relatively confined planes such as those occurring within factories. Second, gradients are currently best applied to internal

---

[5] Gradients also have the potential of shedding new light on old research findings. Proximity and its relationship to communication provides us with one example of a promising area of inquiry which has been stalled because of a lack of appropriate methodologies. A number of studies have found that proximity was positively related to communication (Barnlund & Harland, 1963; Caplow, 1947; Festinger, Schacter, & Back, 1950; Gullahorn, 1952; Merton, 1948). The early interest in this area dissipated partly because the dearth of techniques available for precisely investigating the relation of physical environments to communication, techniques which were rich in their heuristic implications. More recent studies have focused on the impacts of office landscaping, which requires even more precise techniques for linking communication to physical factors, with findings that open-office environments increase communication (Allen & Gerstberger, 1973) and decrease feelings of privacy and satisfaction (Oldham & Brass, 1979; Sundstrom, Burt, & Kamp, 1980). To date most of these studies have been hampered by rather primitive measurement and analytic techniques (except perhaps for Monge & Kirste's, 1980, study). Gradients offer a set of tools for much more sophisticated analysis of the impacts of physical structure on communication.

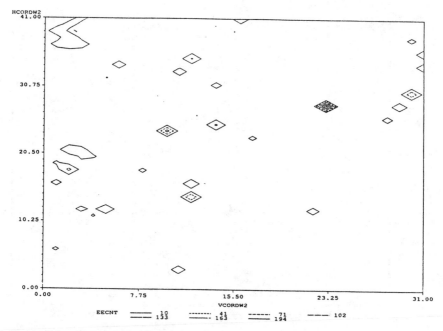

Figure 4-9. Time 2 Sample Gradient for Number of Work Station Contacts

communication, since outgroup communication is typically mediated and geographically diffused. Third, not all of an individual's organizational communication occurs within a confined work space, which limits the range of communication activities which can be directly examined by this technique.

TEMPORAL STABILITY

Gradients offer a number of interesting ways of examining temporal stability, particularly in terms of the continuous motion features of some graphic systems which permits the analysis of communication processes, such as diffusion, over time. Figures 4-8, 4-9, and 4-10 present the results for frequency of contact (EECNT1, EECNT2, and EECNT3) over three points in time in the retail store. While somewhat primitive in terms of causal intervals (1½ months) and number of time points examined, these figures reveal some very interesting temporal differences in retail activities. First, there was a general decline in activity for the right hand side of the store, particularly at the jewelry station. Curiously, the office area had a curvilinear set of contacts, with a peak at time 2, which

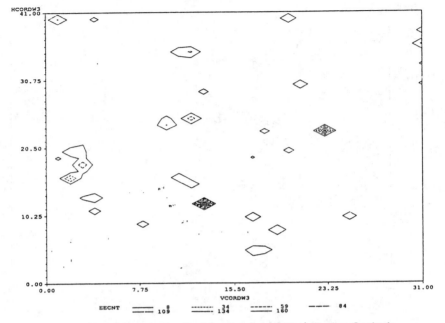

Figure 4-10. Time 3 Sample Gradient for Number of Work Station Contacts

coincided with a series of management interventions, which resulted in substantial layoffs in the store immediately before this time period. The cashiers generally had an increase in frequency over these three points in time.

Perhaps most interesting were patterns involved in the shifts in contacts which appear to reflect seasonal variations in retail activity. At time 1, around Christmas, the peak activity areas were centered around toys, trim-a-tree, and jewelry; at time 2, which was in mid-February, housewear and fabrics became more important, perhaps reflecting the bitter winters in this area; and finally, at time 3, in March, just before Easter, there was a cluster of activity around ladies wear. All of this reflects the seasonal nature of retail operations.[6]

---

[6] While some of the problems associated with network analysis and temporal stability may also be present in gradient research, they should not be as severe. In particular, the statistical analysis of dynamic features of gradients, particularly in the context of work done in geography and meteorology, is much more well developed and appears to present more tractable problems. In addition, methodological difficulties associated with measurement error (e.g., missing values) are less severe. However, the greatest advantage may lie at the substantive level, since, if the context of gradients (e.g., the physical environment) is itself relatively stable, the nature of gradients within them should also be relatively stable.

STRENGTHS AND WEAKNESSES

Substantive Weaknesses

Perhaps the biggest drawback to the use of the gradient approach to communication structure is its difficulty in portraying relationships, at least in the conventional sense.[7] But this drawback is also an opportunity, because it may force us to think about relationships in different, more encompassing ways. Of course, the very communication intensity data itself is an indicator of relationships, but they are not specified in the complete and direct manner that they are in network analysis. When individuals are clustered together, as they were in the shipping and office areas of the warehouse, relationships can be assumed but not really known. Much like network analysis, gradients can reveal cliques and isolates in organizational settings. For example, very much in the manner described by Rogers and Kincaid (1981), the physical structure of a social system serves as an antecedent to the development of network groupings. In fact, gradients and networks can offer complementary views of a phenomenon which could be helpful in achieving method triangulation.

---

[7] The pilot studies point to some potentially promising advantages to the gradient approach over more conventional approaches to analyzing communication structure, such as network analysis. (See Johnson, 1986, for a more systematic discussion.) First, there is not the same limit on the size of the organization analyzed (although there are definite limitations on the physical shape.) Second, the use of gradients demands the use of precise scaling, and there is the possibility, with overlays or color coding, of very rich descriptions of communication linkages. Third, while it certainly is not desirable, gradients are somewhat more robust in regard to missing data. They also offer greater inherent potential for use of sampling techniques. Fourth, the gradient computer packages typically have higher institutional credibility and also have somewhat easier tasks. Fifth, the gradients generated for data sets with large n's can be more interpretable than comparable communigrams (compare Figures 4-3 and 3-3, which picture the same data set).

According to Monkhouse and Wilkonson (1971) several factors directly related to measurement determine the manner in which gradients can be generated. First, the selected value intervals for gradients can lead to data acquisition errors (Stott, 1977). For example, in the illustrative data the communication frequency variable had an extreme range of values, which made the generation of contours problematic. In addition, tying the intensity measures to individual locations produced more dramatic contrasts than would probably occur in purely locationally based strategies. Second, the size of coordinates and their meaningfulness (more or less central to key features and peaks in common) ultimately determine the precision of the mapping and of measurement (Harrison, 1974). The self-report measures used here resulted in crude intervals which mask the sophistication of the graphics capability. Third, the method of interpolation or smoothing between data points can be too gross, which, especially for contours, can be a primary source of errors (Stott, 1977). In these examples the planes which were generated were somewhat misleading because of the large number of points where no communication was reported. Thus, gradients research is not without its problem areas, but solving them may not be so intractable as many of the methodological issues which confront network analysis.

Substantive Strengths

Communication gradients appear to have a more direct tie than network analysis to the underlying contextual factors which determine particular communication structures (Johnson, 1988a). For example, while physical factors have been found to be one of the major contributing factors to communication structure, until recently no approach to communication structure was capable of examining this association systematically. In fact, since gradients are so intimately tied to such organizationally related contextual factors as physical structure and technologies, they offer the potential of generating precise theoretical statements which then can be used to predict the development of particular communication structures (Monge & Eisenberg, 1987). Gradients can also potentially be used to investigate a number of other problems in large social systems, such as the relationship between communication intensity and productivity, satisfaction, privacy, and social density (see Johnson, 1987b). Somewhat relatedly, gradients can provide us with very interesting information on temporal stability and, somewhat relatedly, on the predictability of communication behaviors. However, the very source of the strength of this technique is also a weakness, since gradients can only be applied to communication within defined physical boundaries. Thus it would have only limited usefulness in tackling such problems as portraying communication within telecommunication networks, for example.

Since the growth of a discipline is intimately interrelated with the growth of techniques for examining its unique problems, this approach offers a wealth of potential payoffs. The most direct one is to provide researchers with an alternative means of investigating communication structure. Development of gradient related techniques can lead to conceptual advances, since they provide researchers with new means of thinking about and analyzing communication structure.

chapter 5

Cultural Approaches

Interest in organizational cultures has increased dramatically in recent years within the field of organizational communication (e.g., Putnam & Pacanowsky, 1983). This interest arises partly out of the realization that meanings are created through the social communication people have with each other; they are emergent properties of this communication (Barnett, 1988). Communication thereby constructs the realities of the organization, and in turn organizational culture shapes how members communicate (Pacanowsky & O'Donnell-Trujillo, 1982). Unique corporate cultures are distinguishable through the values, beliefs, activities, stories, language, and so on, which emerge from the intersubjective interactions of organizational members (Deal & Kennedy, 1982; Pacanowsky & O'Donnell-Trujillo, 1982). Employees come to understand the organization and their function within it through their shared consensus on the cultural values and norms of the organization.

Pacanowsky and O'Donnell-Trujillo (1982) talk about organizational culture as how "organizational life is accomplished communicatively." Communication relates to culture in three major ways: it creates it, it maintains it, and it changes it. Theorist in the social sciences have differed on the overall relation between culture and social structure, with Parsons, for example, arguing that culture is distinct from social structure while operating as a major exogenous influence on it, while Levi-Strauss argues that cultural symbols and meanings are the essence of social structure itself (Blau, 1981). Culture emerges out of communication and in turn constrains communication. This circular causal relationship has led some to define culture as a communication phenomenon (Barnett, 1988). Thus, culture can be seen as both process and context. In this chapter the focus will primarily be on the role of culture in providing a context for communication activities in an ongoing organization. In this sense culture is centrally concerned with the routinization of behavior—a subject which is receiving increasing theoretic attention (Rapoport, 1982). The first section will focus on the constraining impact of rules on communication relationships; next, configurations related to rituals and subcultures will be examined; and then temporal and contextual factors will be discussed.

RULE-GOVERNED RELATIONSHIPS BETWEEN ENTITIES

Rules for gathering, storing, communicating, and using information are essential elements or organizational operating procedures. (Feldman & March, 1981, p. 171)

Rules are like an invisible skein which bundles together all the technological and social aspects of organizations. (Perrow, 1972, p. 29)

Rules do a lot of things in organizations: they protect as well as restrict; coordinate as well as block; channel effort as well as limit it; permit universalism as well as provide sanctuary for the inept; maintain stability as well as retard change; permit diversity as well as restrict it. (Perrow, 1972, p. 32)

The major advantage of rules is that they provide predictability. They specify who is to do what, when, where, and sometimes how. (Hage & Aiken, 1970, p. 21)

Cultural approaches promote an in-depth understanding of the substance of communication relationships and of the constraining forces on them. Perhaps the most traditional way of looking at structural relationships is in terms of formal (especially bureaucratic) organizational rules. The notion of *rule* has always been central to theorizing about organizations (Perrow, 1972; Porter, Allen, & Angle, 1981). In fact, the earliest thinking about bureaucracy noted the importance of rules for determining the actions of organizational members and indeed every bureaucratic organization has an elaborated set of formal rules (Rogers & Agarwala-Rogers, 1976).

Formal rules have also been seen as one of the primary means used by organizations to control the activities of their members, and the extent of this formalization has traditionally been considered an important element of organizational structure (Hage & Aiken, 1970; Pfeffer, 1978). Rules have also been viewed as a means of minimizing communication activities and therefore costs, since it can be presumed that rules will be followed most of the time, therefore minimizing the need for direct intervention through communication to control the actions of organizational members (Pfeffer, 1978).

While rules constrain behavior, they can also be enabling. They limit the raw exercise of power in the organization and thus protect lower-level organization members (Pfeffer, 1978), partially because rules also mean workers know what is not expected of them (Morgan, 1986). Since rules often require some creativity in their application and interpretation (McPhee, 1985) they can also preserve the autonomy of organizational members (Perrow, 1972).

"To the extent that regular, habitual patterns of behavior are noted in communication activities...we say that certain rules...are in effect" (Farace et al., 1977, p. 132). Many of the deeper elements of cultural value systems become embedded and reflected in the rules governing organizational members' behaviors (Poole & McPhee, 1983); thus, "at the heart of an organization's rule system is its culture" (Cushman, King, & Smith, 1988, p. 78). These emergent rules are what communication scholars have focused on most in recent years. For our purposes rules will be considered to be followable, prescriptive, contextual, and they pertain to behavior (Shimanoff, 1980). Thus rules provide clear guidelines for action which are embedded in the context of an organization's culture. They are prescriptive in the sense that, if they are not followed, the organization may punish the violator in some manner. Rules may also function to regulate, evaluate, justify, correct, and predict behavior (Shimanoff, 1980). Indeed, a high level of coorientation, or agreement, about rules is a necessary condition for coordination in organizational settings (Schall, 1983).

The first distinction that must be made concerning rules is whether the rule is formally or informally proscribed (Farace et al., 1977). Formal rules are official and written. For example, the Army has a number of formal rules concerning who may initiate conversations with superior officers. Violation of these rules, especially in wartime, can result in a court martial. Informal rules, while not written down, still may contain clear expectations concerning the behavior of organizational members. If they are violated, the resulting punishments may be as severe as those for violations of formal rules. For example, the organization may have the informal rule "Thou shalt not criticize thy boss in public." Violators of this rules may learn that punishments can be quite severe and swift.

Most troublesome for employees is the reality that the formal and informal rules of an organization are often in conflict (Brown & McMillan, 1988). For example, companies often state officially that their managers have open door policies. They expect their managers to be available to employees, so that employees can come in and talk to managers about anything that is of concern to them. However, employees soon find that managers are very busy. If the employee is seen as constantly bothering the boss over trivial problems, then the boss may form a negative evaluation such as "This employee needs too much direction." This evaluation, if included in formal appraisals of the employee, could be extremely damaging. This is but one example of how an understanding of informal rules is more critical to an employee's advancement than an understanding of formal organizational policies.

Cushman and Whiting (1972) distinguish between two general types of rules which are critical to our understanding of organizational communication structure: content and procedural. *Content* rules govern how symbols (e.g., words) are used in organizations. They also can refer to such issues as the topics that are permissible to discuss with a supervisor. For example, I am unlikely to want to discuss at length with my supervisor a perception I have that older people cannot handle stress, especially if my supervisor is nearing retirement age. On the other hand, providing my supervisor with suggestions which might improve efficiency could be highly rewarded content in some organizations.

Procedural rules are perhaps the most central to the development of organizational communication structures. These rules have a major impact on the patterning of communication relationships in an organization. They govern such things as when an interaction will take place, how long it will last, where it will take place, and so on. Most important in this context are interactant selection rules and transmission rules. Interactant selection rules govern to whom I can send messages. These rules will ultimately have a major influence on the form and shape of a communication network. If I cannot send messages to people more than one level below or above me in the hierarchy, my level of vertical communication is severely restricted. Transmission rules govern what I can do to a message that I am sending to someone else in the organization. If I am permitted to substantially modify the content of the message, then it is more likely that the sort of problems in vertical communication discussed earlier in this book will emerge.

Practical force determines the strength of an organization's rule system and the degree to which it can predict individual interactions. There are several factors that determine the degree of practical force in a rule system. First, the degree of coorientation of the interactants determines their level of intersubjectivity. If two parties have a consensus on the nature of a rules and its importance for various goal states, then there is more practical force. Second, the specificity of rules can effect their level of ambiguity. Third, the degree to which rule systems allow multiple paths in the pursuit of goals also influences practical force. Fourth, there is the strength of the sanctions imposed when rules are violated (Poole & McPhee, 1983). Fifth, while rules promote stability, they are not very effective in changing organizational circumstances (Pfeffer, 1978). All of this implies, of course, that there are interactions not governed by organizational rule systems, and that there can be conflicts between multiple rules systems (e.g., management and workers), where interactants have some discretion in negotiating their own rules systems. However, a certain minimum level of rules, and relatedly intersubjectivity, are a necessary ingredient for successful communication.

CONFIGURATIONS

Structural configurations reveal the overall pattern formed by the interaction of relationships, entities, and contexts. At the macrolevel, at least in the sense of the previous approaches to structure, there is not an equivalent holistic view of the configurations of an organization represented in the cultural approach. Especially lacking is the degree of precision and variety of indicators which can reveal overall patterns that are so central to the prior approaches to organizational structure. Work on configurations has primarily examined the group level in cultural approaches, particularly focusing on rituals and the interaction of subcultures.

Rituals

Despite the interest in organizational culture, specific elements of culture have not been comprehensively studied in organizations. Although individual elements of organizational cultures have been identified—relevant constructs, practices, vocabulary, metaphors, and stories (Deal & Kennedy, 1982; Pacanowsky & O'Donnell-Trujillo, 1982)—only a handful of studies have focused on one or another of these elements. One specific element of culture which has a number of potential implication for organizational communication structure is the study of communication rituals. Beyer and Trice (1984) describe *rituals* as events in which much of a culture surfaces due to their behavioral groundings. Rituals are a good focus for cultural studies, in that they consolidate several cultural elements which allows for more in-depth inquiry of other variables (Beyer & Trice, 1984). Rituals also reveal the interpenetration of deep and surface structures (Conrad, 1983). Indeed, communication rituals themselves, in addition to being reflections of culture, are also elements of communication structure, since they represent relatively stable configurations of communication relationships between entities within an organization.

Researchers have identified communication rituals in their own distinct ways, with many combining rituals with organizational rites. Pacanowsky and O'Donnell-Trujillo (1982, p. 126) depict rites and rituals as those behaviors which "members regularly or occasionally participate in." For example, weekly staff meetings, morning coffee gatherings, or bimonthly marketing blitzes. Trice and Beyer (1984, p. 126) define these behaviors as "relatively elaborate, dramatic, planned sets of activities that consolidate various forms of cultural expressions into one event, which is carried out through social interactions, usually for the benefit of an audience." An example might be a presentation of the salesperson-of-the-month trophy before the recipient's work group. Barnett (1988, p. 108) defines rites and rituals as "programmatic and routinized activities of everyday life that enable the organization to accomplish its goals." For our purposes communication rituals are those recurring activities which organizational members participate in, which are communicative, and which are relatively elaborate, since they contain multiple forms of cultural expressions.

More specifically, researchers have begun to categorize various types of rites and rituals. For example, Pacanowsky and O'Donnell-Trujillo (1983) consider four types of rituals: personal, task, social, and organizational. *Personal rituals* refer to unique behaviors of individuals which "are 'trademark' performances that not only solidify the actor's organizational identity, but inform and orient others to those identities" (Pacanowsky & O'Donnell-Trujillo, 1983, . p. 16). For example, a baseball pitcher who stomps around on the mound before delivering a pitch is giving a trademark performance. *Task rituals* are those day-to-day behaviors which revolve around getting the job done; they are the routine practices in which employees engage in the process of accomplishing their tasks. *Social rituals,* including the Friday beer blast, holiday parties, and company softball games, aid organizational members in identifying the membership status or role of themselves or their work group within the organization. Examples of the final type of rituals, *organizational rituals,* include company picnics, board of directors' meetings, and executive succession ceremonies.

The literature has identified many functions that rituals perform in organizations. First, rituals transmit values and norms within the organization (Deal & Kennedy, 1982; Trice & Beyer, 1984). Second, "participation in such events provides access for members to a particular shared sense of reality" (Pacanowsky & O'Donnell-Trujillo, 1982, p. 126). Third, they provide dramatic illustrations of an organization's culture in action (Deal & Kennedy, 1982). Fourth, rituals reveal information about organizational practices, thus guiding behaviors (Trice & Beyer, 1984). Fifth, they can also reveal information about organizational practices, thus guiding behaviors (Trice & Beyer, 1984). Fifth, they can also reveal power relationships within organizations (Trice & Beyer, 1984). Sixth, they can provide emotional support for organizational members (Harris & Sutton, 1986). In sum, rituals help employees make sense of their work environments.

Buster, Eckert, Friedland, and Johnson (1987) conducted a study of rites and rituals in a high-technology organization which points to the relationship between rituals and other approaches to organizational communication structure. This study suggested that one's position within the communication structure of an organization had important cultural implications. Specifically, explicit differences between boundary spanners (e.g., systems engineers), who have links with members of other organizations, and nonboundary-spanning personnel existed in terms of the rites and rituals in which they engaged. When prompted for subjective judgments of the value of organizational events, nonboundary-spanning personnel reported one or more social activities as least preferred. Furthermore, nonboundary-spanning personnel reported a high proportion of task-related activities as preferred, especially meetings of various types (e.g., planning, sales, marketing). In contrast, systems engineers did not express any dissatisfaction regarding social events, while failing to report task-related activities to the same extent as non-boundary-spanning personnel. Indeed, social rituals were frequently mentioned; when asked, "Which activities do you look forward to the most?" system engineers responded with beer blasts, Christmas parties, picnics, and ski trips.

It seems system engineers use these activities to help them feel a part of the company socially, while the nonboundary spanners are functionally integrated more deeply into the organization because of their day-to-day interaction within the company's environment. The main function of the rites and rituals to the system engineers, then, becomes a means of identifying themselves and their positions as part of the organization. In this instance rites and rituals maintain a sense of integration with the organization for the system engineers.

Following up on this exploratory study, Buster, Friedland, Eckert, and Johnson (1988) used self-report questionnaires to examine specific hypotheses which argued that rituals were critical to the level of role ambiguity and commitment among members of this high-tech organization. The results revealed an overall pattern of support for the hypotheses. The extent to which the interest in organizational culture can be translated into in-depth explorations of specific aspects of organizational cultures is perhaps the most important test of the heuristic value of the cultural approach. This research suggests that communication rituals offer a rich area for such studies.

Subcultures

As organizations grow, they tend to develop subcultures. This is a result of well-defined communication networks in which individuals communicate with a restricted group of people within the organization. (Barnett, 1988, p. 105)

One of the most interesting problems for a cultural approach is the presence of various subcultures within an organization. These subcultures are often associated with coalitions and political processes. Subculture-to-subculture relationships form important configurations within the organizations, and the manner in which these groupings relate to each other through various cultural elements has important consequences for the organization. Communication across organizational subgroups is often difficult and subject to distortion because of the different language schemes, goal orientations, and task differentiations (Katz & Tushman, 1979). However, the presence of subcultures also raises the important question of whose culture it is anyway. Is an organizational culture a reflection of the societal culture in which it is embedded, is it the amalgamation of various cultures, or can we speak of dominant cultures (e.g., management) which officially represent the organization to the larger environment?

Much of the interest in a cultural approach stemmed from a recognition that organizational performance was associated with the societal cultures in which an organization was embedded, what has been termed a comparative approach to organizational culture (Smirchich & Calas, 1987). Thus the development of Theory Z, which attempted to systematize the linkages between Japanese organizational forms and the societal-level culture (Ouchi, 1981). These societal differences also produce differences in organizational communication, particularly structures (Chao & Gordon, 1979; Triandis & Albert, 1987).

However, specifying the association between organizational cultures and societal cultures has always been problematic. In the United States democratic principles are valued at the societal level, but authoritarian practices are widely accepted within U.S. organizations. This issue is especially important to our understanding of multinational organizations. Perlmutter (1965) has classified multinational organizations broadly into three types: ethnocentric, polycentric, and geocentric. *Ethnocentric* multinationals are dominated by their home offices and have centralized operations, while *polycentric* multinationals are more decentralized and attempt to accommodate themselves to local differences in business practices. In both of these cases the cultural orientation of the multinational is clear: for ethnocentric multinationals it is the home country, and for polycentric it is the host.

Perhaps the most interesting case, however, is the *geocentric* multinational, which operates from a more truly global perspective. It is often difficult to isolate a geographic home base for these companies; they recruit and promote key personnel from a variety of countries, and they try to develop policies and practices without reference to any one country. These companies want to have uniform organizational practices, including structure and culture. However, the development of this type of multinational in pure form revolves around the possibility of the existence of multicultural men, individuals whose value systems transcend those of nation states. Hofstede (1980, 1984), who has perhaps the most widely recognized research program in this area, argues strongly against this possibility, at least for efficient organizational operations. In effect, he argues organizations and their members are bound to national cultures. He bases his argument on the common frame of reference, the taken-for-granted reality, provided by an orientation to a dominant national culture.

Of course, this is an empirical question and there does appear to be at least suggestive empirical (e.g., Edstrom & Galbraith, 1977; Lee & Larwood, 1983) and anecdotal evidence (e.g., Morgan, 1979) that the existence of multicultural man and geocentric multinationals is possible. This possibility creates some interesting problems for the linkage of deep and surface structures, since, implicitly, deep structures are associated with larger societal frames of reference and are thus embedded in religious, political, and other value systems associated with societies. What possibilities exist for surface structures that are dominated solely by deep structures driven by organizational imperatives?

A partial answer to this question may lie in examining the nature of intraorganizational subcultures. Early approaches to culture tended to assume that there was one culture within an organization, or at least one dominant one, usually identified with management (Deal & Kennedy, 1982). Indeed, from this perspective culture becomes a variable management can manipulate for its own ends (Smirchich & Calas, 1987). While comforting to management, this perspective vastly oversimplifies life in modern, complex organizations. In fact, some of the early classics of organizational research, such as the Hawthorne studies, involved the recognition of subcultures within organizations, which often had direct impacts on such crucial matters as group productivity.

The existence of multiple cultures and their configuration into coalitions can be taken as a given in most organizations (Eisenberg et al., 1988; Morgan, 1986). Perhaps the crucial question relates to whether or not there is a dominant subculture or more of a pluralistic arrangement of subcultures in organizations. The emergence of one form or another may be in part dependent on the duality of concerns related to collaboration and control (Frost, 1987). The weighting on these dimensions can determine the extent of pluralism in an organization, with control associated with the emergence of dominant subcultures and collaboration associated with pluralism.

All of this of course has direct implications for structure. If management is the dominant subculture in the organization, then riefications of the power relationships of this subculture, such as the formal organizational chart, take on added significance. Indeed, in some organizations there will be substantial overlaps between formal and cultural approaches, especially when management dominates through bureaucratic structures. Thus, deeper structural elements become reified in the formal structure of the organization, which protects existing power blocks and gives them the cloak of rationality (Mumby, 1987). Similarly, coalitions form to reinforce and to also subvert this formal structure, and this leads to emergent informal communication networks whose patterns stabilize in part from opposition to the formal structure (Brown & McMillan, 1988). Thus, it is in a subculture's interest that its symbols become a part of the taken-for-granted meanings that structure organizational life. This structure then reflexively mediates and reproduces these interests (Mumby, 1987). However, if there are in reality, as there often are in organizations like hospitals and universities, multiple, more or less equal subcultures, then a formal organizational chart has little real significance for the organization and coactivational approaches to organizational structure take on more significance.

While there have been countless studies on how dominant coalitions, particularly management, exert power and influence, there is not a similar wealth of research concerning how roughly equivalent coalitions relate to each other in more pluralistic organizations, particularly at deeper levels. Some have suggested that organizational structure is the result of the conscious negotiation between subgroups that have defined themselves in terms of shared values and beliefs, and that a political cultural analysis begins with the concept of a negotiated order between these groups (Lucas, 1987). One way in which subcultures may relate to each other at the deeper levels of culture is through the usage of symbols and metaphor.

Meyer's (1984) research on the use of metaphors related to coalitions in a hospital setting is very interesting in this regard. He argues that there are four dominant root metaphors which serve as decision making models for different coalitions: organism (physicians), computation (administrators, government agencies), cybernetics (boards of directors), and pluralism (the interaction of major coalitions) (see Table 5-1). In making decisions concerning medical equipment, it is unlikely that one of these metaphors can totally dominate; what is needed is an overlap of argument that can make symbolic sense in the context of more than one model. Thus coalitions are built on the overlap of symbol systems as well as relationships.

The process by which this is accomplished may relate directly to the concept of strategic ambiguity put forth by Eisenberg (1984). At its heart this concept refers to the intentional omission of contextual cues in messages to promote multiple interpretations of messages in receivers.

Table 5-1.* Models for Hospital Decision Making

	Clinical Model	Fiscal Model	Political Model	Strategic Model
Root metaphor	Organism	Computation	Pluralism	Cybernetics
Espoused values	Maximizing patient welfare, advancing medical knowledge	Maximizing wealth, fiscal stability	Political assimilation of competing interests	Formulating and realizing institutional missions
Typical structuring of decisions	Professional collegia	Embodied in standardized procedures and analytical programs	Shifting issue-specific coalitions within quasi-legislative forums	Long range planning and policy making bodies
Information gathering	Personal experience and professional media	Systematic search, quantitative measurement	Gathered, used, and withheld tactically	Gleaned from diffuse sources, combined intuitively, and extrapolated holistically
Bases of influence	Professional eminence and certification of clinical expertise	Financial and computational acuity	Power based on professional status, hierarchical position, or resource scarcity	Intuitive acuity, credibility, and charisma

*Drawn from Meyer (1984, p. 10)

Power in this context relates to the interpretation of ambiguity; who governs these interpretations and governs the ambiguity can be said to have power (Mumby, 1987). Strategic ambiguity promotes the integration of diverse coalitions, facilitates organizational change, and preserves privileged positions. While it is necessary to achieve some consensus for organizations to be successful, it is not always necessary to achieve high levels of consensus among the operational goals of individuals. Strategic ambiguity is in part accomplished by setting goals that are very abstract. Thus a university president may exhort his or her faculty to achieve excellence. Some faculty members will interpret this as a mandate to redouble their efforts in research, others to establish innovative departmental curricula, and to still others it will mean improving classroom instruction. The point is not that these are conflicting goals, but rather that they are complementary ones, if the entire institution is to achieve excellence. The pursuit of that goal becomes a means of integrating what would otherwise be conflicting coalitions within the institution.

Heimstra (1983) provides an interesting illustration of these points in his examination of changes in organizational coalitions in response to the shared interpretations of subcultures of the term *information technology*. This term encompasses a variety of subterms, and it can be said to be relatively ambiguous, at least in the sense that it is subject to multiple interpretations. In general, these interpretations relate to the impacts of information technologies in terms of speed, efficiency, communication changes, depersonalization, motivation, and revolution. Most interestingly, symbol manipulation relating to information technologies reflected the changing status of various organizational groups. Thus, *clericals* become *word processing operators* and *skeptics* (often older managers) are labeled as *old-timers*.

While cultural approaches have been considered the primary means of understanding the development of configurations related to organizational structures at deeper phenomenal levels, they are not the only means that organizations have of providing a deeper medium for interactions to occur. In an insightful article Wilkins and Ouchi (1983) argue that there are essentially three mediums for interactions within organizations: clans (culture), market, and bureaucracy. Wilkins and Ouchi argue that it is unlikely that an organization will have a single culture which can provide a medium for interaction; rather, there will be many local organizational cultures (subgroups). The interaction between these groups must occur in a medium that transcends their individual cultural orientation. Organizations need some way of determining the value of exchange relationships which serve as the basis for cooperative interactions. In market approaches transactions are governed by price mechanisms, and in bureaucratic approaches they are governed by legal means. In any case certain levels of reciprocity must be met as a universal requirement for collective effort. A cultural, or clan, orientation is perhaps the most difficult of the three to develop in organizations and is the one that is most uniquely associated with idiosyncratic organizational understandings rather than more general societal ones. Clan control of transactions requires the development of shared social knowledge in two areas: an interpretive framework that helps interactants understand what is in the best interest of the entire organization, and a perception of goal congruence for all of the entities in an organization. Thus in this view a strong culture would be one which provides a medium for interaction, metaphoric or symbolic, between diverse subcultures.

CONTEXT AND TEMPORAL STABILITY

In addition to the role of cultural elements like rites and rituals in transmitting culture, often structure itself becomes a means of metacommunicating about cultural elements (McPhee, 1985); "(formal) structure communicates about constraints organizational members face in the communication process" (Jablin, 1987, p. 300). Thus, following the earlier work of Levi-Strauss and the more recent work of Giddens, many organizational communication scholars have become concerned with the deeper processes associated with more surface structures (e.g., Frost, 1987; McPhee, 1985; Monge & Eisenberg, 1987; Poole & McPhee, 1983; Riley, 1983). At the core of this concern is the duality of Giddens's *structuration,* in which every action is argued to both produce and to reproduce structure and the underlying social system (McPhee, 1985). Structures are seen in this perspective as the rules and resources used in interaction (Riley, 1983). These rules and resources provide the medium for interaction, but they are also an outcome of it, since they are only made real in action (Riley, 1983). Thus communication structure is crucial to both the emergence and the maintenance of culture; structure promotes temporal stability but also is a source of change. Culture also has important consequences for temporal stability through its contextualizing properties. The establishment of a culture entails a large range of constraints which act to stabilize communication relationships. Indeed, some have argued that the persistence of cultural elements over time is one of the primary means which can be used to distinguish them from other approaches to organizational communication such as climate (Falcione & Kaplan, 1984).

The relative impact of context on communication may be related to Hall's distinction between low- and high-context cultures. In *low-context cultures* (LCC) most of the information transmitted in a message must be contained in the message itself. On the other hand, in *high-context cultures* (HCC) the interpretation of messages is primarily determined by the implicitly shared social and cultural knowledge of the context of the HCC system. This distinction has important implications for the nature of communication in organizations. Communication in low-context cultures is much more cumbersome, while communication in HCC systems can be rich in meaning and significance (Ting-Toomey, 1985). In fact, the source of a message and who is included in the communication loop may be fraught with significance. Thus, the structural patterning of messages becomes part of the message itself. However, these deep layers of meaning come at a cost; it takes a long period of time and much effort for actors to come to this level of understanding.

Poole and McPhee (1983) have presented an interesting perspective on the successively deeper layers of structure in organizations. First, they argue, are system patterns which constitute observable relationships and regularities (e.g., networks and gradients). Second are practical structures which primarily refer to rules and resources that directly govern interaction. Third are background structures which are rules and resources which provide the basis for interaction and give it meaning. Finally, collective attitudes, which constitute more generalized conceptions of a social system, may be what most organizational members naively conceive of as climate and culture. Poole and McPhee (1983) go on to argue that the degree of structure is determined by the interaction between these levels. They also argue that instability may be a direct result of the relationship between them. Thus, a repressive bureaucratic organization, which is dominated by practical structures, may force change because of internally generated opposition.

STRENGTHS AND WEAKNESSES

Substantive Weaknesses

The major substantive drawback of the cultural approach may come in what it reveals about configuration.[1] Except at the micro level of individ-

---

[1] Most cultural studies within the field of organizational communication have used qualitative methods. One of the key advantages of exploratory, qualitative studies is their ability to uncover the unexpected. For example, in Buster et al.'s (1987) qualitative study of rites and rituals the researchers noted that these methods allowed room for *error and surprise,* in Daft's (1983) terms. Thus, unexpectedly, studying rites and rituals led to the "discovery" of their critical linkage to the more structural, systems-oriented variables associated with boundary spanning and the general issues of cliques and coalition formation. This linkage would not have been discovered in a more narrowly pursued research design.

Cultural studies can also use more unobtrusive data-gathering methods such as content analysis (e.g., Miller, Zook, & Mack, 1987). In this connection Trice and Beyer (1984) have also suggested a number of advantages to studying rites within organizations. Since rites are

ual interactions or the group setting of rituals, cultural approaches have not been too concerned with developing techniques for systematically describing communication behaviors across an entire organization. Thus, no technique is currently available for describing the overall pattern of culturally related communication behaviors at the level of the whole organization. Certainly, no technique is available that has the

---

planned, they grant the researcher the opportunity to more precisely develop a research agenda and study design. Also, many rites are performed for an audience; thus, if the researcher can gain access to an event, his or her observations should have little effect on the organizational activity, and they can be made relatively unobtrusively. Most importantly, since much of the culture of an organization surfaces at these rites, through the many cultural expressions present, the researcher can broaden his or her picture of the organizational culture and the use of communication within it. So some of the more public cultural elements permit the use of techniques which may not, in and of themselves, effect results.

Perhaps the biggest drawback to cultural studies in organizations at the moment is the lack of tools available to examine specific organizational cultural elements. While the examination of organizational cultures has increased in importance in recent years within the field of communication (e.g, Putnam & Pacanowsky, 1983), the specific elements of organizational culture identified by Pacanowsky and O'Donnell-Trujillo (1982)—relevant constructs, facts, practices, vocabulary, metaphors, stories, and rites and rituals—have been explored by at most a handful of studies. One test of any organizing paradigm is its association with systematic, comprehensive research into its major topics (Morey & Luthans, 1985; Redding, 1979). It has yet to be demonstrated that the descriptive studies, which have characterized cultural approaches to date, will be transformed into more rigorous questions and hypotheses that can be used to generate testable theories which advance our general understanding of these processes in organizations.

A series of studies focusing on rituals in a high-tech organization point to the need for this sort of followup (Buster et al., 1987). The initial qualitative study revealed an emphasis on social rituals which was reflected in the company policy of picking up half the cost of any social event organized by employees which was open to all company/branch members. In addition, in informal discussions with executives it became clear that, at the corporate level, social activities were viewed as an important integrating mechanism. Their importance was related to management concerns about the retention of its technically trained personnel, the majority of whom work outside the company environment for lengthy intervals. However, the pattern of results found in the more systematic Buster et al. (1988) study suggest that social rituals occur only infrequently, and that they have a mixed impact on role ambiguity and commitment, with only the correlations associated with formal social gatherings being moderate in size. This pattern of results suggests the importance of following up qualitative studies with more systematic quantitative analysis of organizational phenomenon.

Partly because cultural studies are still in the early development stage, but also because of a substantial bias against quantitative methods (Smirchich & Calas, 1987), the plethora of measurement tools for operationalizing variables and computer/statistical/analytic tools available with the other approaches are just not available for cultural studies. This emphasis on qualitative methods, while appropriate for the early stages of investigation of any phenomenon, raises a host of difficulties associated with reliability and generalizability of findings and, even more importantly, the evolutionary accumulation of knowledge in this area. Even in the qualitative area there is some question concerning the validity of methods used for uncovering successively deeper elements of an organizational culture and discussing the translations between levels (see Deetz, 1982; Eisenberg, 1986; Rogers, 1987).

mathematical and computer sophistication of the network analysis and gradient approaches, although there are sophisticated methods available for describing culturally related values and attitudes (Barnett, 1988).

As in the formal approach, a major source of substantive confusion in the cultural approach comes in attempting to disentangle communication, structure, and culture. Some would argue that they are so inextricably intertwined that disentangling them robs these concepts of their conceptual significance. The resolution of this questions will in large part determine whether the cultural approach leads us to "poetic" insight into particular organizations, or leads to the gradual accumulation of scientific generalizations concerning culture in organizations.

Substantive Strengths

Structure and culture are intimately related to each other. The key advantage of the organizational culture approach comes in its usefulness in explaining the underlying contextual factors manifested in particular communication structures. One of the key factors behind management's interest in organization culture in recent years lies in its use as a tool to increase the predictability, and relatedly temporal stability, of organizational member behavior (see Smircich & Calas, 1987, for an alternative perspective). Management often believes that a strong organizational culture makes behavior more uniform and more in accordance with management's interests. Similarly, cultural approaches promote an in-depth understanding of communication relationships, contributing greatly to our understanding of how they form and what the substance of them is likely to be. In this connection cultural approaches also serve to promote the temporal stability of behaviors. In fact, most organizational socialization efforts are aimed at passing on and continuing the existing cultural behavior patterns of an organization to new members.

part II
Antecedents to Organizational Communication Structure

chapter 6

Spatial Factors

> The physical environment does not determine the structure of the social
> interactions, but rather it sets the limits to the possible variations that may
> occur. (Canter & Kenny, 1975, pp. 156-157)

Spatial dimensions of time-space relations are fundamental to most
scientific inquiry (Giddens, 1985; Sack, 1980; Urry, 1985). While communication science has paid increasing lip service to time in the last
decade (e.g., Monge, Farace, Eisenberg, Miller, & White, 1984), spatial
properties of communication behavior have received relatively little
attention. For a long time the social sciences have been spatially "blind,"
unattuned to the effects of distance and positioning on human interaction
(Massey, 1985; Sundstrom et al., 1980). But "spatial structure is now seen
not merely as an arena in which social life unfolds, but rather as a medium
through which social relations are produced and reproduced" (Gregory &
Urry, 1985, p. 3). In fact, spatial factors also represent a larger movement
in communication and management theory, since some view space as
equivalent to context in providing the medium within which social
interaction is embedded (Hatch, 1987; Pfeffer, 1982). As Pfeffer (1982) has
pointed out, examination of communication structure and spatial factors
serves as a very attractive alternative to traditional approaches to
organizational theory. This is especially so in his view since physical
characteristics are among the most enduring in an organization and
particular activities can come to be associated with particular locations. In
other words, they provide the context within which communication is
embedded.

For our purposes the physical environment will be considered to be
those elements of the built environment which surround and affect, by
their spatial and functional elements, communication behaviors within
organizations. The primary force which determines the impact of the
physical environment is the effect it has on the spatial relationships

between interactants. Indeed, it has been generally suggested that spatial relationships affect communication in organizations, small groups, and different cultural settings in a variety of ways (Monge & Kirste, 1980; Rogers & Kincaid, 1981; Sommer, 1967).

Steele (1973) has defined the physical environment of organizations by six main functions: (a) shelter and security, (b) social contact, (c) symbolic identification, (d) task instrumentality, (e) pleasure, and (f) growth. While Steele's framework was perhaps the first systematic attempt at specifying elements of the physical environment which relate to organizational functioning, it was not directly developed to deal with organizational communication. On the other hand, Davis (1984) provided a framework for directly examining the linkage between the physical environment and organizational communication. He specified three primary dimensions of the physical environment which related to communication. The first dimension Davis identified, *physical structure,* related to architectural factors and semifixed features which act to regulate social interaction. *Physical stimuli,* the second dimension, refers to aspects of the physical setting (e.g., noise) that intrude into the awareness of the individual and thus influence their behavior. Finally, *symbolic artifacts,* such as furnishings and amount of space assigned to individuals, are elements of the physical setting which guide the interpretation of the social setting.

Despite this wealth of potential research areas, the impact of the physical environment on organizational communication has remained a relatively understudied area (Davis, 1984; Johnson & Smith, 1985; Sundstrom et al., 1980). According to Buttimer (1980) there are at least five distinct levels of analysis of social space. First, *sociological space,* at the social-psychological level, investigates a person's position within society. Examples of this sort of analysis include various functional descriptions of the impact of physical space on organizational behavior (e.g., Davis, 1984; Steele, 1973). Second, *interaction space* focuses on the behavioral level investigating activity and circulation patterns. Third, the *symbolic level* investigates images, cognitions, and mental maps (see Evans, 1980; Saarinen & Sell, 1980, 1981, for reviews). Fourth, the *affective level* focuses on patterns of identification and territory. For example, examinations of culture's role in providing a sense of place (e.g., Rapoport, 1982). Finally, there is a *morphological level* which factor analyzes population characteristics to produce homogenous 'social areas.' This chapter will concentrate on interaction space, which focuses on behavior, investigating activity and circulation patterns and examining their implications for communication structure. In particular the focus will be on the impact of space on relationships and on the role of space in providing a context for communication structure. This chapter will conclude with a discussion of the linkage between the approaches to communication structure and spatial factors.

RELATIONSHIPS

Space, like communication, is somewhat of an ephemeral concept, since it is not composed of substances but rather helps define relationships between them (Sack, 1980; Urry, 1985). "The physical environment presents everyone with a set of initial conditions upon which behavior is largely contingent" (Archea, 1977, p. 134). For example, spatial factors associated with location and mobility constrain our selections of interactants. This constraint places limits on the range of individuals we can interact with and, by limiting this range, determines such fundamental relations as friendships (e.g., Evans & Wilson, 1949; Martin, 1974; Nahemow & Lawton, 1975).

In addition to determining with whom we form relationships, the nature of the space within which those relationships are embedded will often determine qualitative elements of those relationships as well (Ashforth, 1985). Qualitative effects include such things as the tension resulting from spatial violations and also feelings of privacy associated with well-being. For example, excessive noise makes polite, subtle instructions nearly impossible, and it can lead to isolation among workers (Ashforth, 1985; Canter, 1983; Mohr, 1971). Physical space can also constrain the meanings given to interactions within it. It is well known that the personal space characterizing an interaction reveals characteristics of relationships (e.g., status differences) (Aiello & Thompson, 1980). For example, some interactions may be viewed as threatening primarily because interactants are impinged on in a way they cannot control (Brower, 1980). Distance in fact can become a way of defining relationships.

The primary force underlying physical structure is the effect it has on the spatial relationships between interactants. Particularly important initially is the dispersion of locations of actors throughout an organization, which is the starting point for any communication gradient. While physical locations may be attributable to a number of factors (e.g., cultural), in organizations these locations are largely tied to technologies. These individual nodal locations provide the basic context for social interaction. Location can determine the information one is privy to and, thus, one's inclusion or exclusion from other organizational processes (Davis, 1984). Thus, physical location provides a static framework within which interaction is embedded. Two variables reveal contrasting dimensions of spatial relationships and their impact on the possible actors involved in interaction: *social density*, or the number of interactants in a space, and *proximity*, which refers to the spatial distances between interactants.

Social Density

Social density has been found to affect a number of organizational behaviors. Since social density refers to the number of interactants within a particular space, it effects the opportunities for communication and it is directly related to different types of technologies (Form. 1972). Increases in social density have often been associated with stress and withdrawal-oriented coping mechanisms, such as avoidance of communication (Baum & Valens, 1977; Brower, 1980; McCarrey. Peterson. Edwards. & von Kulmiz, 1974). On the more positive side, an optimal array of interactants within one's physical environment can promote growth and intellectual stimulation (Sundstrom et al., 1980). The presence of other interactants may also result in social facilitation (Sundstrom et al., 1980). Thus. it has been argued that at least moderate levels of social density are essential for stimulation and the promotion of task accomplishment (Szilagyi & Holland, 1980).

Proximity

Proximity is the dimension of physical structure which has traditionally been most clearly related to communication processes in organizations. The classic work of Caplow (1947), Gullahorn (1952), and Festinger, et al., (1950) identified a relationship between increasing physical proximity and increasing levels of communication in various social systems. Guetskow (1965) referred to this empirical generalization as one of the most common found in the organizational literature. Generally it has been argued that proximity relates to work accomplishment through such factors as increasing information exchange, increasing task facilitation, increasing coordination linkages, job feedback, the use of libraries in R & D laboratories, and decreasing role stress (Allen, 1977; Allen & Gerstberger, 1973; Korzenney, 1978; Szilagyi & Holland, 1980). It has also been found, when examining work flow diagrams, that positions scoring high on organizational centrality were located at the geographic center of an organization (Brass, 1981). In addition, in crosscultural research, it has been found that proximity contributes to the development of strong groupings in R & D laboratories (Keller, 1989).

Access

Social density and proximity could be considered to be primitive terms in our explanations of the impact of the spatial environment on communication. They are also clearly revealed in gradients, with high social density revealed in clusters of actors and elaborate contours. While these factors determine the initial encounters of actors, other physical factors may be needed to understand the maintenance of relationships and what happens after initial intercession. Perhaps the variable which best captures the relationship between communication structure and the physical environment is access. Access may also be the single most important criterion in evaluation by users of an information system (Rice & Shook, 1986).

Increases in social density and in proximity also increase our physical access to others. Thus, physical access provides the opportunity and occasion for interactions (Sykes, 1983). In fact, one of the major problems for individuals in organizations comes in controlling the access of many proximate others to them. Archea (1977) has argued that privacy can best be understood in a framework in which each person is viewed as at the center of a dynamic field of information to which he or she adjusts. The individual's regulation of interpersonal behavior is influenced by his or her access to others for monitoring and the opportunities others have to monitor him or her (exposure). Privacy then becomes inherently a matter of how we present ourselves visually to others; "matching one's spatial and behavioral conspicuousness with one's intentions is a key element of privacy regulation" (Archea, 1977, p. 134).

There are essentially two dimensions of privacy: (a) freedom from unwanted intrusion, and (b) freedom to determine time and place of communication (Canter & Kenny, 1975). Spatial behavior is often used by interactants to control (regulate) their interactions (Canter & Kenny, 1975). Failure to anticipate reactions of individuals to these considerations has led to the many unanticipated problems which have been found in employee reactions to open office environments which generally have not been found to improve efficiency and communication (Becker, 1981; Hatch, 1987; McCarrey et al., 1974; Zalesny & Farace, 1987). Indeed, open office environments are often viewed as a threat to privacy (Bennett, 1977), with attendant negative associations with job satisfaction and performance.

Problems in social density which are associated with crowding reflect a loss of control by interactants of intrusions; they also impact on communication through the process of social withdrawal as a reaction to this overload of social information (McCarthy & Saegert, 1978; Schmidt & Keating, 1979). It has been suggested that managers can increase their control over their physical environment by (a) removing stimuli, (b) manipulating stimuli, and (c) arranging stimuli differentially in the work space (Davis, 1984). People in this context can be viewed as stimuli, which can be arranged in space in such a manner as to promote and to retard task-related communication.

Thus, spatial elements contribute in important ways to the level of satisfaction of organizational members (Pfeffer, 1982). For example, social density has also been found to be associated with increased worker satisfaction (Szilagyi & Holland, 1980), although some would suggest that individuals try to maintain an optimal range of social contacts and that when this is violated, as it can be in modern office landscaping, worker satisfaction decreases (Sundstrom et al., 1980). The quality, satisfaction, and amount of worker interaction is not only associated with these static, embedded elements of the work place, but also with the more dynamic elements represented by mobility (Form, 1972).

Mobility

While both social density and proximity act to determine the access of individuals to each other in organizations, access is also effected by the relative mobility of individuals in the work place. Increasing mobility can be a direct result of transport technologies, but the necessity for this mobility can stem from utilitarian technological imperatives associated with coordination and control as well. Only when movement is introduced does the stasis represented by embedded elements transform itself into a dance which is characterized by relationships between interactants, with network analysis centrally concerned with revealing configurations of relationships. In fact, "the production and reproduction of social life depends upon knowledgeable human subjects tracing out routinised paths over space and through time, fulfilling particular projects whose realisations are bounded by structures of interlocking capability, coupling and steering constraints" (Gregory, 1985, p. 297).

> All social life occurs in, and is constituted by, intersections of presence and absence in the 'fading away' of time and the 'shading off' of space. The physical properties of the body and the *milieux* in which it moves inevitably give social life a serial character, and limit modes of access to 'absent' others across space. (Giddens, 1985, p. 283)

One of the most interesting bases for conceptualizing this dance of actors within the physical environment related to the emergence of human communication patterns is Hagarstrand's time space paths (see Gregory, 1985, for a discussion and critique). The central assumption of time geography lies in its recognition of the routinized character of daily life (Giddens, 1985). "Hagerstrand's approach is based mainly upon identifying sources of constraint over human activity, given by the nature of the body and the physical context in which activity occurs. Such constraint provides the overall 'boundaries' limiting behavior across time-space" (Giddens, 1985, p. 266).

The intersections of these time space paths determines the opportunities for communicative encounters, since they reveal the availability or nonavailability of others (Hagarstrand, 1982). The configurations of these time space paths can then be represented as probability contours which indicate the likelihood that interaction will occur at any particular location (Gregory, 1985). Hagarstrand's work (as summarized in Gregory, 1985, p. 308) can then be summarized in tripartite theoretical grid:

1. Space and time are *resources* on which individuals have to draw in order to realise particular *projects,* subject to:
2. three *constraints:*
   • capability constraints which defines space–time paths;
   • coupling constraints which define space–time bundles;
   • steering constraints which define space–time domains;
3. These constraints are interactive rather than additive, and their prisms delineate a series of *possibility boundaries* in space and time which correspond to (or map out) an underlying and evolving "logic" or structure."

In turn the relatively limited assortment of others with whom there are frequently reciprocated contracts constitute a person's information field (Hagarstrand, 1953). This field sharply diminishes with distance from an interactant's position (Hagarstrand, 1953). This assertion has an interesting corollary. The closer two interacts are, the more their information fields overlap, which could also have a bearing on strength of weak tie notions (Granovetter, 1973), which can be conceived of in terms of shared physical spaces as well as shared interactants.

Spatial factors can determine the pathways, physical or electronic, by which we access others. For example, job pressures, when coupled with distance, can lead to telephone use, and geographic dispersion can lead to the choice of channels such as electronic mail in organizational settings (Steinfield, 1985; Steinfield & Fulk, 1986). As a result spatial factors can determine the method by which we reach other interactants (Conrath, 1973; Hiltz & Kerr, 1980; Klauss & Bass, 1982; Steinfield, 1985). For example, Allen (1977) describes access in research and development laboratories as determined by gradually diminishing communication up to 50 feet away from an interactant, with communication beyond that characterized by a dramatic drop off. Hagarstrand (1953) also describes this in terms of a cone, with probabilities of communication diminishing with increasing distance. This dramatic drop-off may be the point at which an individual chooses to go to another plane, such as electronic channels, in his or her interaction with another. Therefore spatial factors affect channel selection in determinant ways and channels, particularly electronic ones, can be viewed as the communicative surrogate of mobility.

CONTEXT

An irreducable fact of human existence is that individuals are located within a physical world (Seamon, 1980). While individual locations in space may be attributable to a number of factors, they provide the basic context within which all communication occurs (Ashforth, 1985). Many have argued that it might be important to view the relationships in space between individuals at the deeper latent level of culture, especially in terms of an individual's subjective reactions to space (Buttimer, 1980; Rapoport, 1982). The structural impact of culture comes primarily in determining rules for interaction and interpreting and defining elements in the manifest physical environment. It also defines what activities are appropriate in particular spaces. Thus, while open office spaces may be appropriate for routine work, sensitive personal matters may only be appropriately discussed in enclosed rooms outside of public view (Pile, 1978).

Physical factors make visible and often stabilize such cultural elements as status systems (Rapoport, 1982); "the most enduring repetitions are those around particular places and objects" (Collins, 1981, p. 995). Thus, ritualized activities such as brown bag lunches may make clear the "in crowd" of a particular department, and an individual's locations in the lunch room may indicate his or her relative status. The constant repetition of this activity serves to reinforce status relationships within the group and, in this way, defines relationships, including communication and relationships, among its members. Indeed, it has been argued more generally that fixed physical distances among nodes are one source of stability in network structures (Barnett & Rice, 1985).

Physical factors often have symbolic value for organizations and those who interact within them. Thus, increasingly, organizations are using corporate architecture to define themselves to the public (and to their own members). The routinization provided by this architecture is often a crucial factor in the success of franchise operations like McDonald's, since they provide customers with a predictable, comfortable environment in which to pursue their projects (Rapoport, 1982). In addition, members of a culture who share the same physical space are exposed to the same ambient stimuli, thus providing a common experiential base and opportunity to jointly interpret events (Hackman, 1983). Thus, culture, when combined with physical factors in an organization, provides a major source of temporal stability and provides a context within which communication structures are formed.

SPATIAL FACTORS AND THE APPROACHES

As a way of summarizing the antecedent and outcome chapters, each chapter will conclude with a discussion of how the respective factors relate to each of the four approaches to communication structure. These discussions are somewhat limited by a lack of research. Some areas have been examined quite thoroughly, while others have been hardly examined at all, so these summaries are speculative and point to areas of research which would lead to a more balanced view of the relationship of communication structure to other factors.

The relationship of formal approaches to spatial elements has not been adequately addressed in the communication or management literature (Miller & O'Leary, 1989), although industrial engineers and architects have been very concerned with these issues. Thus, there is an extensive pragmatic literature on open office landscaping (Pile, 1978) and a variety of computer programs designed to facilitate physical layouts of plants and office, often explicitly based on communication between units (Bennett, 1977). Naturally, these techniques are heavily rational and share many of the strengths and weaknesses of formal approaches in general. Perhaps the most telling point in this connection is that, when people first move into buildings, they often complain about how formal things have become and how difficult it is to communicate (Canter, 1983). Thus the formal networks associated with physical location need to be 'fleshed out' by the actors to satisfy their individual needs. In this connection Canter (1983) has argued that, while having a minimal effect on formal networks, spatial factors can be expected to have a more pronounced effect on informal networks.

The effect of spatial elements on networks comes primarily in determining the formation of relationships. The impact of physical factors on relationship development is quite pronounced and is associated with such factors as proximity, social density, and access. While much is known about the impact of these factors on dyadic relationships, very few studies have been conducted at the level of the entire network. In one of the few explicit treatments on this topic, Canter (1983) found that open office plans were associated with "loose" networks, while more traditional office arrangements were found to result in stronger, but more exclusive networks. This study does suggest a direct relationship between the overall physical configuration of an office and that of its associated network.

Of course, gradients were designed to represent the linkage between physical location and communication structure. This approach offers much promise as a tool specifically suited for examining research relating communication structure and spatial factors. However, gradients represent a relatively new tool which have only been utilized in a few empirical studies. Part of the hope of gradient research lies in the specific linkage of contextual physical factors with communication structures. This is also the greatest strength of cultural approaches, but at a deeper level of understanding. Cultural factors in general have a significant impact on the development of particular architectures and their meanings (Rapoport, 1982). In turn these underlying cultural preferences determine what can be accepted as a legitimate formal plan and the emergent behaviors of actors within that plan.

As Pfeffer (1982) has suggested, then, it appears that examination of spatial factors has rich potential for increasing our understanding of organizational behaviors. Examination of spatial factors also offers the promise of a fecund ground for future development of theory since it is one of the major, if not the major, source of constraint on the activities of organizational members.

chapter 7

Technological Factors

It is strongly contended that the failure to examine the relationships between technology and communication can leave a major gap in our understanding of organizations. (Randolph & Finch, 1977, p. 1143)

Technology can be viewed, not just in the narrow sense of focusing on machines needed to produce physical goods, but in the broader sense of any systematic set of techniques which leads to organizational outputs. Technology has generally been broadly defined as the organizational process of transforming inputs to outputs (Fry & Slocum, 1984; Pfeffer, 1978). Naturally, an understanding of technology is fundamental to our understanding of organizations, but little is known about the precise impact of technology on communication structure.

Developments in technology have made the modern organization possible. They have permitted the geographic dispersions of organizations across the world and the development of organizations of enormous size. But the development of organizations in the last 150 years has also meant that face-to-face interactions have decreased, and that decision making, messages, and action are often geographically separated from sources. As a result the common core of meanings in organizations has been reduced, so that messages have to be very simple (e.g., numbers in MIS reports) in order to be understood. In short, technology has had an enormous impact on communication in organizations historically and this impact is accelerating with the development of new electronic forms of communication.

Technology also impacts the human composition of organizations, which has direct implications for communication processes. The diversity of skills needed in the modern organization increases the heterophily of its members, and generally heterophily can be associated with a variety of communication problems (Rogers, 1983). Different occupations also have different needs to seek information, and the information acquired has different consequences for their careers. Engineers, for example, are much more likely than scientists to be interested in information that is directly and narrowly relevant to their jobs in a particular organization (Allen, 1977).

Technological factors also have a significant impact on the spatial environment of organizations. In organizations spatial factors often determine the amount of stimulation we receive, a factor which may become very important in organizational design. For example, the organizational structure of Bell Laboratories and other divisions of the old Bell System purposively manipulated these factors. They used organization and spatial bonds to achieve appropriate levels of coordination, so that, for example, application-related development and design was organizationally linked to fundamental development but spatially removed from it, while it was organizationally separated from engineering but spatially proximate. This insured the proper mix of coordination between these units that a focus on one or another forms of relationships would not have achieved (Morton, 1971). Allen (1977) noted similar phenomenon in R & D laboratories he investigated. He found that organizational members tended to communicate only with those with whom they were bureaucratically grouped, but that this isolation could be ameliorated by spatial factors.

The remainder of this chapter will focus on the impacts of technological factors on organizational communication structure concentrating on context, relationships, and configurations. The chapter will conclude with a discussion of the linkage between technological factors and the approaches.

CONTEXT

Technology itself is, of course, a major contextualizing factor for communication structure, but the role of technology is also affected by other contextualizing forces within the organization, which also relate directly to two of the approaches to organizational communication structure: *formal* and *cultural*.

Formal

In general, in organizational settings, a link has been found between technology and formal organizational structure, but there is some controversy over the extent of this relationship (Ford & Slocum, 1977; Mohr, 1971; Porter, Lawler, & Hackman, 1975). However, there is also some agreement that the relationship is stronger at the unit level than at the macroorganizational level (Alexander & Randolph, 1985; Porter et al., 1977; Van de Ven, Delbecq, & Koenig, 1976; Withey, Daft, & Cooper, 1983).

At the macroorganizational level a large number of research programs have examined the linkage between formal organizational arrangements and technology. This research stream started with the classic work of Woodward (1965). The major conclusion of her extensive research program was that technical methods were the most important factor in determining organizational structure and the tone of human relationships inside organizations. Further, she argued that no principle of management (e.g., span of control) was valid for all types of production systems. Thus this research program was instrumental in spurring the development of contingency approaches to organizational theory.

Woodward (1965) identified three major types of technology: unit, mass, and process. Unit or small batch firms produce specialized products which require highly skilled labor (e.g., railroad locomotives). Mass production generates products that have many standardized components, such as the classic assembly line operations of automobile manufacturers. Process production involves continuous flow technologies such as those found in chemical firms.

The findings of Woodward's (1965) study of 100 firms in Great Britain indicated that several formal structural elements differed systematically across the three major types of technology. First, the numbers of authority levels increased with technological complexity. Second, span of control was highest for mass production. Third, administrative intensity was highest for process production. Fourth, written communication was greater in mass production organizations than in small batch or process organizations. Fifth, unit production required day-to-day communication to coordinate activities, while mass and process production systems did not. In sum, Woodward's study found a relationship between formal structure and technology; unfortunately, this study did not systematically examine the other three approaches to organizational structure.

Other studies have also focused on formal organizational structure. For example, Simpson (1952) found that mechanization reduced the need for close supervision and vertical communication, since machines dictated the work pace for subordinates. Mechanization correspondingly increased the need for horizontal communication among first line foreman related to joint problem solving and coordinating the work. Randolph and Finch (1977), more generally, have found that technological certainty decreased the proportion of vertical communication and increased horizontal communication.

Cultural

Perhaps one of the most interesting areas of investigation of the relationship between culture and technology is the limits that an organizational culture can place on the adoption and implementation of new information technologies. Generally, technical (how well the technology matches role requirements) and cultural factors play a crucial role in the level of adoption of information technologies (Kling, 1980; Rice & Manross, 1987). Often, new information technologies threaten existing power relationships within organizations; for example, adoption of MIS systems permits workers to have access to information with which to make decisions that were traditionally the prerogative of upper level management. These threats can lead to decisions not to adopt, or resistance to those technologies that are adopted (Rogers, 1983).

One of the most detailed investigation of this topic to date is found in Johnson and Rice's (1987) exhaustive investigation of the adoption of word processing technologies by organizations. Generally they found that unsuccessful implementation was the rule, not the exception, largely because organizations insisted on implementing technology along the lines of the existing structure of the organization. "Efforts to implement word processing technologies using principles of the industrial bureaucracy *did not work*" (Johnson & Rice, 1987, p. 2).

The other major conclusions of their study were, first, evolution, rather than rational planning, characterized word-processing implementation. Second, managing word processing was a learned skill which required 'unlearning' such traditional skills as typing, data processing, and secretarial pools. Third, conflicts between users and central providers of word processing shaped word-processing implementation. Finally, individuals did make a difference in word-processing implementation.

The most effective implementation of word-processing systems involved high-integration systems which focused on "organized decentralization," often involving microcomputers. Thus, the organization would standardize acquisition and types of equipment available while encouraging units to implement the technology in their own way. Communication in the adaptive systems of word processing was found to be open, topically related to adaptation, and structured to involve appropriate people in the work process (Johnson & Rice, 1987).

Thus, technology, seemingly the most rational of the antecedents, because of its linkage to values of efficiency, is heavily influenced by cultural factors and by existing formal power relationships within the organization (Sept, 1989). These underlying elements of communication structure also effect the surface manifestations of structures revealed in gradients and network analysis.

RELATIONSHIPS

In general, task characteristics have been argued to be the most influential factors in determining interpersonal and group communication patterns in organizations (Jablin, 1987; Penley, 1977). Technological imperatives, especially those associated with the role sender's needs, heavily influence the content of communication that flows within a role set, although the amount of this communication can be mediated by spatial factors (Katz & Kahn, 1978). These communications are some of the most direct indications of interdependencies and coordination requirements existing within an organization. In fact, as Katz and Kahn (1978) note, occupants of the offices to which roles are tied are usually associated with a limited number of others who are adjacent to them in the work flow structure or the hierarchy of authority of an organization. Thus, "Generally, role behavior refers to the recurring actions of an individual, appropriately interrelated with the repetitive activities of others so as to yield a predictable outcome" (Katz & Kahn, 1978, p. 189). This pattern of role behaviors then becomes the throughput that transforms some input into a particular output, thus conforming perfectly to our definition of technology.

Katz and Kahn's (1978) role episode model provides a good framework, then, within which to examine the impacts of communication relationships on task performance. A *role* is defined as the total requirements with which the organizational system faces the employee. A *role set* might constitute the focal person's supervisor, subordinates, and those others with whom the member must work. In other words, the role set is a focal network of relationships emanating from the individual. Each member of the role set has expectations about the focal person's behavior; role sending occurs when these expectations are communicated to the focal person. This type of communication tends to be sustained and frequent between workers and their coworkers and supervisors (Katz & Kahn, 1978). This system of interrelated role behaviors can easily be conceived of as a *technology,* at least in the "soft" sense of the word, and Katz and Kahn (1978) recognize that technology is one of the major determinants of the content of any given office.

A particularly useful framework for examining the interrelationships between communication structure, spatial factors, and technology, which also directly relate to role sets, is Thompson's (1967) classification of differing types of interdependencies associated with technology. Interdependence is a necessary consequence of the division of labor in an organization (Victor & Blackburn, 1987). Thompson (1967) sees structure as facilitating coordinated action among interdependent elements of the organization. In his view, the three different types of interdependence implied by differing technologies are particularly important for organizational functioning. In *pooled interdependence* each part of a system renders a discrete contribution and is supported by the whole (e.g., a bowling team). When one unit of the organization must act before another can, you have *sequential interdependence* (e.g., an assembly line). *Re-*

ciprocal interdependence is found when the outputs of each element of the system become inputs for others (e.g., a basketball team or maintenance unit). Each of these succeeding types of interdependence is generally characteristic of particular types of units, although they can also contain preceding types. To properly coordinate their interdependent relationships, organizational entities must negotiate complementary role behaviors in which they can mutually engage. One of the ways that this is accomplished is by the generation of rules which govern relationships. The development of rules is a key 'soft' technological factor which governs the development of particular communication structures. An individual's role set and interdependence requirements then provide the background for the negotiation of rules and form the basis for many organizational relationships.

CHANNELS

Since channels constitute the means by which we reach other interactants, their characteristics are critical to the development of particular communication structures. Individuals in the modern organization are confronted with a bewildering array of channels from face-to-face communication to electronic mail. How individuals select channels to accomplish particular purposes, and the impact of new information-processing technologies on the process, have received considerable research attention in recent years.

The channels employed vary across different technologies, with a negative relationship found between technological certainty and use of verbal media (Randolph, 1978). As technology becomes more sophisticated, work is differentiated into more and more separate tasks, increasing the need for coordination (Hage, 1974; Jablin, 1985). As we proceed from pooled to reciprocal interdependence, coordination and, relatedly, communication become more costly, and complex and the impact of coordination on output quality and quantity increases (Cheng, 1983). When problems are difficult to analyze and unusual, more interactive modes of coordination—even though costly—are more effective (Dunegan, Green, & Baker, 1987). Face-to-face interaction becomes increasingly important in more complex interactions, further reinforcing the need to examine spatial factors such as accessibility (Allen, 1977; Tushman, 1978).

Channel Selection

A major source of constraint on communication structure lies in the channels used to fulfill relationships. Channels can constitute barriers which shape the flow of communication messages. In turn, channel selection is affected by a number of organizational processes. For example, spatial relationships often determine the manner in which we communicate with others, and channels can determine whether we access other individuals at all (Conrath, 1973; Hiltz & Kerr, 1980; Steinfield, 1985; Klauss & Bass, 1982). For example, geographic dispersion can lead to the choice of electronic mail in office settings (Steinfeld & Fulk, 1986) or videoconferencing across organizational sites (Dutton, Fulk, & Steinfield, 1982). The presence of electronic media can reduce space to a point, however (Hagarstrand, 1967), thus creating a key problem of access to appropriate media channels, with this access determined by the availability of information terminals. In addition to geographic dispersion, job pressures (Steinfeld & Fulk, 1986; Trevino, Lengel, & Daft, 1987), as well as previous media experience and knowledge (Steinfield, Jin, & Ku, 1987), have been found to determine media selection. High-status people may also have more access to an array of channels, while low-status people are systematically deprived of access (Morris, 1988). Indeed, channel selection also impacts on such relational issues as showing respect and consideration for others (Morris, 1988) and concerns for status and self-esteem (Dewhirst, 1971).

While studies relating to technology's impact on organizational structure have been increasing in recent years, most have focused on some derivation of the relatively abstract information-processing typology of Perrow (1970; e.g., Randolph & Finch, 1977; Withey et al., 1983). In general, it has been argued that complex, nonroutine tasks require more information processing than simple, routine tasks (Daft & Macintosh, 1981). As task uncertainty increases, more personal, "rich" forms of communication substitute for more impersonal modes (Heimstra, 1982; Picot, Klingenberg, & Kranzle, 1982; Van de Ven et al., 1976).

Because face-to-face communication uses all of the senses, has immediate feedback, and is more spontaneous, it has become the "standard" against which other channels are evaluated (Durlak, 1987).[1] This emphasis on face-to-face communication is related to the notion of social presence of a particular medium. Social presence refers to the degree to which a channel approximates the personal characteristics of face-to-face interac-

---

[1] Although it has been pointed out that mediated communication through teleconferencing can produce hidden impacts, such as higher quality decisions, because of a dampening of "irrelevant" emotional cues, and that the greater psychological distance of the mediated communication should make it easier to express negative emotions (Culnan & Markus, 1987; Keyton, 1987). Rice and Love (1987) have found that even media considered relatively impersonal, such as computer-mediated communication networks, can have a high degree of socioemotional content. Dutton et al. (1982) argue that videoconferencing, on the positive side, can result in increased numbers of meeting participants and the inclusion of valuable organizational members who might not otherwise be available to attend.

tion (Durlak, 1987) and has its roots in the work of Short, Williams, and Christie (1976) on teleconferencing. Social presence has been found to predict the perceived utility of media by managers (Ruchinskas, 1983).

The preceding research findings have recently been integrated into a theory of media richness articulated by Daft and his colleagues (Daft & Lengel, 1986; Lengel & Daft, 1988). They argue that the information-processing requirements of individuals in organizations are a function of equivocality and uncertainty. Communication media or channels differ in their capacity to process rich information. "Information richness is defined as the ability of information to change understanding within a time interval" (Daft & Legnel, 1986, p. 560). Thus, media of low richness (e.g., impersonal written documents and numeric reports) are effective for processing well-understood messages and standardized data, while media of high richness (e.g., face-to-face meetings) are necessary to process information high in equivocality and uncertainty. The media usage patterns of executives tend to support these arguments (Lengel & Daft, 1988).

Researchers concerned with technological impacts on communication have come to label this sort of approach a *media characteristics approach* and classify both social presence arguments and media richness as two representatives of this school (Fulk, Steinfield, Schmitz, & Power, 1987; Steinfield et al., 1987). They argue that the central assumption of this approach is that individuals select media whose inherent characteristics are congruent with task demands (Steinfield et al., 1987). The other major competing school that they view as being important in this regard is a social information-processing approach, which shares many assumptions with cultural approaches but most closely follows the work of Salancik and Pfeffer (1977, 1978). However, the recent work of Trevino et al. (1987) suggests there may be considerable overlaps across these perspectives. Their newly articulated position is labeled *structural symbolic interactionism* and argues that manager's media choice behavior is a function of constrained, externally determined behavior and voluntary enacted behavior. So, for example, if I wish to communicate with a colleague at another university quickly, I am constrained to use electronic channels, but whether it is by electronic mail or telephone or some other channel depends upon my own preference. They also modify the imperatives leading to communication events, suggesting that content ambiguity results in greater need for rich media because of the greater interpretive needs of organizational members. Daft and his colleagues also suggest that the media themselves contain symbolic cues: The medium chosen is very much part of the message. Some have argued that information-carrying capacity and symbol-carrying capacity represent two fundamental properties of any communication medium (Sitkin, Sutcliffe, & Barrios-Choplin, 1989). Channel selection reflects the subject matter of messages and the status of the participants (Morris, 1988), and face-to-face communication has the hidden benefit of building trust between interactants (Picot et al., 1982).

The key tenet of a social information-processing approach is that workers jointly construct their own interpretations of the workplace, and that an individual's social environment effects media selection. Perhaps most importantly, communication is an activity that implies shared behaviors on the part of workers (Fulk et al., 1987). Thus it is impossible to communicate with a fellow worker by electronic mail if he or she refuse to use the medium. Channel selection is also rule driven (Morris, 1988; Ruchinskas, 1983); thus a perception of a strong information sharing norm in an organization resulted in a greater use of internal communication channels among scientists and engineers (Dewhirst, 1971).

While empirical research examining these perspectives is relatively slight, the few studies which have been conducted have not been unequivocally supportive of any of the above positions. There is evidence that different functional specialties within an organization have different patterns of usage of communication channels, with general management personnel much more likely than finance people to use face-to-face interaction in the headquarters of a multinational organization, for example (Pondy & Mitroff, 1979). Rice, Grant, Schmitz, and Torobin (1988) report results that argue against the substitutability of the media assumption implicit in media richness and provide only minimal support for social information processing perspectives. Steinfield et al. (1987), in reviewing the literature on social presence, have found some moderate support in laboratory contexts, but, in general, they found social presence only accounts for small proportions of the variance in media behavior. Markus (1988), in a study focusing on email, a form of electronic media which should be considered low in media richness, found, contrary to media richness arguments, that, as hierarchical level increased, managers did not demonstrate increased media sensitivity, that use of email did not decrease at higher hierarchical levels, and that email was often used for ambiguous, equivocal communication. Markus suggests that medical richness theory does not adequately account for the possibility that managers will choose channels based on motivations to avoid sending rich cues and to employ new capabilities of electronic media. This study, and a study by Schmitz (1988), suggest that email is often employed by managers, even thought it is a lean medium, because of the high volumes of messages it enables them to send efficiently. The recent work of Trevino, Lengel, Bodensteiner, and Gerloff (1988), which found that low-equivocality situations provide managers more choice, suggests that theoretical work is still evolving, with researchers in this area showing a commendable capacity to incorporate new research findings and theoretical arguments.

Impacts of Information Processing Technologies

> Other things being equal, then, information technology should permit the development of more elaborate and complex organizational structures. (Pfeffer, 1978, p. 74)

The impact of information-processing technologies on organizational communication structure have been a matter of some controversy in recent years. While it appears obvious that the impact of technologies would be dramatic, both structurally and spatially (Morgan, 1986), especially in relation to the enhanced ability to control and coordinate organizational process, this has not been the case in actual practice, with many promising technologies being used to do the old jobs in old ways (Carter & Cullen, 1983; Johnson & Rice, 1987). Thus, a word processor is treated as a fancier version of a typewriter and used for essentially the same functions as a typewriter. However, the promise of electronic media lies in the new capabilities they offer organizations, particularly in areas such as new ways of addressing communication (e.g., public bulletin boards), memory, storage and retrieval of communication (e.g., automatic storage of transcripts of electronic meetings), and control over access to and participation in communication. There is a general consensus that, eventually, often after a considerable lag-time, new information technologies have an impact on organizational structures (Huber & McDaniel, 1986), often as a result of competitive pressures.

Rice et al. (1988) detail the sorts of impacts that one information-processing technology, electronic message systems, could possibly have on organizational communication structure. First, it reduces the necessity for synchronous communication such as telephone calls. Second, it can increase the frequency of communication through a widening of professional and social connections. Third, it can increase efficiency by reducing media transformations (e.g., data files on disk to computer tape) and shadow functions (e.g., time wasted on unanswered telephone calls). Fourth, users may perceive they have greater control, improved communication, and greater access to information.

One area where two competing positions concerning the impact of information-processing technologies have been fully articulated is in the manner in which information-processing technologies relate to the degree of centralization present in organizations (Pfeffer, 1978). Some have found support for the position that enhanced information-processing capabilities lead to greater centralization of decision making and control by management (Reif, 1968; Whisler, 1970), while others have found a negative relationship between more centralized information processing technologies and decentralization (Carter & Cullen, 1983) when size was controlled (Pfeffer & Leblebici, 1977) or when computers were geograph-ically dispersed (Blau & Schoenherr, 1971).

This issue is particularly critical, since it relates directly to the information-processing capacity of management. Computers can serve to increase this capacity, if they present information in a comprehensible manner (Carter, 1984; Carter & Cullen, 1983), but there are real limits to the capacity of individuals managers to process information and com-puters can also serve to vastly increase overload problems for upper level management.

Computers might serve to decentralize decision making in two ways: by providing an extensive array of control mechanisms (e.g., automatic warnings when activities monitored by the computers go outside certain boundaries), and by routinizing work activities (Carter & Cullen, 1983). Some computer technologies do increase administrative intensity by increasing the efficiency with which managers can monitor the activities of workers (Carter & Cullen, 1983). This raises the issue of what decentralization really is, since management substantially constrains activities in these instances (Pfeffer, 1978).

It is possible that both views may be simultaneously correct. Centraliz-ation may have increased, not at the level of upper management, but at lower levels, with an especially functional locus. Thus, lower-level decision makers in the MIS department, or editors in a newspaper office, for example, may now be at the nexus of organizational information flows (Carter & Cullen, 1983). Centralization may also be contingent on an organization's environment, with more centralization in relatively stable environments and less in unstable ones, and the impact of computerization determined by the extent to which it mediates uncertainty (Carter, 1984).

The effects of new technologies on centralization relate to the more general arguments concerning the impact of new media on the democra-tization of the work place through changes in authority relationships. While it would appear that these technologies offer the potential to empower lower-level organizational employees in a variety of ways, in actual practice existing rules and norms tend to limit the use of new technologies for this purpose (Komsky, 1989).

CONFIGURATIONS

In this section we will attempt to integrate some common themes related to space, technology, and communication structure. Spatial positioning and features are often heavily dependent on the nature of the work to be done. These antecedent factors interact to determine in large measure the manifest communication structures of an organization.

Table 7-1. Technological and Spatial Factors and Communication Structure

Technological Factors	Spatial Factors	Communication Structure
Embedded Elements		
Physical Features	Dispersion of Actors	Gradients
–Fixed	–Proximity	–Surfaces
–Semi-fixed	–Social Density	–Bounded Planes
–Information	–Access	–Fields
Terminals		
Utilitarian Elements		
Role Sets	Mobility	Networks
Rules	–Pathways	–Linkages
Coordination	–Channels	–Relationships

Table 7-1 details the basic distinction between embedded and utilitarian elements of communication structure related to technological and spatial factors. Embedded elements are static and contextual, constraining interactions by their presences. Communication structure can be thought of as occurring within the context provided by these elements. Utilitarian elements relate more directly to the information processing requirements of positions, individuals, and/or organizations. These requirements often transcend the embedded elements of the organization and compel individuals to seek information wherever it might be, not only from convenient, proximate sources. Thus, in this sense, organizational members act strategically to achieve their own ends and, in doing so, construct local communication structures that more closely mirror their own interests.

Embedded Elements

Technology, at least in part, determines how actors position themselves vis-á-vis other actors; in other words, technology provides actors with a map of coordinates in which to operate within a gradient of other actors. Technology also plays a key role in defining the dance of actors within a bounded microphysical space. In this connection, coordination of activities is directly related to the manner in which location enables an individual to monitor the sociospatial dynamics of the situation (Archea, 1977).

Technology also affects our settings by shaping the fixed and semifixed features of our environments which in turn constrain communication activities. Particularly important here are such features as the presence of intrusive fixed barriers (e.g., walls), presence of semifixed features (e.g., partitions, work benches), placement of office equipment and ownership/ territoriality, all factors which may impede and regulate the flow of interaction in an organization (Allen, 1977; Davis, 1984; Sommer, 1967). Semifixed features directly impact the flexibility of the space, which has many implications for organizational performance (Pfeffer, 1982). For example, Allen (1977) has noted the impeding influence that stairways represent, even though in terms of pure distance two interactants may be very proximate one to another. Similarly, elements of technology, such as conveyor belts, can constitute absolute barriers to interaction, even when interactants are relatively proximate to each other. A particularly important impact of these features is their effect on the visual access of interactants, which leads to increased understanding and also is a precursor of social interaction (Archea, 1973; Johnson, 1986) and has been found to be crucial to innovation in R & D laboratories (Liebson, 1981).

The physical environment of the organization can also be seen as a space containing a set of locations or places, each differing in their access to information (Canter & Kenny, 1975), particularly information from outside an immediate physical location. In this regard interpersonal behavior can be considered as occurring within an information field, which has rich implications for communication processes (Archea, 1977). To understand interpersonal situations, we should be concerned with the means by which the environment transduces, amplifies, contrasts, or otherwise mediates the appearance of available information (Archea, 1977). "An information *terminal* is a point within an informal social setting at which information is either entered into or retrieved from a formal communication network or information storage system" (Archea, 1977, p. 126). Thus, "the arrangement of the physical environment regulates the distribution of information upon which all interpersonal behavior depends" (Archea, 1977, p. 121). For example, the placement of such features as photocopiers and water coolers is also used by organizations to increase desired or decrease undesired communication relationships (McCann & Galbraith, 1981).

Information terminals are technological features which considerably increase communication levels and thus are major explanatory factors underlying certain levels of communication at particular places within an organization. However, they also serve as major ways of expanding someone's information field. If a terminal is located within someone's field, then the range of interactants they may come in contact with is vastly expanded and spatial limitations can be overcome to a certain degree.

The configuration of information systems, and their associated information terminals, can also impact on the development of organizational communication structures. These systems can generally be classified by four different configurations. Online systems have a central processor and dumb, interactive terminals. *Distributed* systems have a central processor and smart terminals which can do their own computing. *Networked systems* have no central processor, but messages can be sent throughout the network in an interactive mode. *Stand-alone* systems consist of PCs which are not coordinated or standardized. Each of these systems implies different network configurations and mediating impacts of spatial factors. For example, research conducted by Leifer and Triscari (1987) found that network information systems were associated with decentralized organizations and greater information-processing capabilities. These systems create new possibilities for the development of emergent communication networks, particularly in relation to utilitarian factors, all of which raises the policy issue of who should have access to these information networks (Culnan & Markus, 1987).

Utilitarian Elements

The types of interdependence implied by particular technologies have direct implications for spatial positioning of groups and individuals within organizations, which in turn effects communication structure (Thompson, 1967). In terms of spatial distributions, pooled interdependence implies relatively isolated actors working on autonomous tasks. Pooled interdependence, which is coordinated by standardization, also implies low levels of communication (e.g., stock control clerks responsible for different classes of goods). Typically, sequential interdependence (e.g., characteristic of assembly line operations) requires that workers be bound to work stations and/or equipment for much of the day. Coordination by plan characterizes sequential interdependence. It requires more communication, particularly with adjacent individuals and to control adherence to the plan, but it implies a one-way flow of communication messages. Reciprocal interdependence units (e.g., surgical trauma teams), should be much more fluid in their operations, with less formally directed links and less routine, directed tasks. The coordination by mutual adjustment necessary for reciprocal interdependence requires high degrees of feedback and thus implies a two-way flow of messages. Or, stated in another way, complex, nonroutine tasks require more information processing than simple routine ones (Daft & Macintosh, 1981).

These types of interdependence can also explain the imperatives that drive members of role sets to engage in different levels of role sending and compliance with the wishes of others in their role sets. Figure 7-1 represents a situation of overlapping role sets with relationships characterizing different types of interdependencies. For the focal person B, these different types of relationships imply a direct priority for dealing with others' expectations. For an organization to operate in a timely fashion, the sequential interdependencies characteristic of relationships 2 and 3 must be fulfilled. On the other hand focal person B realized that his or her own

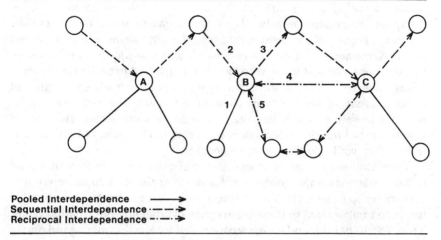

Pooled Interdependence ———➤
Sequential Interdependence ·——·➤
Reciprocal Interdependence —·—·➤

Figure 7-1.   Interdependence and Role Sets

work may be impaired if the reciprocal interdependencies represented by relationships 4 and 5 are not fulfilled. As a result, interdependencies imply priorities for dealing with members of a role set. This suggests, controlling for other factors, that members of a role set who have pooled interdependencies with the focal person are going to receive the lowest priority. Figure 7-1 also reveals the direct linkage of these factors to traditional network analysis representations of the communication structure of an organization, what Monge and Eisenberg (1987) have termed the *positional approach* to network analysis.

While Thompson's approach has been criticized in recent years for some of its assertions concerning relationships (McCann & Galbraith, 1981; Victor & Blackburn, 1987), its spatial implications have not been adequately examined in the literature. However, the types of interdependence implied by particular technologies, in addition to being related to utilitarian elements, have direct implication for spatial positioning of groups and individuals within organizations (Thompson, 1967) and, thus, for the embedded features of organizations. This is one area where both gradient and network approaches may offer different insights into communication structure. In terms of spatial distributions, pooled interdependence implies relatively isolated actors working on autonomous tasks. This is exactly the sort of structure revealed in the gradient of communication activities within the retail store found in Figure 4-7. There is little overlapping of information fields among the individuals in the store and a diffused pattern of communication, except for the checkout area. It is also interesting to note the impact of fixed and semifixed features, particularly in terms of the total absence of communication in the areas where the aisleways are. However, the network analysis results revealed one large group encompassing nearly all of the organizational members (see Johnson, 1986). These results suggested that, while there were not intensive connections around any one task which would result in differentiated groups, the members were loosely enough tied to each other to form a large aggregate. Thus, while the gradient results leads us to think of isolated areas of peak communication activities, the network results reveal a loosely bound collectivity of organizational actors. Both views give us partial insights into what is occurring in the store, but either view in isolation would be somewhat misleading.

Typically, sequential interdependence requires that workers be bound to work stations and/or equipment for much of the day. In assembly line operation this is not a block to all interactions, but rather the assembly line limits communication to those others with overlapping information fields. Thus, Form (1972) found a high frequency of interaction among proximate others in an assembly line operation, but the nature of the technology resulted in short, relatively shallow interactions. Overall, sequential interdependence implies a patterned spatial distribution of communication activities.

The gradient found in Figure 4-2 demonstrates clearly that communication intensity is associated with the sequential flow of the work in the warehouse and the constraining influence of fixed and semifixed features. One area of communication is clustered within the office area, with very little leakage outside because of the constraints of fixed walls; relatedly, the highest peak is represented by the warehouse managers cubicle at coordinates 10, 10. The areas in the warehouse associated with shipping are in the lower middle of Figure 4-2, and it is the location of another cluster of communication activity. The other clusters toward the rear of the store are associated with departments (10, 20, 30, 40) where the goods are initially left by forklifts to be stocked in bins.

The network analysis results revealed groups which formed at three clusters. Within these network groups there was a pattern of linkage which revealed reciprocal interdependence with less formally directed coordination links between members of various statuses. The accomplishment of the work under reciprocal interdependence generally requires a high degree of overlap of information fields resulting from high social density, and the visual access to other promotes an understanding of what is occurring in the organization (Johnson, 1987b). Thus, a highly spatially clustered pattern of communication activities would be expected to be associated with reciprocal interdependence. In this organization there was essential similarity in results with both the network analysis results and communication gradients providing some sense of convergent validity, but they came to these similar conclusions through different pathways and there was not total similarity of results. For example, one prominent member of the office network group was a worker who was physically located in the warehouse. Given this worker's pattern of relationships, it is apparent that he or she served a crucial liaison function which the gradient results would not have revealed, but the gradient results also help to explain why the group, formed around department 30, was by far the most isolated in the organization. Thus an understanding of both embedded and utilitarian elements is needed to explain he manifest communication structures revealed in gradients and network analysis.

TECHNOLOGY AND THE APPROACHES

The previous discussion highlights two general categories of effects relating to the impacts of technologies and the spatial environment on communication structure: embedded and utilitarian. This in turn necessitates different analytical approaches to detailing the impacts of technological and spatial factors on communication structure. This chapter has adopted the view that gradients have more inherent linkages to embedded contextual factors, while network analysis has potentially greater linkages to technological factors associated with utilitarian imperatives. Making these linkages to contextual factors clearer offers the potential of moving communication structure research, particularly network analysis research, from the descriptive level it has been operating on to a more theoretical level.

In general, the overwhelming strength of network analysis lies in its sophisticated description of the overall pattern of communication relationships within an organization. It can develop rich descriptions of individual dyadic relationships and then reveal the overall configuration of these linkage across an entire organization. As we have seen, these linkages often arise out of technological imperatives. However, at the same time technology stimulates the development of certain relationships, it also constrains them: Network analysis offers the most complete picture yet developed of the overall pattern of communication relationships, both formal and informal, which makes it eminently suited for tackling the flow of communication related to technology.

The biggest drawback to the use of the gradient approach to communication structure in its difficulty in portraying specific dyadic communication linkages. This also relates to the various levels of analysis of structure research: "The aggregate is merely the sum of the elements, but the structure depends on their relationships in the broadest sense, including under relationships relative positions and indirect influences as well as direct connections" (Blau, 1981, p. 9). Network analysis tends to focus on a more narrow sense of relationships involving direct linkages. Gradients can move us in the direction of broader thinking about relationships, since gradients relate to the more probablistic world of forces and fields. When individuals are clustered together in physical space, linkages can be assumed but not really known. For this sort of situation, as we have seen, communication gradients and network analysis can be viewed as complementary techniques, each of which provides unique perspectives on communication structure. For example, they both can provide unique insights into the boundaries of groups which may represent high levels of reciprocal interdependencies. Thus high levels of social density in a physical environment may result in high densities of communication relationships within a network. In sum, an overall view of technology and communication structure require analysis by both the network analysis and gradient perspectives.

While gradients and network analysis offer us different views of communication structure, formal and cultural approaches offer us a view of deeper factors underlying the emergence of manifest structures. Technology, of all the factors examined in this book, is perhaps the most heavily influenced by formal planning. In fact, the very raison d'etre for formal structures is that they promote the accomplishment of work through the control of organizational activities and members. In this sense the formal structure of the organization can be regarded as a technological tool, and it thus becomes very hard to separate formal approaches from technological factors.

Investigating the intersection of the approaches related to technological factors offers some hope of the development of a synthesis of the planned vs. emergent views of structure, one that also offers the hope of pragmatic benefits to practicing managers who find that their best laid plans often go awry because of a failure to consider emergent structures. Thus, embedded elements provide a basic context for interaction, but utilitarian elements may determine more precisely which of many possible structures occur within this set of constraining factors. Thus, in essence, formal structure provides a plan for action, but it should be realized that this is a plan to deviate from, a standard by which to evaluate later action.

Although less studied or thought about in organizational contexts, the classic findings of diffusion studies suggest that culture substantially limits the kinds of technologies which can be implemented and their relative efficiency (Rogers, 1983). The formal and informal rule structures of organizations can also substantially limit the adoption of particular innovations. If managers are prohibited from typing, then the efficacious implementation of modern information-processing technologies in organizations will be severely hampered (Johnson & Rice, 1987).

In sum, technological factors go to the core of what an organization is. A closer examination of them also reveals the different contributions of each of the approaches to structure. The rich interplay of the approaches related to these issues highlights the importance of a more pluralistic approach to what structure is.

chapter 8

Human Environment

The human environment of organizations provides a macromedium, or context, for the development of particular communication structures. There are many elements of the larger organizational context, such as pay and promotion systems, which can impinge on human relationships. However, the focus of this section will be on how the human composition of the organization effects the development of particular structures. The impacts of spatial and technological factors are somewhat more readily thought of as environments for interaction, because of their tangible character. The human environment of organizations also has pervasive impacts, but its nature is somewhat more intangible and often difficult to grasp. Generally researchers have focused on the macronature of the human environment, either in terms of climate or cultural impacts, regarding these phenomena as the macromedia which flavor any interactions embedded within them. For example, while there were many similarities, cross-cultural differences have been found in *supervisor- -subordinate communication relationships* (SSCR) (Page & Wiseman, 1988). It has also been found that SSCR-style variables, like argumentativeness, are affected by larger cultural variables (Infante & Gordon, 1987). In addition, certain organizational climates are more likely to result in certain structures. For example, closed climates could be associated with particularly constrained structures. Thus, climate and culture are both seen as providing the context for interactions.

Recently several new approaches to research in this area have developed, approaches which focus clearly on the nature of the human environment of organizations. One example of these trends is a concentration on the impact of demographic factors on various organizational processes. Thus, the nature of the human membership of organizations is seen as determining various communication outcomes. Somewhat relatedly, issues of proportions of human membership are also seen as crucial to the development of individual communication patterns. Thus, minority groups have special difficulties in their communication which could be attributable primarily to the proportion of their members in an organization. In addition, it is increasingly recognized that dyadic relationships are affected by the interpersonal environment of linkages with others that the two parties are embedded in. This chapter will focus on all of these concerns, highlighting the importance of another crucial class of antecedents to communication structure in organizations: the nature of the organization's human membership.

ORGANIZATIONAL DEMOGRAPHY

Organizational demography refers to the composition of the human membership of the organization in terms of such basic attributes as sex and age (Pfeffer, 1982). It has been argued that the distribution of such attributes in an organization's population has important consequences for organizations and their members—particularly so in terms of communication, because of the natural tendency of people to communication mostly with others like themselves (Rogers, 1983; Tsui & O'Reilly, 1989; Zenger & Lawrence, 1989). There is some suggestive evidence that demographic factors, particularly ones associated with larger societal trends (e.g., competitiveness stemming from a particularly large age cohort), impact on dyadic relationships, such as the supervisor–subordinate communication relationship, in several ways (Jablin & Krone, 1987). First, demographic factors may effect recruitment practices and the degree to which an organization will defer to members once recruited. Second, they may effect modes of control. For example, a large number of new members represented in a growing organization may insure bureaucratic vs. cultural forms of control, since the new members have not had the time to be properly socialized. In any event the higher the ratio of new members to old, the greater the proportion of communication which needs to be directed to the socialization of new members (McNeil & Thompson, 1971). These issues may also impact on the number of supervisors needed and their span of control (Pfeffer, 1982). A third issue related to demography is intercohort conflict. If a supervisor is a member of a different demographic grouping, as well as in a privileged position, this might further impede the development of relational qualities such as openness in his or her relationships with subordinates.

Finally, these factors in turn can influence turnover within the organization. For example, the presence of a dominant cohort and substantial gaps among cohorts in university departments were found to be characterized by increased rates of voluntary retirements, resignations, and expired appointments (McCain, O'Reilly, & Pfeffer, 1983). One of the most interesting studies that has been conducted, related to turnover and communication networks, concerns the impact of friends leaving on stayer's attitudes (Krackhardt & Porter, 1985). The results indicated that the closer a stayer was in a friendship network to those who left, the more satisfied and committed he or she was afterward to the organization. This result was explained from a classic dissonance reduction framework which argued that an individual's staying when a friend leaves requires more justification on the part of the stayer. This strengthens the individual's ties to the organization.

A common theme related to demographic research, which bears directly on communication structure, is the relative isolation of certain groups. For example, Allen (1977) has found, in research and development laboratories, that non-Ph.D.'s were relatively isolated from Ph.D.'s. This isolation was due primarily to status differences, while non-Ph.D.'s could enhance their status by communicating with Ph.D.'s, Ph.D.'s would suffer a decrease in their status. Similarly non-Ph.D.'s communicating with each other reinforced their low status position. As a result, non-Ph.D.'s did not communicate widely in these organizations.

The most researched issues related to organizational demography and organizational communication focus on proportional imbalances in organizational membership, particularly related to attributes such as gender. Kanter (1977) has argued that the integration of organizational members whose attributes are different from the work group majority is a function of their relative minority status. Thus tokens who represent a small minority, say 15%, of organizational members are subject to considerable pressures because of their visibility and uniqueness. However, as the balance becomes more even, the impacts of different attributes becomes less pronounced. Perhaps one of the most important impacts of tokenism is the isolation of token individuals from informal communication networks composed of majority members (Fairhurst, 1985). Brass (1985) has found, in a newspaper publishing company with roughly equal numbers of men and women, that men and women were not well integrated into each other's communication networks, and that women in particular were not well integrated into the dominant coalition. A follow-up indicated that, in this organization, promotions were significantly related to an individual's centrality in departmental, men's, and dominant coalition interaction networks.

While Kanter's research stream is provocative, it has been systematically criticized. For example, Fairhurst and Snavely (1983) argue that power and status attenuate these relationships and decrease the potential impacts of token status. Thus, tokens can offset numerical disadvantages by increasing the importance of their power bases, their influence on decision making, and their individual power skills (Fairhurst & Snavely, 1983). In research designed to assess their critique of Kanter,

Fairhurst and Snavely (1983) found that male tokens were not isolated communicatively from their organizational networks. Jablin (1980c) has also found only weak evidence for male/female differences related to superior/subordinate relationships.

A central question related to proportion concerns the impact of the distribution of relational states (see Kanter, 1977; Pfeffer, 1982). For example, Can I be open when all others in my environment are closed? While this issue could be related to a variety of relational characteristics (e.g., trust and credibility), here the focus will be on openness, a variable which has received considerable attention in the literature (e.g., Jablin, 1978) and which cuts across multiple levels of analysis (Dansereau & Markham, 1987). Despite the fact that openness is crucial to organizational effectiveness, there is considerable evidence that subordinates are unwilling to be open in their SSCR (Jablin, 1978), with recent arguments that openness may not be beneficial in all circumstances, especially in term of individual consequences (Eisenberg & Whetten, 1987).

If individuals enter the organization with an essentially open approach to their relationships with others, what factors can cause this approach to change? One factor which might lead to change is the experience of asymmetry; that is, some of the alters with whom the person has relations act in a closed manner. Now, the key issue is, at what point does the perception of closed relationships cause an individual to change his or her own behavior. Does just one particularly devastating experience cause change, or is it likely that a substantial proportion of relationships with others have to be closed to lead to a negative reaction. Or is the person more discriminating? Does he or she reciprocate and behave towards others as these others behave towards him or her? Does the person have closed relationships with only those people with whom he or she is at risk (e.g., I want something from them, or they can punish me in some way)? This guardedness might dissipate over time if a certain level of trust has been built up.

Issues of proportion, both of relationships and of prior experience, can have a substantial impact on the formation of informal networks. Naturally, if a person has had consistently negative experiences, or consistently positive ones, he or she can be expected to respond with less or more openness respectively and contract or spread his or her contacts narrowly or widely. The really interesting issue is, at what point in between these extremes does the individual tendency to react become more negative.

Jablin's (1978) study, which examined the content of messages within the SSCR, suggests that only a minimum amount of negative messages, especially those concerning the underlying relationship between the two parties, can act to close off a SSCR in some instances. Jablin (1978) argues that reciprocal acceptance by both parties is crucial to an open relationship. Thus, individuals must perceive that both their messages and who they are as people will be responded to positively before they will choose to be open. However, in an atmosphere of closed relationships the individual may not feel that this essential precondition is being fulfilled. Thus, subordinates are more likely to distort information when they perceive their supervisors are actively withholding information or are politically motivated (Jablin, 1981). This of course has substantial implications for the flow of communication through formal channels.

The factors discussed in this section may also help explain why researchers often find much less informal communication than would otherwise be expected in actual communication networks (Farace & Johnson, 1974). Indeed, it has been suggested that one of the reasons liaisons are sought out by others is that they are open with, and trusted by, other organizational members; however, liaisons are also very rare in actual communication networks (Reynolds & Johnson, 1982). Indeed, the human environment within which communication relationships are embedded may discourage widespread communication, except for certain unique individuals.

DYADIC RELATIONSHIPS

if we are to ever understand the microsystem of superior–subordinate communication, we must first explicate its relationships with variables in the organization's macrosystem. (Jablin, 1979, p. 215)

In many cases the supervisor operates within an organizational framework that allows him little freedom of action. (Tannenbaum, 1966, p. 82)

In this section we will focus on the supervisor–subordinate communication relationship, since it is by far the most heavily research dyadic communication relationship in organizations. Superior–subordinate communication relationships (SSCR) are the most common interpersonal relationships within organizations (Jablin, 1985), and many would argue it is the relationship of greatest importance because of its impact on productivity (Downs & Hain, 1982; Downs, Clampitt, & Pfeiffer, 1988) and job satisfaction (Downs et al., 1988; Goldhaber et al., 1978). For our purposes this relationship "is limited to those exchanges of information and influence between organizational members, at least one of whom has formal (as defined by official organizational sources) authority to direct and evaluate the activities of other organizational members" (Jablin, 1979, p. 1202).

SSCR constitutes one of the few areas in the organizational communication literature which can be said to be relatively mature, with a well-developed body of research findings. However, most of this literature examines relational states of the SCCR such as trust (see Jablin, 1979, for a thorough review of this literature), without reference to the organizational environment within which these relationships are embedded or the micro structures of the interaction (Fairhurst, Rogers, & Sarr, 1987). Historically the literature on SSCR has recognized the impact of external factors on this relationship, even if this area of the literature has not been adequately explored (Dansereau & Markham, 1987), and several calls for research on the impact of situational factors have been made (Jablin, 1985, 1987).

In the case of SSCR perhaps the most important structural research has been done on the Pelz effect. An essential part of the supervisory function is to manage relationships between his/her unit and other entities within the organization (Pfeffer, 1978). The Pelz effect argues that, to have influence over subordinates, a supervisor must be perceived by them as having influence outside of the work unit (Pelz, 1952). This notion has been supported in a variety of contexts (Kanter, 1977; Wager, 1962) without uncovering any major moderators of the effect (Dansereau & Markham, 1987). However, some have suggested that this effect is curvilinear (Jablin, 1979, 1980b), because with increasing influence the supervisor becomes more distant from workers, although the bulk of the literature does not support this argument (Jablin, 1985). Jablin (1980b) also argues that it is strongest for strategic influence (e.g., promotions), as opposed to work-related influence (e.g., assignment to particular tasks), and when the supervisor exhibits a supportive leadership style. Jablin (1980c) also suggests that male employees who are autonomous and structurally aware depend less on their supervisors, thus weakening the Pelz effect.

Another, somewhat related, issue, is that of plateauing. A supervisor who has occupied a position too long without prospect for promotion is effectively blocking his subordinates from promotion as well. In addition to this leading to resentment on the part of subordinates, it can also contribute to the perception of powerlessness on the part of the supervisor (Bardwick, 1984). This of course directly leads to the Pelz effect. In general, the stronger the mobility aspirations of a subordinate, the more problematic the SSCR is in any case, especially in terms of distortion, although this effect is moderated by trust levels (Read, 1962).

More generally, in the interpersonal communication literature, there has been a growing recognition that our relationships are affected by the relationships we have with others (Milardo, 1983). Thus, our dyadic relationships are seen as being affected by their embeddedness in social contexts. The work of Parks and his colleagues has been particularly important in this regard (e.g., Parks & Adelman, 1983; Parks, Stan, &

Eggert, 1983). For example, Eggert and Parks (1987) found general support for hypotheses connecting relational development factors (e.g., sociability, intimacy, and commitment) and communication network factors among adolescents. In addition, Parks and Adelman (1983) have found that the more enmeshed individuals were in each other's romantic networks, and the more support for the relationship they received from them, the less uncertainty romantic partners felt and the more likely they were to stay together.

As in other dyadic relationships, the overall communication structure in which supervisor–subordinate relationships are embedded can potentially impact their relationship. These impacts relate to the concept of communication proximity (Rogers, 1983). In Figure 8-1, Case B reveals a situation of low proximity and Case C reveals a situation of high proximity. Measures of proximity have been used to characterize the social distance between interactants and to describe their interpersonal environment (Alba, 1982). A strong argument can be made that the dyadic relationship of supervisor/subordinate is affected by the network of relationships in which both parties are embedded. Indeed, the sort of integration into an organizational communication network typified by Case C has generally been related to greater satisfaction with the supervisor (Albrecht et al., 1982).

Somewhat relatedly, two general network patterns central to the theoretical work of Ron Burt (1982, 1987), structural equivalence and cohesion, could also serve to highlight the impact of different interpersonal environments on the SSCR. These two general patterns have a great deal to say about the relative influence of two parties on each other. Figure 8-1 graphically portrays the different possible configurations of relationships. The traditional view (Case A) focuses on the SSCR in isolation. Structural equivalence argues that processes such as organizational commitment are determined by the unique patterns of an individual's relationships, which are affected by factors such as role sets (Case B). Thus, if the two parties in a SSCR communicate with different sets of people, their views will reflect these overall patterns of communication, rather than their direct communication with each other. Cohesion perspectives imply a great deal of mutual influence, resulting from direct communication contact, which can be further reinforced by overlapping with other communicators (Case C in Figure 8-1). Structural equivalence explanations are antithetical to the development of commonalities between supervisor and subordinates. These different configurations of relationships with others may explain how the two parties in an SSCR can maintain different perspectives despite frequent communication with each other.

CASE A: TRADITIONAL VIEW

CASE B: STRUCTURAL EQUIVALENCE, LOW PROXIMITY

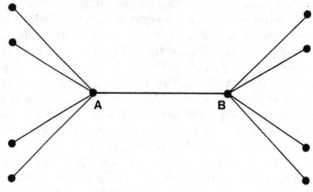

CASE C: COHESION, HIGH PROXIMITY

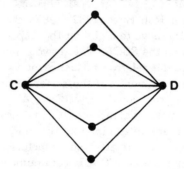

Figure 8-1. Different Levels of SSCR Embeddedness in an Organizational Communication Structure

Contextual Impacts

Context discussions inevitably lead to discussions of levels of analysis, since the context for one process lies at the next highest level of aggregation in a system (Blau, 1981). If we are to avoid pure reductionism, we must systematically account for the impact of higher order processes in organizations. For example, supervisor–subordinate dyadic relationships cannot be understood without reference to higher order organizational processes such as authority systems (Blair et al., 1985; Dansereau & Markham, 1987). At the level of the whole organization, structural variables such as size, hierarchical level, span of control, and centralization all have been found to effect openness within the SSCR (Jablin, 1982; Jablin & Krone, 1987).

In this regard, a key issue is the extent of impact of the larger organizational environment on SSCR. In somewhat analogous reasoning to open systems approaches (Katz & Kahn, 1978) and the impacts of organizational information environments at the macrolevel, it could be argued that the very permeability of the boundaries surrounding a SSCR have important consequences for its unique impacts. There may indeed be instances when a SSCR is relatively isolated from the larger organization and its members are permitted to develop the relationship without intrusive influences from the larger organization. Such relationships can be expected to develop into a steady-state relationship that reflects the idiosyncratic dynamics of the two parties. It can also be expected that minimal amounts of change will be needed in the relationship and communication related to mutual adjustments would be minimal. However, such relationships are probably becoming increasingly rare in the modern organization.

For a variety of reasons, legal, bureaucratic, technological, and humanitarian, the larger organization intrudes on the SSCR (Viega, 1988). There is a wide array of both formal and informal rules which governs the behaviors of the members of the SSCR. This level of intrusion partly reflects the value placed on this relationship by the modern organization. The greater the degree of environmental impact, the less the unique impacts of the SSCR and the more constraints on their behaviors toward each other members feel. A relationship so central to the effectiveness of the organization and the lives of its members must be monitored and controlled. Interestingly, Japanese managers deal with employees in a systemic manner (as part of an interrelated unit), while American managers treat employees as more of an isolated unit (Hirokawa & Miyahara, 1986).

Thus, the nature of the larger organizational context also determines the extent to which the parties are uniquely constrained by the actions of the other. The nature of multiplexity within a whole series of relationships determines the extent of impact. If they depend on each other exclusively for a wide variety of things, supervisors and subordinates are heavily constrained by each other. But in the modern, more pluralistic organization individuals can develop a patchwork of uniplex relationships each of which provides a piece of their larger array of needs. For example, for information within a communication structure, the degree to which parties in a dyad must go through each other to reach others determines their level of dependency on each other. They also may occupy positions which essentially replicate their relationship with each other, which may entail a redundancy between them that clouds formal organizational differences.

Levels of Analysis

An issue of growing importance in communication, management, and social science research is that of levels of analysis (Berger & Chaffee, 1987; Dansereau & Markham, 1987; Granovetter, 1979; Monge, 1987). Dansereau and Markham (1987) have developed the most sophisticated approach for examining levels of analysis in relation to SSCR and thus organizational dyadic relationships. They argue that there are four basic levels of analysis: (a) the person, (b) the dyad, (c) the group, and (d) the collectivity. In the person tradition the SSCR reflects differences between individuals, and it also reflects processes occurring within individuals. The dyad tradition views the parties to SSCR as members of dependent pairings. The group tradition focuses on a supervisor's relationship to an entire group of subordinates. Finally, the collectivity tradition focuses on the embeddedness of superiors and subordinates as members of larger collectivities. Naturally, each of these levels implies different approaches to measurement, statistical analysis, and conceptualizations. They also imply a different focus for communication research. For example, approaches to dyadic relationships may be very concerned with issues of relational control (Fairhust et al., 1987), an issue which is by and large irrelevant to collective approaches.

Dansereau and Markham (1987) argue that, given these distinctions, analysis can proceed at several different levels. Level-specific formations can focus on differences between similar entities or on relationships within similar entities, but only pertain to that level. For example, high levels of dominance in a relational control study might be linked to lower levels of satisfaction within that relationship. Cross-level formulations suggest that relationships between variables hold at two or more levels. For example, it could be hypothesized that information overload results in deterioration in performance. An emergent formulation suggests that relationships between variables hold at a higher level of analysis, but not at lower ones.

As Dansereau and Markham (1987) suggest, network analysis can be used as a systematic means of linking the micro- and macroperspectives represented by these different levels within organizations. However, they

Table 8-1.   The Role of Supervisor-Subordinate Communication Relationship in Other Organizational Processes

| | Relational Type | |
	Affective/Affiliative	Informational/Work
Individual	Cell 1 Social Support Committment Satisfaction	Cell 2 Information Load Role Ambiguity Career Advancement
Locus		
	Cell 3 Integration Turnover Coalition Formation	Cell 4 Coordination Control Innovation
Organizational		

also imply that relationships at the various levels (e.g., supervision reflecting the collectivity and exchange representing linkages) may be qualitatively different, with supervision being much more autonomous and remote, for example. This also suggests that multiplex relations across these levels has important implications for individuals. Its sophisticated means of handling these complex configurations of relationships in fact accounts for the popularity of network analysis (Farace & Mabee, 1980; Knoke & Kuklinski, 1982) as well as its promise for bridging micro- and macroperspectives (Alba, 1982; Tichy et al., 1979).

Multiplexity. Perhaps the most interesting issue related to multiplexity for SSCR, in a more informal sense than we discussed in relation to network analysis, is the mix of work and nonwork relationships, particularly concerning affective (e.g., friendship) relationships and/or affiliative (e.g., political coalitions) ones. The SSCR plays a role in many organizational processes, as Table 8-1 reveals. This table classifies a selected list of these processes based on relationship type and the locus of impact of the relationship: either individual or organizational. This is a list of possible impacts; however, not all SSCR are going to impinge on all of these relationships. Obviously, the more cells a particular SSCR impinges on, the more important it is, both for the individuals involved and the organization. The SSCR is the only organizational relationship which has such far-reaching potential impacts. Most other relationships are much more uniplex, being relatively easily categorized into one or another of the cells in this table.

Cell 1 reveals a combination of affiliative/affective impacts whose primary locus is the individual. Variables such as social support, commitment, and satisfaction would be included in this cell. The SSCR can mediate this relationship for both parties. However, it must be remembered that, although it probably is the most important relationship, it is only one relationship of many which may have such impacts. Perhaps the crucial issue for an integrated understanding of organizations is how the SSCR relates to and interacts with other relationships in the organizational communication structure.

Similarly, in Cell 2 we find various informational impacts of the SSCR on such variables as decision support, information load, and role ambiguity. It has been argued that supervisors serve as a central source of information for employees (Daniels & Spiker, 1983). Perhaps the most critical issue here is the extent to which parties serve as unique sources of information for each other. If there are other, alternative channels available, then this relationship becomes less important in determining impacts for both parties.

Cell 3 indicates organizational level affective/affiliative outcomes. Here the locus is not the individual but the emergent effect of this relationship on the organization. Effective SSCR can speed integration of individuals into ongoing organizational processes and diminish turnover. However, on the darker side, supervisors can recruit subordinates into coalitions which contest for power and increase the level of conflict in an organization. Jablin (1981) has found that supervisors who are perceived to be highly involved in politics are perceived to be less open, and that their subordinates are less satisfied in general with their SSCR.

Cell 4 stresses the importance of SSCR in the systemic processes of coordination and control. Here the relationship becomes crucial in maintaining the organizational system. It is at this level that such factors as hierarchical distortion become so critical to organizational operations. Since the SSCR is the primary link in this hierarchical chain, it has a determinant impact on whether or not long-linked chains become so distorted as to diminish the capacity of an organization to effectively coordinate and control its operations. Jablin (1979) has also stressed the important impacts of technology on SSCR which could operate at this level.

Even a cursory examination of these cells reveals that the SSCR is an important mediator of other organizational processes. Its relative importance is determined in part by its degree of embeddedness in the structure of communication relationships of an organization. This structure can constrain the parties in the relationship, limiting their range of action. Thus a supervisor's worst impulse for dominant behavior may be restricted by the rules governing his or her behavior.

In addition, the structure may determine the amount of redundancy in other relationships which can offset the harmful consequences of a bad SSCR. It often seems to be forgotten that a supervisor naturally has relationships with multiple subordinates. So when a relationship with one subordinate turns sour, the most likely outcome is that a supervisor will seek a more satisfactory relationship with another subordinate. Thus, the easiest course for a supervisor is not to repair a relationship, or to terminate it, but simply to let it wither. A subordinate, on the other hand, has more difficulty in finding a qualitatively similar substitute, but through a patchwork of many relationships, can recover many of the things that are lost from a poor SSCR. A bad SSCR is definitely not a good thing for the individuals involved or for the organization, but it need not be a devastating thing, since an individual's relative embeddedness in a larger organizational structure provides alternative means for accomplishing various ends. Thus a series of uniplex relationships with persons other than one's supervisor could substitute for a rich multiplex one.

On the other hand a strong SSCR may actually hurt the organization in a number of ways. One finding from the interpersonal literature is telling in this regard. It has been found that, as couples become more involved with each other, their separate focal networks shrink in size and their mutual networks grow (Milardo, 1983). This finding, if generalized to the organizational situation, has important implications, since, among other things, it reduces an individual's weak ties, with important consequences for the access of the two parties to a diverse array of information. Thus, an individual's communication proximity, which has been associated with the concept of the strength of weak ties, can be related to such issues as his or her relative innovativeness (Rogers, 1983).

HUMAN ENVIRONMENT AND THE APPROACHES

The human composition of the organization often determines formal rules governing relationships, as well as emergent cultural ones. In turn, these rules often are represented in manifest communication gradients and organizational networks. Thus, each of the approaches can be related in various ways to the impact of the human environment. In turn these factors can be related to contextual factors which influence both, such as organizational demography. For example, an aging, long-tenured organizational cohort may have developed elaborate cultural norms concerning member behavior. These norms may have been embodied over time in the formal rule structure of the organization and, as a result, become sacrosanct. This cohort, as it rises to more and more powerful positions, can effectively block newcomes from contending for power. They can manipulate communication networks to deny access to information, as well as physically isolate new members.

In this chapter the human environment has primarily been viewed as an antecedent to the development of structures, but of course the existing communication structure of an organization can impact individuals and their relationships with others. In Chapter 9, the focus will be more specifically on such individual outcome variables as commitment and social support. Naturally, cultural and formal rules and norms can, in effect, set parameters around our relationships with others. In some organizations a supportive male/female relationship will not be an occasion for any remarks or discussion, while in others assumptions may be made about underlying, latent characteristics which determine this manifest relationship. As we have also seen, especially in the Pelz effect, our relationships with others may impact on specific dyadic relationships. How others view our relationships often determines how we view them as well. Thus, the human environment in which structure is embedded affects the nature of our dyadic relationships and, through them, the structure of communication. However, central to these arguments concerning levels of analysis is the notion that higher level social phenomenon (e.g., group and whole organizational) cannot be explained just by combining the attributes of individuals who make up a system (Monge, 1987); the whole is more than the sum of the parts, although, as we have seen in this section, the whole also effects the nature of the parts.

part III

Outcomes of Organizational Communication Structure

chapter 9

Individual Outcomes: Satisfaction, Commitment, and Support

Communication structure can be related to a number of individual outcomes in organizations. These outcomes can be linked to affective states of individuals and also are related to what has been termed *human relations* or *climate* approaches to organizational theory. Thus research in this area tends to focus on how the overall configuration of the organization at the macrolevel is linked to individual reactions to the organization. Most often this research has posited that structure determines these individual processes, and that will be the major thrust of this chapter. However, these processes can also be viewed as being recursive; that is, variables like commitment can be determined by structural factors, but the ensuing level of commitment can affect things like participation in communication networks. These processes themselves also relate to a number of other individual outcomes, such as career advancement/mobility, turnover, and absenteeism, which are beyond the scope of this chapter.

In this chapter the focus will be on three variables which are representative of these processes and which have been extensively examined in the literature: satisfaction, commitment, and social support. Interestingly, these variables can also be linked to the temporal development of investigations into organizational structure. The earliest research in this area examined the linkage between formal structure and satisfaction; then, an intermediate set of studies represented a transitional phase between formal and informal views of structure in relation to commitment. Recently, active research programs have examined the linkage between communication networks and social support. Gradient and cultural approaches, relatively recent advents to structural approaches, have not been as systematically examined in relation to individual outcome variables.

FORMAL STRUCTURE AND JOB SATISFACTION

Perhaps the most extensively researched area which considers the relationship between structure and individual outcome variables is that concerning the relationship between formal structure and attitudes, particularly those relating to job satisfaction. Since several classic literature reviews have systematically reviewed this area (Berger & Cummings, 1979; James & Jones, 1976; Porter & Lawler, 1965), the focus here will be on the most important issues relating to the central themes of this book.

Porter and Lawler's (1965) review of the literature found that hierarchical level related strongly to both attitudes and behaviors, with job satisfaction increasing as one goes up the organizational hierarchy. Berger and Cummings's (1979) systematic literature review was designed to follow up on the extensive review of Porter and Lawler (1965), focusing on studies conducted after Porter and Lawler's (1965) review and including nonbusiness organizations. Although Berger and Cummings (1979) also found general support for the relationship between hierarchical level and job satisfaction, they noted that there was only limited support for this proposition in military organizations. Berger and Cummings (1979) also found that work attitudes other than job satisfaction systematically varied by hierarchical level.

It might be the case that only satisfied individuals are selected for higher-level positions, thus accounting for this finding. Another more interesting possibility for communication researchers is that the nature of normative communication behaviors changes dramatically as one advances in status in organizations (Porter & Lawler, 1965), becoming more uncertain, personalized, novel, and potentially interesting. As a result this finding might be linked to attendant changes in the communication environment of satisfied individuals. This contention is buttressed by research conducted by Rice and Mitchell (1973) which found that job satisfaction increased for individuals at higher organization levels because of the increased attention of other people, and because interpersonal relationships were more likely to be symmetrical.

It appears that the impact of the number of hierarchical levels is moderated by organizational size, with workers more satisfied in small organizations which have a flat structure. However, there is some evidence suggesting that, in large organizations, workers might be more satisfied with a tall structure (Porter & Lawler, 1965), which has the effect of decreasing subunit size. Berger and Cummings (1979) found general support for a relationship between complexity, particularly vertical complexity, and an organizational member's attitudes and behaviors.

Similar to other controversies concerning centralization, such as those in the area of new technologies, there does not appear to be clear evidence relating centralization to an individual's level of satisfaction (Porter & Lawler, 1965). However, Berger and Cummings (1979) were slightly more encouraging, suggesting that there was evidence that, as decentralization increases, positive attitudes increase as well as the frequency of verbal communication.

The level of horizontal differentiation or complexity, particularly related to the line and staff dichotomy, have been found to relate to individual attitudes and behavior (Porter & Lawler, 1965). People in different types of organizational units do tend to have different levels of satisfaction, with staff people being less satisfied than line people, partly because they are less autonomous (Porter & Lawler, 1965). However, a subsequent review of the literature has found this relationship to be far more muddy (Berger & Cummings, 1979).

The smaller the size of the subunits an individual is a member of, generally the greater his or her level of satisfaction. This has been attributed in part to the generally poorer communication in large organizational subunits (Porter & Lawler, 1965). There is also some evidence for a smaller effect for the overall size of the organization, but this effect may be moderated by subunit size (Porter & Lawler, 1965) and a host of other variables, including such communication ones as the nature of an organization's information processing and communication systems (Berger & Cummings, 1979).[1]

Oldham and Hackman (1981) have attempted to provide a theoretic base which offers the hope of ameliorating some of the confusion in this literature. They examined two competing frameworks which explain the relationship between organizational structure and employee attitudes and behaviors. The attraction–selection framework suggests that organizations with certain structural properties attract and/or select employees with particular personal attributes, which in turn affects employee reactions. The job-modification framework posits that structural properties affect the characteristics of an employee's job, particularly the level of challenge and complexity, which are then associated with employee reactions. Data

---

[1] This area of the literature can be criticized on several grounds. Perhaps most important is the degree to which these formal organizational properties can be defined in terms of communication or are related to communication process, which in turn raises some concern with the relationship between communication and the level of satisfaction in organizations. There also appear to be complex interactions among most of the formal structural variables and attitudes, and very few multivariate studies have been conducted which directly assess the nature of these interactions (Berger & Cummings, 1979; Porter & Lawler, 1965).

from 36 organizations showed that job modification framework was a superior explanation, but that a synthesis of both might be needed to explain the relationship between employee attitudes and formal structure.

NETWORK GROUPS AND ATTITUDE FORMATION

The formation of attitudes in human communication networks has long been a crucial concern in a number of the social sciences. Indeed, there have been a number of mathematical models which in essence argue that greater amounts of communication result in more attitude similarities within networks. These discrepancy models have received empirical support in a number of contexts (e.g., Danes, Hunter, & Woelfel, 1978; Goldberg, 1954; Zimbardo, 1960) and essentially hypothesize that attitude change is a function of the distance between initial attitudes and the rate of contact between any two communicators. This leads to the notion that, if an individual communicates intensively within a group, he or she will, over time, converge on the group's consensus. However, if the individual has ties outside of the group then his or her attitude will be some linear combination of the proportion of time he or she spends communicating with others, and the nature of their disparate attitude positions. Danowski (1980) found some support for these notions in studies of groups within a large Eastern financial institution, although the relationships between group connectivity and member attitude uniformity were somewhat counterintuitive and more complex than expected. One major limiting condition to these processes is the amount of information that an individual already possesses relating to a particular attitude. Woelfel, Cody, Gillham, and Holmes (1980) argue that the greater the amount of information that has been previously communicated to an individual, the less the likelihood that future messages can induce attitude change.

In organizations, partially because of their differentiation into functional groupings, individuals within disparate groups will come to adopt unique perspectives often associated with their functions (Lawrence & Lorsch, 1968). It might be expected that, if there were enough ties present between groups, a whole organization network would eventually come to reflect a common position on a particular attitude (Abelson, 1964; French, 1956). The underlying assumptions of this particular perspective have been empirically supported in the work of Albrecht (1979), who found that key communicators were more likely to be cognitively and attitudinally integrated into their organizations. However, recognizing the openness of organizations to communication from other organizations, other institutions within the society (e.g., professional associations), and the mass media, it is unlikely that any organization will be isolated enough or long enough lived for the entities within it to come to convergence (Taylor, 1968).

The underlying thrust of these ideas is helpful in understanding a number of critical issues related to subgroups and coalitions within cultures and climates, and other organizational issues as well (e.g., Abelson, 1979). For example, they may help to explain why technological impacts have always been clearer at the work-unit level (Withey et al., 1983). Perception of organizational climate has also been found to vary among subgroups within an organization (Drexler, 1977; Jones & James, 1979; Payne & Mansfield, 1973), as well as by positions within networks (Falcione, Sussman, & Herden, 1987), with the assertion that collective perceptions of members have a much clearer relationship to such outcome variables as job satisfaction and job performance (Joyce & Slocum, 1984).

Similar arguments can also be advanced in the field of organizational culture. Erickson (1982), while developing arguments from a different conceptual base, especially those related to structural equivalence and related processes of social comparison, has suggested that a somewhat similar notion can be found in the development of belief systems of individuals in networks. A *belief system* is an organized diversity of attitudes which can be directly related to notions underlying organizational cultures. Erickson contends that too many ties between groups will result in a commonality of positions, but she offers an interesting twist to the previous arguments. She contends that a moderate number of ties between divergent groups is likely to result in stronger opposing belief systems, since these groups can now define themselves more clearly in their opposition to other groups.

Her arguments have direct implications for the development of coalitions and subcultures within organizational cultures, particularly in terms of the political processes within organizations, which have been the focus of most work in this area (e.g., Lucas, 1987). According to Stevenson, Pearce, and Porter (1985), the following are the defining characteristics of coalitions: interacting group, deliberately constructed, independent of formal organizational structure, lack of formal internal structure, mutual perception of membership, issue oriented, external focus, and concerted member action. Most of these dimensions directly relate to communication structure, particularly concerning the emergence of communication networks. Stevenson et al. (1985) have argued that coalitions are more likely to occur in times of major organizational change, when social comparison indicates that one's own position vis-á-vis others is unfavorable, when the opportunities for interaction are greater, when members have a fair degree of discretion in carrying out their responsibilities, and when coalitions have greater visibility within the organization. All of these conditions are remarkably evocative of the previous work reviewed in this section.

COMMITMENT

Commitment has been subject to extensive review over the past 20 years within the framework of traditional organizational theory (for example, see Bateman & Strasser, 1984; Becker, 1960; Hrebiniak & Alluto, 1972; Mowday, Porter, & Steers, 1979; Sheldon, 1971). Despite this scrutiny, there has been little consensus on the conceptualization of commitment. Reichers (1985), for example, lists 11 different ways in which organizational commitment has been researched as a determinant of other organizational variables. Likewise, he also cites 17 definitions of *commitment* as a dependent variable. Although the construct of commitment has been defined in many ways, the most common and extensive investigations of commitment have employed Mowday, Steers, and Porter's (1979) definition (for example, Blau & Boal, 1987; Farrell & Peterson, 1984; Randall, 1987). Consequently, *commitment* is defined for our purposes as:

> 1) a strong belief in and acceptance of the organization's goals and values;
> 2) a willingness to exert considerable effort on behalf of the organization; and
> 3) a strong desire to maintain membership in the organization. (Mowday et al., 1979, p. 226)

It has been generally argued that structural characteristics of an organization are antecedents of commitment (Steers, 1977; Morris & Steers, 1980). Social integration, a concept intimately related to communication networks, has been found to be an antecedent to organizational commitment, especially in relation to a strong desire to maintain membership in the organization (Buchanan, 1974; Lodahl, 1964). Thus, positive relationships have been found between commitment and membership in informal cliques (Becker, 1960), overall patterns of participation (Antonovsky & Antonovsky, 1974), and group attitudes towards the organization (Buchanan, 1974; Patchen, 1970). A lack of integration seems to be associated with the development of negative attitudes towards the organization (McLaughlin & Cheatam, 1977).

More specifically related to organizational communication structure, previous studies have indicated that a positive relationship exists between network involvement and organizational commitment (Buchanan, 1974; Eisenberg, Monge, & Miller, 1983; Lodahl, 1964; Salancik, 1977; Salancik

& Pfeffer, 1977). Network involvement has been defined as the extent to which people establish and maintain direct and/or indirect communication contacts with others in their organization (Eisenberg et al., 1983). Research studies on this aspect of commitment have primarily focused on the role of cohesion, or direct communication contact, in developing within networks 'a strong belief in and acceptance of the organization's goals and values,' thus directly relating to element 1 of the definition of commitment.

Following up on these ideas, Hartman and Johnson (1989) conducted a study which focused on the relationship between commitment and Burt's (1982, 1987) theory of social contagion. Burt's (1982, 1987) social contagion theory addresses how members embedded within the social context come to share similar perceptions based on their communication relationships. Social contagion theory seeks to explain how network structure affects emergent social pressures to conform. It specifies how the social context of individuals affects their attitudes and behaviors. This social context is determined by the configuration of relationships that exist in a particular social structure. Cohesion and structural equivalence serve as competing theoretical explanations of the impact of social context (the structural configuration of communication relationships) on social contagion processes.

Cohesion perspectives essentially argue that communication contacts determine the development of norms (Friedkin, 1984). Thus, cohesion focuses on the socializing effect of discussions. The central assumption of the cohesion perspective is that the more frequent and empathetic the communication between the ego (focal individual) and the alter (comparison individual), the more likely the ego's opinions and behaviors will resemble that of the alter's (Burt, 1987). The ego is able to come to a normative understanding of the costs and benefits of specific actions and opinions in terms of the people with whom the discussions are held, thus reducing the ego's level of uncertainty. The cohesion perspective predicts contagion between the ego and alter when they have strong relations with each other (Burt, 1987). The ego and the alter are expected to act similarly even though they may have different configurations in their relationships with others. Thus, if I have strong ties to my supervisor, my relationship with him or her could "override" his or her ties to other managers.

Structural equivalence focuses on competition.[2] The more the alter is able to substitute for the ego in the ego's role relations, the more likely it is

---

[2] Of course, structural equivalence has been the object of intensive investigation in the other social sciences, particularly in sociology. It can also be tied to other areas of communication research, such as interpersonal (Eggert & Parks, 1987). In network analysis

that the ego will conform to the behavior or opinions that characterize competitors (i.e., structurally equivalent alters) (Burt, 1987). In this view my supervisor could be expected to hold views similar to other managers' at his or her hierarchical level because of their similar positioning in the network. Structural equivalence details similarity in patterns of relationships that the ego and alter have with others. The ego comes to a normative understanding of the costs and benefits of the alter filling his or her role and a social understanding which is shared by others in similar roles. So physicians may adopt a new drug because they think that it is the proper behavior for people in their position, regardless of their direct discussions with others (Burt, 1987). This suggests a slightly different interpretation of structural equivalence than that offered by Burt, and a restatement of its central assumption. Individuals may be the focus of similar information, requests, and demands from members of their role set, creating an information field in which they are embedded which, when internalized, creates even more powerful pressures to conform than discussions with other alters. Thus, two academics who read the same journals may come to hold similar views of the world, even though they never actually discuss them with each other.

Since cohesion explanations of network impacts have been the norm within communication (see Rogers & Kincaid, 1981), some adjustment is required to rethink past results in terms of structural equivalence, but, as Burt (1987) establishes, some classic studies in the social sciences might be best reinterpreted in structural equivalence frameworks. Burt's work on innovation processes (Burt, 1987) and on perceptions of academic journals (Burt, 1982) leads him to conclude that structural equivalence explanations are superior. While there is a very interesting pattern to these results, social contagion has not been widely examined in organizations.

Hartman and Johnson's (1989) study hypothesized that cohesion perspectives of social contagion would provide a better explanation of the relationship between communication networks and commitment than would structural equivalence explanations. This study systematically compared cohesion and structural equivalence explanations of social contagion by examining multiplex functional communication networks. It was conducted in an Eastern, state wide, nonprofit lobbying organization. The results, which generally supported the hypotheses, suggested that

---

research this interest is especially reflected in the work of White and his colleagues (1976) in block modeling, which constitutes an alternative approach to structural equivalence. White's research has focused on network programs, which determine the homogeneity of patterning of actors across several different types of relationships. However, this approach has not been systematically tied to nonnetwork variables and tends to be less suited to communication problems than Burt's (Alba, 1982).

commitment was a broad-based concept in network terms, which significantly related to cohesion explanations of social contagion.

While there was general support for this hypothesis, involvement in networks related to job duties did not have as much impact on commitment as was expected. Krackhardt and Porter (1985) have suggested, from a social information-processing framework, that job-related functions would have a more immediate impact on employees than discussions related to organizational goals. While the general pattern of results does not support this argument, there does appear to be a different pattern for job duties than for the other networks. The explanation for this might be associated with the previous communication-network-related findings that job involvement can mediate commitment-related processes (Moch, 1980; Eisenberg et al., 1983).

Moch (1980) found that people who were isolated in work networks looked to their jobs as alternative sources of meaning and identity. Thus, job duties and commitment (defined as network involvement) may serve as distinct sources of individual gratification relating to separable organizational processes. Eisenberg et al. (1983) found that, for employees who were not involved in their jobs, involvement in job-related communication networks tended to lead to commitment. However, they also suggested that commitment could be increased by involvement in other networks. This contention was supported by the findings of the Hartman and Johnson (1989) study, particularly in the biplex network of job duties and goals, which when multiplexed was closer to Eisenberg et al.'s (1983) operationalization. In sum, commitment appears to be related to an individual's integration into communication networks.

Boundary Spanning and Culture

The integration and commitment of boundary spanning personnel have always been problematic for organizations. *Boundary spanners* are individuals who, while members of one social system, have links to another. Usually, these linkages are discussed in terms of individuals who have communication ties to people outside their organization as a result of their formal organizational position. However, boundary spanning has also been applied to individuals who link different groups within the same organization (Tushman, 1977), and this variant of the definition can overlap with a number of other structural roles such as the liaison (Womack, 1984). Central to the definition of boundary spanning is the idea that these individuals process information from diverse sources and represent the organization externally (Womack, 1984). These positions are critical to innovations and the diffusion of ideas between and within organizations (Czepiel, 1975; Daft, 1978). Both of these aspects of boundary spanning can interfere with an individual's integration into the organization and with his or her resulting level of commitment, since commitment can be reduced by the inherent uncertainties of these positions.

While many cultural elements can effect the level of an individual's integration, the structural features of culture which relate most directly to these processes are rites and rituals. A study conducted by Buster et al. (1987) addresses precisely these concerns. Based upon a content analysis of interview data, as well as document analysis and researcher observations, it was found that, as a function of structural position, individuals' participation in, and preference for, rites and rituals differed within a high-tech organization.

Specifically, organizational members who were employed in a position which entailed high boundary-spanning behaviors (e.g., systems engineers) showed a tendency to devalue task-oriented rituals while expressing a strong liking and desire for socioemotional rituals. In contrast, non-boundary-spanning support personnel (e.g., accountants) expressed dissatisfaction with socioemotional rituals and indicated a preference for task-related rituals. This relationship may be tied to differential needs for social integration for individuals occupying boundary-spanning and non-boundary-spanning roles. It seems systems engineers use such activities as beer blasts, Christmas parties, picnics, and ski trips to help them feel socially integrated into the company, while the nonboundary spanners, who are functionally integrated more deeply into the organization because of their day-to-day interaction within the company's environment, do not value these rituals as highly. Thus the different emphasis on social activities exhibited by systems engineers appears to be a function of their roles in the organization. In a follow-up quantitative study conducted in the same high-tech organization, Buster et al. (1988) found a significant relationship between ritual importance, which reflected the value orientation of organizational members, and commitment. These results bear out the importance of culture and structure in relation to organizational processes such as commitment, integration, and involvement.

SOCIAL SUPPORT

Social support is seen as being "inextricably woven into communication behavior" (Albrecht & Adelman, 1987d, p. 14). In their extensive review of the social support literature Albrecht and Adelman (1987b, p. 19) define *social support* in the following manner:

> *Social support* refers to verbal and nonverbal communication between recipients and providers that reduces uncertainty about the situation, the

self, the other, or the relationship, and functions to enhance a perception of personal control in one's life experience.

Generally, two crucial dimensions of support are isolated, informational and emotional, with informational associated with a feeling of mastery and control over one's environment (Friemuth, 1987), and emotional support crucial to feelings of personal coping, enhanced self-esteem, and needs for affiliation (Albrecht & Adelman, 1987b). Support has been associated with such critical organizational outcome variables as stress, absenteeism, burn-out, turnover, productivity, and morale (Ray, 1987). Support has also been directly tied to communication structures, although it is usually most strongly related to network analysis approaches.

Informational Support

Informational support has not been the subject of extensive investigation in organizations, but it would appear to offer a wealth of potential research opportunities, particularly in the context of organizational decision making processes. Although not typically conceived of as a form of support, informational support is implicit in training programs, and many organizational design decisions revolve around a determination of the information which an individual needs to perform adequately in his or her position. In fact, formal structural relationships may be designed primarily to satisfy the informational support requirements of particular positions. Often, formal organizational programs, such as socialization programs, performance evaluations, and organizational change efforts, stimulate the need for support (Ray, 1987).

Weak ties. The strength of weak ties is perhaps the most well-known concept related to network analysis. It refers to our less-developed relationships, which are more limited in space, place, time, and depth of emotional bonds (Adelman, Parks, & Albrecht, 1987; Weimann, 1983). This concept has been intimately tied to the flow of information within organizations and, by definition, is removed from stronger social bonds such as influence and multiplex relations (Weimann, 1983). Weak ties notions are derived from the work of Granovetter (1973) on how people acquire information related to potential jobs. It turns out that the most useful information comes from individuals in a person's extended networks—casual acquaintances and friends of friends. This information is the most useful precisely because it comes from infrequent or weak contacts. Strong contacts are likely to be people with whom there is a constant sharing of the same information; as a result, individuals within these groupings have come to have the same information base. However, information from outside this base gives unique perspectives and, in some instances, strategic advantages over competitors in a person's immediate network.

Weak ties are also crucial to integrating larger social systems, especially in terms of the nature of communication linkages between disparate groups (Friedkin, 1980, 1982; Weimann, 1983). Granovetter (1982) now maintains that this bridging function between different groups is a limiting condition necessary for the effects of weak ties to be evidenced. However, weak ties may be discouraged in organizations because of concerns over loyalty to one's immediate work unit and questions of control of organizational members. Strong ties may also be preferred, because they are more likely to be stable and because, as a result of the depth of their relationship, individuals may be willing to delay immediate gratifications from the other person associated with equity demands (Albrecht & Adelman, 1987c). Individuals to whom an individual is strongly tied may also be more readily accessible and more willing to be of assistance (Granovetter, 1982).

Weak ties provide critical informational support, because they transcend the limitations of our strong ties and because, as often happens in organizations, our strong ties can be disrupted or unavailable (Adelman et al., 1987). Thus, weak ties may be useful for discussing things you do not want to reveal to your close work associates, providing a place for an individual to experiment, extending access to information, promoting social comparison, and fostering a sense of community (Adelman et al., 1987). While weak ties have been primarily related to networks, they can be legitimated by the culture in which our relationships are embedded, and they can also be linked to communication gradients. Individuals need proximate, accessible others for support, but they also need them for understanding, a process in which visual access also plays a major role (Ray, 1987).

Emotional Support

Social support studies in organizations have tended to focus on the affective side of organizational life. This is reflected in the three fundamental conclusions Albrecht and Adelman (1987a) draw from the literature on social support in both organizational and non-organizational settings. First, supportive interactions are seen as a search for human contact as well as a search for meaning to interpret the world. Second, social support is needed to reduce uncertainty and thus to produce feelings of control and mastery. Finally, reflecting most of the research literature in this area, they conclude that support occurs within an individual's communication network.

Networks are often viewed as the infrastructure of social support (Albrecht & Adelman, 1987b). For example, Albrecht, Irey, and Mundy (1982) found that workers who spent much of their time outside of the organization needed to be highly integrated into their organizations. The literature on the relationship between integratedness (couched in network terms), support, and burnout is probably the most developed in this area. However, the results of the studies which have been done to date are somewhat mixed (Ray, 1987), providing some interesting insights into the dysfunctional aspects of support. Interestingly, the conclusions of this literature also bear on strength of weak ties notions.

Early studies in this area tended to argue that the more integrated networks were, the more supportive they were (Albrecht, 1982). Indeed, high-density networks tend to lead to positive social identity and the acquisition of tangible services from others with whom the individual has strong ties (Albrecht & Adelman, 1987c). However, it turns out that less dense networks of relationships may be more supportive, since they provide access to a wider range of information sources (Ray, 1987). High-density networks can also be stifling, and even devastating for individuals who are rejected by their groups (Albrecht & Adelman, 1987b). They may also be stressful because their maintenance requires more energy (Ray, 1987). These assertions are supported by a study conducted by Kirmeyer and Lin (1987) which found a negative relationship between communication with peers and social support. In terms of larger system consequences, highly integrated networks run the risk of dysfunctional social contagion effects, since, for example, stressed individuals may increase the stress of others (decreasing the support they in turn can give), putting the whole system at risk (Albrecht & Adelman, 1987c).

The conclusion drawn now is that individuals in low density, heterogeneous networks, partitioned into discrete subfunctions, fare better in terms of social support. In particular, ties to others outside the immediate work unit are much more likely to reduce burnout and stress (Albrecht, 1982; Ray, 1983). These networks facilitate coping, role transition, and access to needed information (Albrecht & Adelman, 1987b). They also contribute to a greater sense of personal control on the part of individuals, since they are not dependent on any one group of individuals (Albrecht & Adelman, 1987b). Not so paradoxically then, Leiter (1988) has found that, at higher levels, work-related contacts may be associated both with increased feelings of personal accomplishment, and increased emotional exhaustion among members, of a multidisciplinary mental health team.[3]

---

[3] In general, given the presumed positive benefits of supportive relationships, there are considerable dysfunctions of social support both for the organization and for individuals. For individuals receiving support, it can produce illusions of control and an inflated sense of self-

While the social support literature focuses on communication networks, this is a somewhat limited view of the array of supports offered by the communication structure of an organization, particularly because such organizational features as the length of tenure of employees and the extent to which a particular position permits interaction limit the role networks play in social support (Ray, 1987). Many formal organizational programs, often fostered within the perspective of human relations approaches, are specifically designed to achieve social-support-related outcomes. Employee assistance programs, affirmative action programs, t-groups, and mentoring programs are all formal organizational mechanisms designed to support the employee. Effective supervisor–subordinate communication relationships also contain many supportive elements.

Communication networks themselves can represent convergence of network members around symbolic meanings of support (Albrecht & Adelman, 1987b). This highlights the importance of context in the development of supportive relationships, since supportive relationships may be best provided by those who share a particular organizational context and stable relationships are also more likely to be supportive (Ray, 1987). These networks can in effect constitute elaborate feedback processes through which individual behavior is regulated and maintained. At times, such as with drug addicts in larger societal settings, the enmeshment of individuals in these networks may not be to anyone's benefit (Albrecht & Adelman, 1987b). Communication rituals can also be viewed as a key means of maintaining emotional support for organizational members, especially those that must spend considerable time outside of the organization (Buster et al., 1987).

Other elements of an organization's culture may also play a role in the development of supportive relationships. Support within organizations can exist only to the extent organizations are committed to a supportive climate symbolically and tangibly (Ray, 1987). For example, root metaphors of an organizational culture can greatly influence whether or not support is offered and what type will be given. A family metaphor is inherently a supportive one, while other metaphors, such as the machine, where an individual is viewed as an interchangeable part, are antithetical to support. Also, the normative rule structure of an organization may

---

worth (Albrecht & Adelman, 1987a). The process of seeking support can increase stress resulting from the uncertainty of another's reactions, especially since support is most often sought from those higher in status and credibility (Albrecht & Adelman, 1987a), and often their reactions are negative and result in a poor impression of the seeker (Albrecht & Adelman, 1987c). For the source of social support, the act of giving it to another may drain personal resources (e.g., psychic, time, etc.) and it could potentially worsen his or her relationship with the seeker (e.g., invalidating seeker perceptions of the organization and his or her role within it) (Albrecht & Adelman, 1987c).

effect the willingness of others to give support. In addition, except perhaps at the initial stages of socialization, continued appeals for social support on the part of workers may be looked upon unfavorably, especially by supervisors, and as a result they may threaten an employee's upward mobility and even retention (Ray, 1987).

INDIVIDUAL OUTCOMES
AND THE APPROACHES

The relationship between the four approaches to communication structure and individual outcomes shows, perhaps more clearly than any other area, the role of trends in the social sciences in the development of a field. The approaches to communication structure have followed a clear historical pattern, with formal approaches coming first, followed by network approaches. Only recently have cultural and gradient approaches been systematically introduced. These approaches appear to have been related to whatever individual outcome variable was "hot" in the organizational behavior literature at the time that they were the primary approach to structure. So we have a preponderance of studies relating to formal structure and job satisfaction, then a transitional era when network involvement was related to commitment, soon followed by an emphasis on networks and social support. Thus this area of structure research has developed in a very ad hoc fashion. As a result there are a wealth of research opportunities emerging today, especially in terms of culture and gradients, and the opportunity to return to some traditional questions with new approaches.

While the job satisfaction literature has become moribund, in part because of a failure to find a clear relationship with productivity, the significant relationships often found between it and formal structural indices points to some opportunities for structural research. First, it suggests a general relationship between structure and attitudes (see Porter & Lawler, 1965), which, especially in terms of cultural approaches, may be well worth investigating with more precise techniques, which encompass a range of culturally related attitudes (see Barnett, 1988). Second, given the conceptual muddiness of most of the formal structure research (Porter & Lawler, 1965), more precisely conceived studies, which more clearly incorporate communication properties, offer a wealth of research opportunities. There also are a number of opportunities for investigation of particular research questions which have been suggested in a few limited studies. For example, the reinforcing or moderating influence of spatial properties on attitude formation has not been adequately investigated. Johnson (1987b) reports that physical proximity relates to understanding; might it relate to shared attitudes as well?

Commitment, and the associated issues of involvement and integration, also need to be grounded in more empirical network studies. They also could be fruitfully explored with other techniques as well. The Buster et al. (1987, 1988) research studies suggest one line of research relating cultural approaches to an individual's structural position in organizations. But the early work of Etzioni (1961) suggest yet more fundamental questions: What is the relationship between attitude structures of individuals and those represented in the culture of an organization? The high congruence suggested by a normative involvement in organizations (a strong belief by the individual in the goals of the organization) has been argued to result in high levels of commitment. What is the role of communication structure in promoting this high level of congruence between individual and organizational goals?

Social support is the individual outcome most intimately associated with communication structure, but social support is almost exclusively conceived of in terms of network analysis. The Johnson (1987b) research findings linking understanding to physical positioning could also be associated with the possibilities an individual has for informational support, and certainly Allen's (1977) work in research and development laboratories discussed in Chapter 6 suggests that there is a strong tie between informational support and spatial proximity within organizations. Community-based studies have also found linkages between emotional support and proximity, but, except for some research on burnout, this research topic has not been systematically examined. On the other hand, increased social density can increase stress and the need for social support, as well as decrease the possibility that those who are proximate can offer social support for individuals. Similarly, the role of culture both in shaping the kinds of support that will be expected and offered, and in providing occasions, such as rituals, when it can be obtained, has not been systematically investigated.

At a more abstract level, the major theoretical contribution that research in this area could make is in specifying the transformation processes by which macro-organizational properties (e.g., size) become translated into individual-level effects. Most studies have tilted to the psychological level of explanation rather than focusing on how characteristics of the organizational levels above the immediate work group influence behavior and attitudes (James & Jones, 1976; Oldham & Hackman, 1981). Many of the translation mechanisms between macro-level properties and individual outcomes are represented in the various approaches to communication structure, particularly network analysis (Danowski, 1980; Payne & Mansfield, 1973). As Moch et al. (1983) have pointed out, there is little detailed theory to directly measure the structure vs. individual behavior linkage and the various transformations that must occur. Focusing on relationships (e.g., network analysis) might offer the best hope of doing just this. Indeed, some have argued that organizational characteristics which are remote from someone's experience require more numerous and complex linkages to influence individual perceptions than those characteristics which are more directly experienced, such as organizational reward structures (Jones & James, 1979).

Perhaps the most interesting study in this area is the one conducted by Indik (1965), which focused on the linkage between organizational size and member participation. Essentially, Indik argued that size was a structural variable which influenced member participation indirectly through such organizational processes as communication, control, task specialization, and coordination. These organizational processes then affected the ties (e.g., job satisfaction) that bind individuals to organizations and which directly affect organizational member participation behavior. A total of 96 organizations in the broad classes of package delivery, automobile dealerships, and voluntary membership educational political organizations were used to examine four alternative models derived from this basic framework. Interestingly enough, the explanation which worked best across three types of organizations was the one that most explicitly incorporated communication. Essentially, the argument for this alternative ran that, in larger organizations, there were more possible communication linkages, which reduced the possibility that adequate communication would be achieved. In turn, less adequate communication among members reduced their interpersonal attractiveness to each other, and, as a result, member-participation rates declined. Indik's (1965) research provides a foundation for thinking about the specific linkages between formal structural properties of an organization, communication structure, and individual reactions to the organization. Regrettably, in spite of the crucial theoretic importance of research in this area, his initial foundation has not been built upon.

As we have seen, there are a wealth of research opportunities related to structure and individual outcomes. This wealth of opportunities, and the ultimate payoffs of a focus on individual outcomes, is seen in the history of strength of weak ties, social support, and boundary spanning notions. These concepts are arguably the structural variables which have most directly captured the imagination of social scientists.

chapter 10

Organizational Outcomes: Innovation and Productivity

The two organizational outcomes examined in this section are critical to the success of the modern organization. In today's environment an organization which cannot innovate will soon find its products and services obsolete, and one which cannot increase its productivity will find that the goods and services that it does produce will not be offered at a competitive price. While the outcomes examined in the previous chapters can all contribute to the relative effectiveness of organizations, the processes examined in this chapter in a very direct way spell out the "bottom line" for the organization. These outcomes do this because they determine how well the organization is doing vis-á-vis other organizations.

Somewhat similarly to the individual outcomes examined in the previous chapter, these variables can also determine other organizational outcomes. For example, it is quite possible that the relative success of an organization can be a major contributor to variables such as job satisfaction. That is, I can take some vicarious satisfaction from how well my organization is doing independent of my perception of how well I am doing in my organization. This is somewhat akin to the thrill that even the lowliest student within a university can get from the fact that that university's football team is ranked number 1. There may also be a contagion effect which increases my willingness to share information with others in a growing, vibrant organization. In this situation a rising tide raises all boats, and the success of my peers can contribute to my success as well. Organizations which are no longer growing become more characterized by zero sum games; that is, I only succeed at the expense of others, which can have disastrous consequences on the flow of information in informal networks. In this chapter, however, the emphasis will be on the impact of structure on innovations and on organizational outcomes.

Much is known about the relationship between formal organizational structures and innovations, but very little work has been done on the relationship between innovation and the informal structures of organizations. Similarly, while it appears obvious that both cultures and spatial factors have important relationships to innovation processes, very little empirical research has examined this relationship systematically.

While on the surface it may appear that there is a clear link between communication and productivity (Downs et al., 1988), somewhat disconcertingly very little is known about the relationship between communication structure and productivity. This can be partially attributed to the general emphasis of the social sciences on psychological processes such as attitude formation (Pfeffer, 1978, 1982). As a result, much less is known about people's actual behavior than about what they think they will do. This lack of knowledge is also attributable to the complications which soon arise when one tries to explore what at first would appear to be a relatively straightforward outcome variable such as productivity. "Productivity is simultaneously one of the most important and most difficult variables for communication researchers to study" (Downs et al., 1988, p. 173).

INNOVATION

Modern organizations must constantly adapt to survive in today's rapidly changing environment. An organization which cannot change, which cannot innovate to meet changing environmental conditions, eventually will find itself no longer competitive in an increasingly complex and technologically sophisticated economy. As a result innovation processes are crucial to organizational success in terms both of establishing new directions for a company (Wager, 1962) and for organizational effectiveness generally (Rogers & Agarwala-Rogers, 1976).

Innovation can be related to: (a) a product or service, (b) a production process, (c) organizational structure, (d) people, and (e) policy (Zaltman, Duncan, & Holbek, 1973). A number of factors can potentially determine the success of innovation processes, including the interdependence of components of the system, their diversity, the nature of the formal management system, external conditions (Galbraith, 1973), the general organizational cultural norms towards innovation (Deal & Kennedy, 1982), and the openness of the organizational system (Rogers, 1983). Although these factors are all important, communicative processes, particularly those related to reducing uncertainty and persuasion, can ultimately determine the extent to which an innovative idea is assimilated into the preceding constraints of the ongoing organizational system.

An increased understanding of the central role communication plays in innovation has both important theoretical and pragmatic implications. The nature of the information transmitted concerning an innovation can be grouped into three general categories: (a) information concerning the innovation, (b) information related to influence and power, and (c) information concerning operationalizing the innovation (Schramm & Roberts, 1971). Face-to-face channels are crucial to the formations of coalitions which support an innovation. Most prior research has focused on the implementation by management of innovations through formal channels (see Rogers, 1983) rather than the more informal communication processes which are linked to the initiation of innovations in large organizations (Kanter, 1983). Indeed, it has been argued that the matching of oral communication patterns to the structure of a particular task is critical to innovation in research and development laboratories (Tushman, 1978). In fact, "innovation flourishes in organizations when information flow is wide spread, feedback is rapid ... and both mechanisms cut across traditional lines of authority" (Albrecht & Ropp, 1984, p. 78).

Formally Generated Innovations

Considerable research attention in the 1960s and 1970s was devoted to the relationship between formal structure and innovations, with a disheartening array of mixed findings, for reasons similar to the ones we have noted in previous chapters (see also Rogers, 1983). For example, the mixed findings related to organizational size and innovation have been attributed to two offsetting processes. While size increases occupational diversity, it stifles innovation through the institution of more bureaucratic controls (Daft, 1978; Kim, 1980). There does appear to be support, with some cross-cultural verification in Korea, for the hypotheses that complexity and integration are positively related to innovation and formalization and centralization are negatively related (Kim, 1980). Thus, adoption of technological innovations is more prevalent in organizations which are large, specialized, functionally differentiated, and decentralized (Kimberly & Evanisko, 1981; Rogers, 1983), factors which have also been found to relate to innovation adoption by lower-level decision makers in organizations (Moch & Morse, 1977).

   Formally generated innovations are ones originating in upper management using the traditional authority structure as the primary impetus underlying adoption. This is a unique feature of innovation within organizations; an entity of higher status and authority can decide to adopt an innovation that another segment of the organization must implement. In organizations the former unit has been termed the *adoption unit* and the process as a whole has been called *authority innovation decision* (Rogers & Shoemaker, 1971).

   Successful implementation of an innovation can be conceived of as the routinization, incorporation, and stabilization of the innovation into the ongoing work activity of an organizational unit. For organizations, "the bottom line is implementation (including its institutionalization), and not just the adoption *decision*" (Rogers & Adhikayra, 1979, p. 79). Advocating change necessarily results in increased uncertainty, which can lead to resistance to innovation by adoption units (Coch & French, 1948; Katz & Kahn, 1978). Communication plays a key role in overcoming resistance to innovations and in the reduction of uncertainty. Complexity and risk are elements of uncertainty which are crucial to the ultimate implementation of innovations (Bennis, 1965). Complexity in this context relates to the number of potential alternatives perceived in an innovation adoption. Risk is the perceived consequences to the adoption unit associated with the implementation of an innovation adoption (Lowrance, 1980).

The reduction of uncertainty inherent in communication can decrease resistance to innovations, but usually decision units also must exert some degree of power and influence to facilitate innovation implementation. In fact, the various types of power, and the communication channels available to transmit them and information concerning innovations, are the primary structural characteristics which affect innovation implementation. The commonly used types of power in organizational settings have different communication costs associated with them, and they also result in different levels of involvement in adoption units (see Figure 10-1).

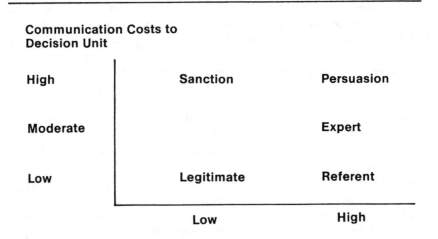

Figure 10-1.   Communication Costs and Levels of Involvement Associated with Various Types of Power*

* Fidler & Johnson (1984, p. 706)

These communication costs are determined by the amount of resources expended in the transmission of a message (Farace, Taylor, & Stewart, 1978). Some combinations of power, complexity, and risk can overload available channels, creating an upper limit to the capacity of an organization to implement certain innovations successfully (Fidler & Johnson, 1984). The complexity and perceived risk inherent in innovations interact with types of power to determine the communication costs associated with the implementation of a particular innovation.

The perception of risk often is a result of a lack of knowledge concerning the implications of an innovation (Strassman, 1959), which necessitates additional information transfer to reduce uncertainty. The more risky the adoption of an innovation, the more likely it is that an adoption unit will be resistant, requiring more rewards or influence attempts on the part of the decision unit before the acquiescing of the adoption unit in the implementation of an innovation (Zaltman & Duncan, 1977). The various types of power used to overcome resistance to innovations are crucial in determining the success of innovative processes generally, since acceptance can be hindered through both passive and active resistance (Zaltman et al., 1973).

Complexity also affects the types of power that will be used to promote innovation implementation. For example, the more facets to an innovation, the more actions that have to be rewarded and, somewhat relatedly, the greater the volume of information related to persuasion. Thus, the high communication costs of persuasion and sanction—and also, in this case, expert power—increase almost exponentially with greater complexity; however, the communication costs of other types of power increase more linearly, because the invocation of these types of power is inherent in the messages concerning innovation (Fidler & Johnson, 1984).

One of the primary structural features associated with the diffusion of innovations within systems is the number and arrangement of recurring communication channels. These channels have differing capacities for handling particular types of information, and their combined capacities limit the raw volume of information in any system. Communication channel efficacy within organizations refers to the ratio of resources expended to the utility of a transmission event (Farace et al., 1978). The efficacy of a channel is important. It determines, in part, the ultimate cost effectiveness of the process of innovation implementation.

Generally, two channels have been focused on in innovation research: *interpersonal,* involving primarily face-to-face modalities; and *mediated* (often referred to as *mass media*), which typically are interposed in some way between source and receiver (Rogers & Shoemaker, 1971). The capacity of interpersonal channels to provide social support and enhanced confidence in the outcomes of an innovation can be crucial to the ultimate adoption of innovations (Katz, 1957, 1961). Interpersonal channels generally have been found to be more useful in transmitting highly complex subject matter (Chapanis, 1971; Conrath, Buckingham, Dunn, & Swanson, 1975; Picot et al., 1982; Tushman, 1978). They are more flexible than mediated channels, they can activate more senses, and they can be more attuned to the specific problems of receivers (Picot et al., 1982; Rogers & Shoemaker, 1971; Tushman, 1978). Interpersonal channels are also able to carry more information through a variety of codes; as a result of this "richness" of channel, they are in a better position to reduce uncertainty caused by the complexity of organizational settings (Holland, Stead, & Leibrock, 1976; Picot et al., 1982). However, the communication costs associated with the use of interpersonal channels generally are quite high. In situations of low complexity a minimum of activity is necessary to relate dimensions to the experience world of the adoption unit. Thus, mediated channels can widely distribute the essential information concerning the innovation with a minimum of effort (Picot et al., 1982; Rogers & Shoemaker, 1971) (see Figure 10-2). In addition, the more modalities an innovation is communicated through, the more likely it is to be diffused by managers to workers (Hoffman & Roman, 1984).

Figure 10-2 details the interactive effects of risk, complexity, and the communication costs of power on communication channel load. Even a

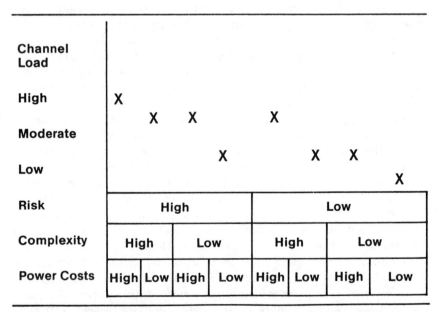

Figure 10.2.   Relationship Between Risk, Complexity, and Communication Costs of Power and Channel Load*

* Fidler & Johnson (1984, p. 710)

cursory examination of this figure reveals some substantial barriers to innovation implementation in some situations. There appears to be a direct inverse relationship between the amount of information load associated with particular conditions and the presumption of the relative success of implementation. Certainly with a highly risky and complex innovation, which requires high volumes of communication to effect, the chances of successful implementation become problematic. These contingent situations suggest that there is a practical upper bound to formally implementing innovations within organizations. In recent years, it has become obvious that innovation adoption does not occur solely on the level of top management. Indeed, the very limitations on communication capacity outlined in this section entail that, if innovation is to flourish, it cannot be limited to management.

Informally Generated Innovations

The initiation of innovations in organizations is more likely to occur in an internal environment where people have easy access to information; there are permeable boundaries between organizational units, rewards for sharing, seeking, and utilizing new information, and for risk taking, accepting, and adapting to change; and the organization encourages its members to be mobile and to develop interpersonal contacts (Goldhar, Bragaw, & Schwartz, 1976). Burt (1980) has argued that one of the motive forces for innovation is the presence of competitors who occupy structurally similar positions in a communication network. Since, if competitors adopt an innovation and it is successful, this would put another individual at a competitive disadvantage, the other has a structural interest in adopting innovations. This entails an individual adopting an innovation when a structurally similar alter will, even if they are not in direct communication contact. All of these factors reflect the market-driven forces of a coactivational view of structure.

In general, informal coalition building is critical to the development of innovations (Albrecht & Hall, 1989; Kanter, 1983), if for no other reason than because some innovations, such as electronic messaging, need a substantial number of adopters for successful implementation (Rice et al., 1988). For informal channels persuasion, or influence, is the primary means available to secure participation in an innovation. Persuasion rests on the capacity of an individual to cause changes in another's behavior by the use of more subtle, informal, and often cognitively oriented means than those associated with sanction or authority (Fidler & Johnson, 1984). In utilizing persuasion, an individual communicates evidence, arguments, and a rationale advocating acceptance of an innovative idea and participation in an innovation. Since innovations within large organizations generally are initiated by an idea generator who must convince others to participate (Galbraith, 1982), the willingness to participate in the implementation of innovations, it usually entails less resistance to the eventual implementation of innovations as well (Kelman, 1961) and is more likely to insure active involvement (Bennis, 1965).

Reducing uncertainty is central to processes of innovation within organizations (Fidler & Johnson, 1984). Uncertainty is a function of the number of alternatives (complexity), the risks associated with them, and the extent to which an individual can be sure of the alternatives (Johnson, 1990). Overcoming perceptions of risk and complexity is crucial to inducing the level of involvement needed for successful innovation (Bennis, 1965). Because new ideas are risky, workers initially share their ideas first with members of their immediate network, which can provide the support individuals need to reach others with whom they do not have strong ties (Ray, 1987). Advocating change necessarily results in increased uncertainty, which can lead to resistance to innovations (Coch & French, 1948; Katz & Kahn, 1978). Communication plays a key role in overcoming resistance to innovations and in the reduction of uncertainty.

Johnson (1990), in one of the more systematic attempts to investigate informally generated innovations, tested a structural equation model of the effects of persuasiveness, salience, and uncertainty on participation in innovations. This research focused on the role of informal communication channels in the transmission of influence attempts related to a new component of an existing program, and examined the initial stages of the development of innovations at lower levels in an organization. The communication channel typically used in this phase is primarily interpersonal, and these subformal channels reflect the informal authority structure of an organization (Downs, 1967). Typically, these more personal channels are more likely to be effective, since they meet the specific needs and questions of the receivers because of the immediacy of feedback and the situation specificity of the channel. As a result there is an inherent reduction of uncertainty involved in the use of these channels, since they lead to increased understanding of a proposed innovation, which may in part account for the somewhat more moderate impact of uncertainty in the model. Indeed, the very complexity of most innovations may require more intensive interaction to arrive at high-quality decisions (Tushman, 1978).

The model developed by Johnson (1990) was tested on data gathered from a large financial institution. In general, the results were supportive of the model, with an acceptable overall goodness of fit and measurement model. The results suggest that the classic communicative variable of persuasion had a paramount impact on participation, reinforcing the notion that communication is central to innovative processes within organizations. Generally, persuasive strategies have been found to be the

most effective means of ensuring the successful implementation of innovations, especially highly risky and complex ones (Bennis, 1965; Zaltman &
Duncan, 1977). Effective persuasion can best overcome resistance attributable both to lack of understanding and to fear; in addition, the use of
persuasion results in a higher level of involvement (Bennis, 1965). The
path between uncertainty and willingness to participate showed a moderate, negative relationship, which confirms the view that firms must build
in an ethos of risk taking, a system of rewards for accepting and adapting
to change, for innovation to prosper (Goldhar et al., 1976). At least in the
early stages of innovation a maximum amount of diversity and freedom is
needed to be innovative; later, in the implementation stage, greater
certainty is required, at least in terms of formal authority and design
(Galbraith, 1982; Rogers & Agarwala-Rodgers, 1976).

The Impact of Culture on Innovations

It is generally assumed that culture plays a significant role in innovation
processes, although the specific nature of its impacts has not been heavily
researched (Rogers, 1983). It has been argued that, at a formal level,
management can effect innovation by setting goals and priorities (Daft,
1978), and that a cultural emphasis on the diffusion of innovations helps
(Hoffman & Roman, 1984). Perhaps the most direct assessment of the role
that organizational culture plays is in issues related to the compatibility of
the innovation with existing values, past experience, and the needs of
adopters (Rogers, 1983). The more compatible an innovation is along these
dimensions, the more likely it is to be adopted. For example, some
innovations such as word processing are often "sold" to an organization on
the basis that they are a more efficient replacement for current practice or
technology (Johnson & Rice, 1987). It is only later that an organization
discovers the truly innovative features of such technologies. However, in
the relation of innovations to organizational communication structure,
perhaps the most telling issues deal with the rules structures related to the
diffusion and generation of innovations.

Kanter (1983) has offered compelling arguments that organizations
which are segmented into different functional groups with strong barriers,
especially informal rule structures, between them, are not going to be
capable of generating or diffusing innovations. Differentiation is necessary for the synergy essential to the creation of ideas, but it also makes it
difficult to insure the consensus necessary for their implementation. In
this regard it is important that several distinctions be made when
discussing innovation in organizations. First, innovation processes often
need to be considered separately from the operating side of the organization (Galbraith, 1982). Second, the rule structure governing the initiation

of innovations may be considerably different than those governing its implementation (Rogers, 1983; Rogers & Agarwala-Rogers, 1983). Thus, while it's known that cultural factors affect innovation processes, currently only the grossest sorts of distinctions can be made about the differential nature of those impacts by function and staging of innovative processes.

PRODUCTIVITY

For the organization and its ultimate survival there is probably no more important issue than productivity. However, surprisingly little research has been done in this area. While there is some evidence that communication relates to productivity (Lewis, Cummings, & Long, 1982), it is often based on anecdotal evidence, on case studies, or on limited, one-shot research efforts (Downs & Hain, 1982). However, improvements in worker effectiveness, since a substantial amount of organizational costs are associated with labor, linked to communication, offer much potential for improving productivity (Downs et al., 1988).

Match, Fit, Congruence, and Contingency

"Organizational architects" design their structures to match functions. While there will be variations in the structure of organizations, they may remain within a "reasonable" range in which there will be no difference in performance attributable to structure. (Dalton et al., 1980, p. 61)

The concepts of match, fit, congruence, and contingency have been used rather loosely in the literature to capture an essential idea related to structures; there is some optimal arrangement of structural elements which promotes the accomplishment of particular functions. For example, Tushman (1978) found in an R & D laboratory that effectiveness is a function of matching communication patterns to the nature of a project's work, particularly at the subunit level (Tushman, 1979). Specifically, high-performance research projects need more intraproject communication than high-performing technical service projects (Tushman, 1978). This idea permeates most of the literature related to organizational outcomes and has become a cornerstone of organizational theory, partly in reaction to the overly simplistic focus of classical management theory, which sought to discover the *one* best way of doing things in organizations (Lawrence & Lorsch, 1965; Woodward, 1958). This notion has been applied to a number of organizational outcomes: the congruence between rules (both perceptual and actual) of the two parties in the supervisor--subordinate communication relationship and job satisfaction (Downs et al., 1988); the relationship between organizational strategy and structure (Egelhoff, 1982; Fry & Smith, 1987); and the relationship between technology and structure (Fry & Smith, 1987). In this section the idea of *match* will be explored in more detail in relation to small group communication networks and the more macrostructural patterns of differentiation and integration.

Small group communication networks. Perhaps more research has been conducted on small group communication networks than on any other area of research related to organizational communication structure. The research results related to task performance and structure are also fairly clear, and they appear to fit quite nicely into a contingency theory framework (Lawrence & Lorsch, 1967) and the idea of a match between structure and performance.[1]

The experimental situation in small group network studies (typically five individuals) constrained the written messages that could flow between group members (e.g., Leavitt, 1951). The primary distinction was between centralized communication networks, where some individuals were clearly more central in the communication flow and could, in effect, act as gatekeepers for other individuals, and decentralized structures, where there was more than one way of routing a message and no one individual dominated the communication flow within a group. Key men would be likely to be selected as leaders of centralized groups by other members (Leavitt, 1951; Shaw, 1971). In addition, there was also clear evidence that central members were more satisfied than peripheral ones, and that the overall level of satisfaction was higher in decentralized groups (Shaw, 1971).

Most of the research studies in this area focused on the performance of groups with different structures on simple and complex tasks. In reviewing this literature, Shaw (1971) found clear evidence of a relationship between effectiveness in the performance of particular types of tasks and the relative degree of centralization of these groups. For simple problems, such as symbol identification, the centralized groups were more efficient in terms of time, sent fewer messages, and made fewer errors. For complex

---

[1] However, this area of research has also been heavily criticized because of the artificiality of the laboratory setting, the lack of realism of the tasks engaged in, the lack of embeddedness of groups in a larger organizational system, the difficulty of capturing temporal effects (Dennis, Goldhaber, & Yates, 1978), and because they make the complex world of communication in organizations too simple (Downs et al., 1988). Despite these criticisms, many of the research findings related to small group communication research speak directly to current organizational experience. For example, even though, for simple tasks, a centralized communication structure is more efficient, it may not be more effective, particularly in terms of worker satisfaction issues, which are often assumed to be linked to innovation and product quality.

problems, such as sentence construction, decentralized groups took less time and made fewer errors, but they still sent more communication messages.

Shaw (1971) adopts the concept of *saturation* to explain these findings. For complex problems the most central person quickly becomes overloaded with both information and the burden of relaying information to other group members. When the group is faced with a simple task, the volume of communication can be easily handled and there is a benefit to having a central repository of information. However, the independence possible in decentralized groups permits the sharing of the relaying burden of information among group members, and it also results in a better match of individual capabilities to the problems confronting the group.

Guetskow and Simon (1955), in an interesting twist on these experiments, speculated that one of the reasons centralized groups were more efficient was that they had in effect been provided with a plan of action for making decisions. They discovered that, if decentralized groups had an opportunity to discuss group organization after they had some experience in the task, they became just as efficient as more centralized groups in performing simple tasks. Thus, decentralized groups became more efficient by reducing the number of linkages that were used within the group. Other research studies have also suggested that there is a general trend over time for efficient groups to reduce the number of communication linkages used, to in effect become more structured or to match their structure to the task at hand (Katz & Kahn, 1978). Indeed, some have argued that these processes can be generalized to a broad range of systems, that hierarchies are inevitable (Krackhardt, 1989).

Differentiation and integration. Perhaps the most well-known research study done relating to the contingency perspective is the classic research of Lawrence and Lorsch (1967) relating to differentiation and integration. In this study companies that varied in their level of performance in three different industries—plastics, food processing, and container—were examined to determine which factor led to high performance in these industries. In general, Lawrence and Lorsch found that high performers matched their levels of differentiation and integration to the demands of their environment.

Differentiation refers to the tendency of organizations to divide into more and more groups in order to specialize their labor, become more sophisticated, larger, and competitive (Katz & Kahn, 1978). Differentiation is often a response to environmental pressures, with some of the groups (e.g., public relations) reflecting new environmental relationships of the organization (Katz & Kahn, 1978). As the organization becomes more and more divided into functional subgroups, a corresponding pressure arises to integrate all of these groups with common organizational goals. Depending on the imperative an organization feels to control the activities of its members, integration may put a limit on the extent to which an organization can grow, since it represents increased administrative costs, information-processing demands, and complexities related to coordination. Thus integration is an area where improved communication can make a substantial difference to an organization:

> The capacity of an organization to maintain a complex, highly interdependent pattern of activity is limited in part by its capacity to handle the communication required for coordination. The greater the *efficiency of communication* within the organization, the greater the tolerance for interdependence. (March & Simon, 1958, p. 162; emphasis in original)

Differentiation of organizations, in Lawrence and Lorsch's (1967) view, is associated with four major dimensions which distinguish subgroups in organizations, although they might most properly be considered consequences of the division of the organization into functional subgroupings: formality of structure, goal orientation, interpersonal relations, and time pressures. These differences exacerbate conflict between subgroups. Resolving conflicts also becomes more complex as environmental demands increase, which in Lawrence and Lorsch's (1967) view can best be resolved by confrontation. A confrontational approach to conflict resolution is more likely to result in the emergence of the best solution, providing the organization has a nonthreatening internal climate.

Integration is accomplished by various linking mechanisms. Lawrence and Lorsch (1967) identified the following integrating mechanisms: the use of teams, direct managerial contact, the managerial hierarchy, and the paper system of the organization. What they found is that organizations which were most successful matched their levels of differentiation and integration to their environments. Organizations in the container industry, which had the most stable environment, had the lowest level of differentiation and only used three integrating mechanisms: direct managerial contact, managerial hierarchy, and the paper system. On the other hand, organizations in the plastic industry, which had the most competitive environment, had, in addition to these three integrating mechanisms, integrative departments and permanent cross-functional teams at different levels of management. Most interestingly, they found that organizations in the container industry which had too many integrating mechanisms were lower performers, because of increased conflict, delays, and waste of resources.

While the general ideas of match, contingency, and congruency are powerful heuristic concepts which have been supported empirically in a number of contexts, they are not without problems. Fry and Smith (1987) have developed a very systematic conceptual critique of this literature. Essentially, they argue for consistent definition and careful distinction of these concepts within the framework of a general approach to theory building. They argue that *congruence* is a concept which is defined by the relationships of a theory's variables. On the other hand, *contingency* is defined by system states where the integrity of the system is maintained, but in markedly different condition. So Lawrence and Lorsch's (1967) work in relation to the match between differentiation and integration and an organization's environment would most clearly fall at the level of contingency, while their discussion of the importance of certain styles of conflict resolution is more of an example of congruence. Congruence is a prior requirement for contingency and a necessary, but not sufficient condition, for contingency. Thus, an organization in Lawrence and Lorsch's (1967) theory must have appropriate conflict resolution strategies if the match between differentiation and integration and the environment is going to occur, but this is not sufficient; the appropriate levels of differentiation and integration must also be in place.

Several other problems exist in this literature. First, many times a contingency view is taken to explain research findings after the fact, but a true perspective on congruence and contingency requires specification of relationships before research is undertaken. Second, and somewhat re-latedly, contingency perspectives often suffer from tautological or circular reasoning: It works because it works. It does not work because the proper match did not occur. Third, the fundamental systems notion of equi-finality immensely complicates this picture. That is, many congruent systems might be established to maintain the system within the same contingent state (Fry & Smith, 1987). Thus, it is possible that both a centralized communication structure coupled with authoritarian manage-ment, and a decentralized structure coupled with democratic manage-ment, can maintain a productive organization within the same general environment. Fourth, only really gross differences in structures may make a difference in performance, and (somewhat akin to catastrophe theory notions) there may be drastic change in organizational perfor-mance when certain thresholds are reached. Thus a change from de-centralized to centralized decision making, or vice versa, may result in dramatic reductions in performance, at least initially.

However, institutionalization theory suggests that organizations cannot operate with radically different structural forms because of normative pressures (Meyer & Rowan, 1977; Pfeffer, 1982). Arguing from an institutional theory perspective, Euske and Roberts (1987) suggest that there are two ideal types of organizations. Technical organizations use structure to become more efficient, while "institutional organizations use structure to demonstrate conformity to social and cultural expectations/'myths' of what is rational and efficient" (p. 58). Thus, some organizations may not be permitted the requisite variety needed to truly assess the impacts of different structures on productivity.

ORGANIZATIONAL OUTCOMES AND THE APPROACHES

The organizational outcomes discussed in this chapter are crucial to the very survival of modern organizations. However, surprisingly little research has been done related to these processes, except perhaps as they relate to formal structural elements. In addition, these variables pose somewhat paradoxical demands on structures. The contingencies necessary to innovate may be antithetical to efficient production systems. How an organization resolves these paradoxes may have a lot to do with its ultimate survival.

Innovation in organizations is a complex process involving all of the approaches to structure. Except for the work of Allen (1977) in research and development laboratories, the effects of spatial factors have been ignored or considered only superficially. For example, Galbraith (1982) notes in passing that spatial coupling is often used to overcome barriers to innovation associated with the differentiation of the organization. Cultural research has been concerned with issues of compatability and match— somewhat similarly to the issues of match in production research. The influence of subcultures on innovations is reflected in Daft's (1978) dual core model of innovation. In the technical core of the organization, innovations tended to occur from the bottom up, while in the administrative core they tended to be from the top down, a finding which has been supported in other research (e.g., Kimberly & Evanisko, 1981).

Because of the dearth of research relating productivity and communication generally, it is difficult to establish definitive conclusions concerning productivity's relationships to particular approaches to organizational communication structure. One area where there has been significant volumes of research is in the relationship between formal indices of structure and productivity. While, at the subunit level, there is evidence of an inverse relationship between size and performance, at the organizational level there is no clear systematic relationship (Dalton et al., 1980), although earlier reviews of the literature have suggested there was no clear relationship between subunit size and productivity (Porter & Lawler, 1965). For other formal indices things are much less clear: there is no evidence that span of control relates to performance in an uniform way (Porter & Lawler, 1965; Dalton et al., 1980), mixed relationships with flat vs. tall hierarchy, and no clear relationship between administrative intensity and performance (Dalton et al., 1980). In general, Porter and Lawler (1965) suggest that the relationship was clearer between formal indices and attitudes than it was for behavior. Aside from some theoretical work, there has not been much systematically done to assess the relationship between specific cultural elements and productivity. Somewhat similarly, gradients have not been very systematically related to productivity, although there is certainly evidence that physical factors have an impact on organizational effectiveness (Allen, 1977).

Perhaps the key issue related to this area is the different types of structures necessary for different outcomes. For example, at different phases of the innovation process, different structure may be emphasized. Zaltman et al. (1973) have argued that organizations need one type of structure to generate ideas (low formalization, decentralization, and high complexity), which reflects the market-driven forces necessary for informally generated innovations, although Papa (1989) has found that network size and diversity were related to how quickly employees became productive after the implementation of a new computer system. This is also reflected in the work of Aiken and Hage (1971), which suggests that organic organizations, with decentralized decision making, a number of occupations, slack resources, and a history of innovation are more likely to be innovative.

However, implementation requires high formalization, centralization, and low complexity, the sorts of structure characteristic of configurational approaches. This distinction also reflects the general historical trend of research studies related to innovation. In the 1960s and 1970s researchers focused on formal approaches and the implementation of innovation sanctioned by top management (Rogers, 1983). More recently research has focused on more informal approaches and the initiation of innovations. These informal processes, in effect, add to the capacity of the organization to innovate by increasing the volumes of information which can be handled by the organization.

Accomplishing both innovation and productivity poses a difficult problem for an organization, since both appear to require different structures (Kanter, 1983). Some organizations choose to emphasize either innovation or productivity, recognizing the inherent difficulties in trying to accomplish both. For example, organizational efficiency can be improved, not by producing more information, but by reducing the amount of information any one subsystem must handle (Johnson & Rice, 1987). However, this strategy will be deleterious to the development of innovations within the organization. In addition, Hage and Aiken (1970) have argued that the greater emphasis on efficiency, the slower the rate of change.

Another strategy which many organizations adopt is to compartmental-ize these processes with very rigid structures in production processes, and those with more flexible ones, in R & D labs. However, although there is no research evidence to speak to this point, the most effective strategy in the long term may be to try to adopt a dynamic synergism between two differing structures, which sometimes overlap in messy and troublesome ways. In this regard organizational incongruence may be related to overall organizational effectiveness, since it may establish the creative tension necessary to move to more productive organizational systems (Fry & Smith, 1980). Indeed, the more market-driven relationships characteristic of the coactivational approaches to organizational communication struc-ture may be a partial answer to this dilemma. This argument is borne out by research evidence which suggests that individuals in liaison positions in informal networks are more productive (Downs et al., 1988) and also more innovative (Reynolds & Johnson, 1982). These findings, when coupled with those about the structuring of small group networks, suggest that, when left to their own devices, organizational members will create the structures most appropriate to the task at hand (Pacanowsky, 1989). Somehow, organizations must achieve a balance between stability and flexibility (Weick, 1969); how to strike that balance is still very much open to question.

chapter 11

Summing Up

As this book reveals, the study of organizational communication structure can be deep and rich, offering a myriad of possible approaches to specific problems. Each approach to examining communication structure has a different set of strengths and weaknesses relating to the major underlying dimensions of communication structure. Table 11-1 contains a rough ranking of the relative strengths of each approach for each of the major underlying dimensions of structure.

In terms of relationships, network analysis, which is fundamentally based on a rich specification of linkages, is obviously the premier approach. It can develop rich descriptions of individual dyadic relationships and then reveal the overall pattern of these linkages across an entire organization; thus, it receives a superior ranking in the table. Second comes cultural approaches, which promote an in-depth understanding of communication relationships, contributing greatly to our understanding of how they form and what the substance of them is likely to be. Another useful area of inquiry for cultural approaches comes in detailing the content of relationships proscribed by various communication rules. In a more limited sense, the formal approach is also useful in detailing

Table 11-1. Relationship Between Approaches and Underlying Dimensions of Structure

Dimensions	Formal	Approaches Network Analysis	Gradients	Cultural
Relationships	1	2	1	1–2
Entities	1	2	1	1–2
Configuration	0–1	2	2	1
Context	1–2	0–1	1	2
Stability	2	0	1	2

2 = Superior
1 = Useful
0 = Limited utility

formally proscribed organizational linkages, but it has obvious weaknesses in trying to account for the informal linkages in an organization. However, the formal approach's focus on authority relationships might be quite appropriate, since arguably these relationships form the foundation for any organization. Perhaps the greatest weakness of the gradients approach lies in the area of relationships, at least when they are viewed in the traditional sense. At best it only implies their presence when there is a cluster of interactants in a proximate physical space. Of course the very communication-intensity data itself is an indicator of relationships, but they are not specified in the complete and direct manner that they are in network analysis.

A substantial advantage of network analysis lies in its ability to provide information related to entities concerning communication structure across a number of levels of analysis including: interpersonal, group, whole organization, and extraorganizational. Culture defines entities and their relative importance in an organization. The formal approach deals directly with a narrow range of concrete entities, specifying positions and formal divisions within organizations. In doing this, predictability and control, especially in terms of vertical communication, is enhanced. Gradients force us to broaden our thinking about the nature of entities, since physical location itself can become an entity in this approach.

Gradients and network analysis, because of their association with sophisticated graphics and mathematical expressions, both excel in revealing configurations. Indeed, development of gradient-related techniques could lead to substantial conceptual advances, since, in general, it has been argued that some of the most useful discoveries in the history of science have been associated with visual imagery and visual representations (Klovdahl, 1981). Network analysis also offers very sophisticated computer tools and mathematical expressions for specifying configurations of communication relationships, such as connectedness, within an organization. It offers the most complete picture of the overall configuration of communication structure yet developed, and certainly a much more complete view than that offered by formal approaches alone (Monge & Eisenberg, 1987). In a much more restricted sense, the formal approaches have some potential for graphically and mathematically portraying configurations. The only major drawback of the cultural approach may come in what it reveals about configuration. Except at the micro level of individual interactions, cultural approaches have not been too concerned with developing techniques for systematically portraying configurations of communication behaviors. Thus, no technique is currently available for describing the overall pattern of culturally related communication behaviors at the level of the whole organization.

The key advantage of the organizational culture approach lies in its usefulness in explaining the underlying contextual factors manifested in particular communication structures. Thus, cultural approaches offer great potential for examining context, since the various elements of culture operate to constrain an individual's behavior, often serving as a guide to action in the organization. The formal approach, which after all is based on management's desire to control the organization, offers compelling advantages for examining context. In essence, formal approaches represent management attempts to set up a pattern of control for crucial organizational relationships, often proscribing penalties for a failure to institute these relationships. This formal structure is intimately related to the overall context of the organization and could be considered to be its most direct manifestation. Gradients reveal the linkage between one of the prime causal factors in human interaction, the context provided by the physical environment and associated technological factors. While physical factors have been found to be one of the major contributing factors to communication structure, until recently no approach to communication structure was capable of examining this association systematically. However, the very source of the strength of this technique is also a weakness, since gradients can only be applied to communication within defined physical boundaries. Thus it would have only limited usefulness in tackling such problems as portraying communication within telecommunication networks, for example. Network analysis offers very little in terms of context, beyond the social context of network configurations. Indeed, factors which determine the predictability of communication linkages, and thus also their causes, may lie outside of the scope of network analysis, which some have argued is best suited for describing existing patterns of communication relationships. Divorcing network analysis from context may be partially responsible for the noticeable lack of theoretical work relating to network analysis (Blau, 1982; Smith, 1980), particularly concerning organizational processes (Blair et al., 1985; Fennell et al., 1987; Monge & Eisenberg, 1987).

Both the cultural and formal approaches offer crucial information related to temporal stability for two reasons. First, they both can be used to reveal the status quo, since they formalize already existing relationships. Indeed, the organizational chart often reflects rationality after the fact (Weick, 1969) and acts to promote temporal stability. Second, once relationships are formalized, cultural and formal factors act to constrain organizational interactants to continue in them. Gradients are directly tied to the physical environment, one of the major underlying conditions promoting stability in an organization (Johnson, 1988a). A major reason for management's interest in organizational culture lies in its use as a tool to increase the predictability, and relatedly temporal stability, of organizational member behavior. Indeed, management often believes that a strong organizational culture makes behavior more uniform and more in accordance with management's interests (Deal & Kennedy, 1982). In fact most organizational socialization efforts are aimed at continuing and passing on the existing cultural behavior patterns of an organization to new members. Unless network analysis is conducted over time or its linkages are defined in terms of stability, it offers very little information on temporal stability (Aldrich, 1982).

Overall, this discussion of the strengths and weaknesses of the approaches reveals the necessity for multiple approaches to communication structure. No one technique is universally superior or, for that matter, inferior. Perhaps most interestingly, network analysis, the overwhelming focus of most investigators today, is of only limited utility for context and temporal stability. Its popularity is most attributable to its superiority in revealing configurations of relationships. While culture and gradient approaches are viewed as having major strengths, these are more projections of their potential than accomplished facts. This book also suggests it might be useful to go back to our roots; to more systematically investigate some of the formal approaches which have by and large been left behind (Jablin, 1987), they offer real strengths in terms of context and stability, without major weaknesses in other areas.

The Approaches and the Antecedents

Table 11-2 summarizes the relationships between antecedents and the approaches to communication structure which have been discussed in detail in the preceding chapters. While spatial factors have been found to be one of the major contributing factors to communication structure, only one of these approaches, gradients, systematically reveals this linkage, which is why it is rated so highly in the table. At times organizations have incorporated a concern for physical factors and communication structure in their design decisions. This is revealed particularly in open office landscaping. Industrial engineers have also been traditionally concerned with designing plants to minimize distances between units which interact substantially. Culture also has an impact on physical factors relating to communication, especially in determining the spatial boundaries and limits to interaction. Network analysis has not been related to physical situations very systematically in organizations, with the possible exception of Allen's (1977) work in research and development laboratories. The few attempts which have been made, suggest that overlaying networks onto physical contexts can seriously distort both.

Table 11-2. Relationship Between Antecedents and Approaches

Antecedents	Formal	Approaches Network Analysis	Gradients	Cultural
Spatial	1	1	2	0–1
Technology	1–2	1–2	1–2	0–1
Human Environment	1	2	1	1

2 = Strong relationship
1 = Moderate relationship
0 = Weak relationship

One of the major shortcomings of the field of organizational communication, historically, is its failure to explicitly assess the linkage between technology and communication. While recent years have seen a growing interest in information technologies, a comprehensive survey of the role technology plays more generally in contributing to the development of particular communication structures has not been attempted. These factors are partially reflected in the low scores for the approaches in relation to technology found in Table 11-2. The 1–2's given to formal, network analysis, and gradients, indicate more the promise of these techniques than their actual performance. Formal structures are often dictated by particular technologies, but what the exact contingencies are, are only poorly understood. Formal networking of information technologies is receiving increasing attention, but often the research findings are mixed and/or contradictory. In addition, the accommodations and modifications which need to be made to more clearly link technologies to network analysis, without robbing the technique of some of its sophistication, are only glimmers in someone's imagination now. However, as was suggested earlier, in the more limited domain of utilitarian concerns, especially related to role sets, network analysis holds much promise for investigating the relationships between technology and structure. Gradients can potentially link the spatial location of technology to the development of structures, particularly in terms of their embedding characteristics. Regrettably, however, the gradient approach is limited to those technologies which are spatially bound, rather than the perhaps more interesting technologies which overcome spatial boundaries. In general, the relationship between organizational cultures and technology is only poorly understood, although in the international development literature, cultural factors are seen as crucial to the diffusion of innovations (Rogers, 1983). There is also some suggestive evidence that cultures can impede the spread of technology in organizations in some sectors, and promote it in others (Heimstra, 1983).

Formal and cultural approaches are often dictated by the human composition of the work force. So in an organization composed of professionals who have been educated to expect supportive, open communication relationships, there will likely be, at least informally, a supportive set of communication rules. Similarly, the restrictions, especially in terms of control, of the formal structure may arise based on management's assumptions concerning the human membership of the work force. The interpersonal environment reflected in our network of relationships with others will also have an impact on whom we communicate with and the nature of the relationship. Similarly, status requirements of individuals and perceptions of crowding may have more to do with how space is used in the organization, than with more functionally related concerns such as promoting closeness desired relationships for coordination.

The Approaches and the Outcomes

The relationship of the approaches to our understanding of selected organizational outcomes reveals a somewhat different pattern than the one found for antecedents. Table 11-3 points to one of the prime reasons for the popularity of network analysis—its usefulness for studying a wide range of outcomes. Individual outcomes have been the focus of perhaps more research than any other issue concerning structure. Both formal approaches and network analysis have a substantial impact on individual attitudes, especially job satisfaction. Gradients also impact on job satisfaction issues, but it is not clear yet whether the association is as strong. The relationship between cultural elements of structure, such as rules and rituals, and job satisfaction is not as clear, and this is an area where very little research has been conducted.

Table 11-3.   Relationship Between Outcomes and Approaches

Outcomes	Formal	Approaches Network Analysis	Gradients	Cultural
Individual				
Satisfaction	1–2	1–2	1	0–1
Commitment	1	2	0–1	1
Support	0–1	2	1	1
Organizational				
Innovation	1	2	1	1
Productivity	1	1	1	1

2 = Strong relationship
1 = Moderate relationship
0 = Weak relationship

The impact of culture on commitment is probably much stronger than the other approaches, especially since this variable may directly relate to consonance between an individual's and an organization's value structure. There is also evidence that structural factors related to cultures, such as rituals, are related to the development of commitment within organizations. Culture can effect commitment in a variety of complex ways, offering a fecund area for studying the impacts of organizations on the level of an individual's commitment. However, perhaps the strongest evidence exists for a tie between network integration and commitment. Formal structures also could serve to integrate individuals into organizations, but perhaps not in quite as powerful a way. There is also some evidence that an individual's positioning in space, especially as it relates to the integration of an individual in an organization, could lead to commitment.

Network analysis has been seen as a crucial means of examining social support in a number of disciplines. It is quite understandable that supportive relationships are crucial factors in the overall level of support an individual derives from an organization. Increasingly, organizations are designed so as to promote supportive work relationships for individuals. Examining rules in a cultural framework can certainly help us to understand what sorts of support, informational or emotional, are sanctioned by the organization. These factors are reflected in the inference that support is almost antithetical to traditional views of the organizational hierarchy, which don't recognize the needs of individuals for emotional support. Surprisingly, some fascinating insights have emerged in early exploratory studies of the physical environment on the relationship between communication embedded in physical environments and support, particularly in terms of informational support. A study conducted by Johnson (1987b) suggests that an individual's understanding of other's positions were linked to proximity. Similarly social density has been found to be linked to levels of support in community situations.

Since formal approaches give most weight to operational systems and control, using them to stimulate innovativeness is inherently contradictory. The formal structure is designed for control; deviations from the ideal pattern defeat its very purpose. Recognizing this, organizations have tried to establish alternative designs which foster creativity and innovativeness. While somewhat successful, these design factors still heavily embed notions of organizational control which may impede high levels of innovativeness within the organization. Management designs for innovativeness, but only within certain boundaries. Network analysis can capture the coalition-building processes and individual initiative which are increasingly seen as central to such innovative processes as intrapreneurship within organizations. Thus a complete picture of innovation requires the more sophisticated and holistic picture of organizational relationships only possible with network analysis. Allen's (1977) work in research development laboratories also points to the critical impact of physical factors on innovation, particularly in terms of providing people with stimulation from others. As Kanter (1983) points out, the culture of an organization can also play a critical role in promoting the structural communication patterns essential for innovation processes, but little is known specifically about what the nature of relationships are.

While little is known empirically about the direct linkages between communication structure and productivity, there is some suggestive evidence which can allow us a tentative assessment of the strengths of the major approaches. All of the approaches have at least some linkage to productivity, but the exact nature of the linkages are still very much open to question. Even in areas where there has been a fair amount of research, such as that dealing with formal structural indices, no clear set of findings have emerged. This is especially troubling, since one of the purposes of the formal approach is the control of organizational processes in the service of productivity. Network analysis has been examined in terms of the match between informal network structures, especially those related to coordination. However, not much is known about the exact contingencies which lead one informal network structure to be superior to another in terms of productivity. Gradient approaches can offer clues to the visibility of interactants, a central factor in direct management control, and physical access often determines the quality and extent of coordination which is possible in an organizational setting. This factor is often explicitly included in organizational design decisions; however, again much more needs to be done to determine what the linkages are. Culture, at least as viewed by management, is fundamentally a vehicle for control. Thus, rules related to it can formally determine communication and impact the kinds of coordination which are permissable in large organizations. Certainly, dysfunctional communication rules are legendary, and there is considerable anecdotal evidence that they can directly impact on productivity. However, as with the other outcomes, there are still major gaps in our understanding of their relationships to the approaches to structure.

New Approaches to Structure

A casual examination of the preceding tables reveals many areas where there is not a wide array of excellent approaches for particular problems. Until the last several years the same could have been said for physical factors. The advent of gradients gives us a tool for specifically examining the relationship between physical factors and the development of particular communication structures. New approaches to structure are often needed to tackle particular theoretical problems. For example, recent years have seen a resurgence of interest in cognitive approaches, partially because of a heightened interest in the individual's place in communication research (Hewes & Planalp, 1987). In the field of organizational research there has also been great interest in cognition (Weick, 1979), especially in terms of organizational learning (Daft & Huber, 1987; Duncan & Weiss, 1979) and as it relates to information processing. There even has been a tendency to characterize the entire organization as a thinking entity.

Traditionally, the role of structure in information processing, particularly in the context of systems theory, has been one of the major foci of structural research (e.g., Farace et al., 1977). How well an organization handles varying levels of information load is often determined by its communication structure (Downs, 1967). Organizations which severely constrain their structures substantially reduce their level of information load. The communication network in which an individual is embedded is also a critical part of decision-making processes (Connolly, 1977). It influences the diversity of an individual's information sources as well as the volume of information an individual will be exposed to. Perhaps most interestingly, cultural norms and expectations also have an impact on the level of information processing in organizations. Thus, organizations often gather more information than they need to, to make decisions as a result of social norms (Feldman & March, 1981).

In another research stream related to cognition, communication network roles have been linked to notions of cognitive complexity (Schroder et al., 1967). Schreiman and Johnson (1975) found moderate support for a linkage between cognitive complexity and the amount and variety of communication in social networks. Albrecht (1979) has found that key communicators (individuals occupying linking roles in networks) have more coherent cognitive spaces than do nonkey communicators. There also is empirical evidence that entrepreneurs structure their businesses' information environments according to their integrative complexity (McGaffey & Christy, 1975). Sypher and Zorn (1986) found that cognitive differentiation accounted for substantial variation in job level and upward mobility in an insurance firm. Walker (1985), in research conducted on a software firm, found that network position was a stronger and more stable predictor of differences in cognition than the type of function an individual had and the type of product worked on. Weak ties have also been associated with more cognitively flexible individuals (Granovetter, 1982).

Perhaps the most interesting research study in this area was done by Zajonc and Wolfe (1966). Unlike the previous studies, they viewed this problem from a formal, configurational perspective. They argued that the formal structure of organizations resulted in an imbalance in the nature of information flowing into certain positions, particularly in terms of its diversity. Employees of an industrial company who held different administrative positions at different status levels were examined. The essential argument of this study was that an individual's "cognitive structure is influenced by the individual's access to information" (p. 144). Importantly, they found that high vs. low levels of formal communication was more likely to lead to cognitive differentiation, complexity, segmentation, and organization. They also found no significant relationship between the levels of informal communication and these variables. In part, this suggests that individuals may be compelled to broaden their cognitive structures as a result of certain role requirements. Thus there is empirical evidence that individuals' cognitive structures are related to their positioning in organizational structures. The nature of this relationship is complex, and the processes are so intertwined it may not be possible to conceive of one without the other.

Recently there has been tremendous interest in the social sciences in the general notion that our cognitive structures provide us with a routinized set of procedures for operating in the world. While this body of work has not been extensively explored in organizations, it offers much potential for explaining the regularly recurring communication relationships that make up an organization's communication structure.

> Organizations exist largely in the mind and their existence takes the form of cognitive maps. Thus, what ties an organization together is what ties thoughts together. (Weick & Bougon, 1986, p. 102)

Cognitive maps represent the patterns of personal knowledge individuals derived from their experiences in organizations. One form of such a map is a *strip map*, which specifies a routinized pathway to get from one point to another. These strip maps may be directly related to the routing of messages through formal and informal structures in organizations.

Another, more complex form of mapping is a *cause map*, which represents concepts tied together by causal relations. These maps remove equivocality by placing concepts in relation to one another and by imposing structure on vague situations. Individuals can interact with each other on the basis of an assemblage of their maps, a composite, or an average. The general aims of analysis of cause maps of individuals within an organizations are to discover structural regularities. Cause maps have been directly related to two basic components of cognitive complexity: differentiation and integration. The concepts contained in cause maps can also serve as a means of linking individuals together in organizations (Weick & Bougon, 1986).

At a somewhat lower level of complexity and abstraction scripts have also been used recently to explain the behavior of individuals in organizations. A *script* is a knowledge structure held in memory which specifies sequences of behavior which are appropriate in familiar situations (Gioia & Poole, 1984; Lord & Kernan, 1987). Scripts can be applied unconsciously to particular situations, especially conventional, predictable, and frequently encountered ones (Barley, 1986; Gioia & Poole, 1984). This scripting is intimately related to the performance of organizational rituals, such as staff meetings (Gioia & Poole, 1984). Scripts are said to serve two roles for organizational members: they aid understanding of organizational events, and they provide a guide to appropriate behavior. Scripts often incorporate multiple paths to goals which can be incorporated in hierarchical means–ends structures (Lord & Kernan, 1987).

Figure 11-1 contains a script for responding to a budget cut. This figure also reveals the different possible tracks of a script (Gioia & Poole, 1984). While such figures are typically discussed in terms of paths to goals and subgoals, they can also be discussed in terms of at least implied communication behaviors. That is, implicit in the attainment of goals are communication strategies which need to be implemented to attain these goals. This is revealed in the figure in such communication activities as having meetings, writing memorandum, and documenting the efficiency of the department. Thus, scripts form the underlying basis for many structural communication behaviors.

These scripts are important because they also reveal the normative base of information to which individuals will expose themselves; the

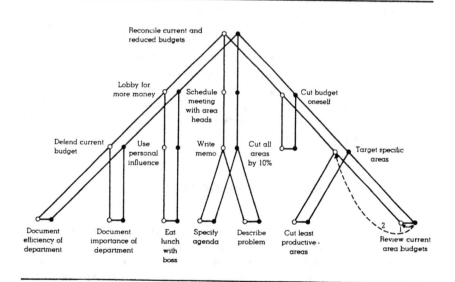

Figure 11-1.   Script for Responding to a Budget Cut*

* Lord & Kernam (1987, p. 270)

habitual patterning of sources they consult in particular situations (Lord & Kernan, 1987). Weak scripts are ones which specify particular behavioral events which are expected in a given situation, while strong scripts specify the sort of progressive sequencing of behaviors contained in this example (Gioia & Poole, 1984). Scripts and maps provide clear antecedents to people's communication behaviors, and thus structures, within organizations.

At any one time a person's existing cognitive structure may influence the more observed, surface manifestations of communication structure. However, a person's cognitive structure may develop in part as a result of the various communication events he or she has been exposed to. So someone who occupies an isolated spatial location and is also isolated in the communication network may develop relatively simple cognitive structures.

Aspects of formal structure and of culture are more difficult to cast as consequents of cognition. Indeed, rationality, especially as represented in formal structures, may occur only after action (Weick, 1969). Rather, the deeper elements represented in these approaches may constitute substantial limits on cognition. They in effect may provide an interpretive framework through which an individual views the world. Interpretive frameworks are heavily influenced by individual cognitive processes; since meaning is determined by cultures, implicitly cognition is as well (Weick, 1987). This interpretive framework in turn will limit the development of particular surface manifestations of structure.

Cognition is one of the most poorly understood areas of structure research and contains many possibilities for future growth and development. In many ways it also stands apart from the other factors examined in this book. It is of a different character and nature and as such may eventually contain the seeds of another major alternative approach to structure. Indeed, some have argued that cognitive processes related to decision making cannot be separated from the social structures which frame them (Carley, 1986).

METATHEORETICAL ISSUES

In this section the focus will be on four metatheoretical issues which focus on structure qua structure: context, the nature of relationships, the linkages between deep and surface levels of structure, and planned vs. emergent views of structure. These issues have constituted recurring themes throughout this book and point to some major unresolved problems which should guide future inquiry into organizational communication structure.

Context

> Despite repeated appeals for contextual inquiry and sensitivity to context
> ... no one is exactly sure what is being requested or how to produce it.
> (Weick, 1983, p. 27)

While context is an integral part of the definition of structure, the extent to which it can be systematically related to other issues is limited by the dearth of literature related to it at any meaningful level. In addition, context and temporal stability are heavily conceptually inter-twined, so the failure to consider context also leads to diminished attention to issues related to temporal stability. Earlier in this book it was argued that gradients have more inherent linkages to spatial contextual factors, while network analysis has potentially greater linkages to technological factors associated with utilitarian imperatives. Making these linkages to contextual factors clearer offers the potential of moving communication structure research, especially network analysis, from the descriptive level it has been operating on to a more theoretical level. Thus, greater understanding of context isolates crucial explanatory variables and thereby suggests theoretical propositions between contextual and struc-tural variables which are generalizable across organizational situations.

Somewhat similarly to physical factors, cultural and formal elements of organizations are often considered the context for structure. Because of its recent advent it is fairly easy to see that gradients constitute a structural approach which relates communication to the physical environment. This points to the necessity of making clear conceptual distinctions between organizational communication structure and other phenomenon which are intimately related to it. Analyzing the formal structure literature is particularly difficult because of a lack of clear distinction between communication structure and the formal features of an organization's bureaucracy. While organizational communication structures develop within a particular context, they are not equivalent to that context.

Relationships

The second theoretical issue is the nature of relationships. Relationships have been the primary focus of most recent empirical investigations into communication structure within the field of organizational communica-tion. Often in the network analysis approach, which has become the premier approach for investigating structure, relationships have been the exclusive focus, slighting other dimensions of structure (see Johnson, 1989). However, recently there has been increasing concern over what the nature of relationships is in network analysis research. Network analysis tends to approach relationships in a binary sense; either relationships exist or they do not (Johnson, 1989). However, there are obviously gradations in the strength of relationships, and even more interestingly, there are various probabilities that a relationship may or may not occur. Network analysis tends to focus on a more narrow sense of relationships involving direct linkages between human entities. Gradients can move us in the direction of broader thinking about relationships, since they move us into a more probabilistic world of forces and fields where locations may be entities as well as individuals. Gradients might be better thought of in terms of relative intensities which are spatially bound. Thus, considering a wide range of approaches also compels us to expand our view of what relationships are, a compelling topic for future theoretical inquiry. In addition, relationships which do not occur (e.g., no communication between two interrelated work units) may be almost as important as those that do (Knoke & Kuklinski, 1982), especially in the context of constraints. The examination of missing relationships may be more fruitful in identifying underlying factors which shape structures than examining relationships which do exist.

Deeper vs. Surface Levels

The results of a network analysis and/or communication gradients are typically manifestations of powerful forces which constrain the communication structures of organizations. These forces often operate at different levels of analysis and can represent the underlying functions which need to be performed by an organization. For example, most graduate programs find it necessary to establish structures beyond the classroom to insure the education of graduate students to professional norms and standards. The rituals by which this end is accomplished are many and varied: brown-bag lunches, Friday afternoon informal drinking sessions, colloquia, and formal defenses of theses, papers, and dissertations which a significant proportion of students and faculty attend. All of these specific manifest forms have the same underlying, latent function.

The problem for structural research is the linkage between function and form, between deeper and surface levels. The nature of these linkages, and their consequences for organizations, are only poorly understood. This is one area where qualitative, critical approaches are making a substantial contribution to our knowledge of structures, particularly in terms of domination, exploitation, and the decline of organizations.

Planned vs. Emergent Views of Structure

The fourth metatheoretical problem lies in whether or not structure should be thought of as planned or emergent. Increasingly, market-oriented views of structure may compel us to recant the underlying determinism of structure conceptualizations. That is, structures may be an expression of individual needs, and while these needs are predictable and temporally stable, the level of agency is still the individual. Thus the configurational view's emphasis on formal authority leads in Dow's (1988) view to theoretical omissions, particularly concerning the forces of the "market" underlying many informal relationships in organizations. It is then the joint activity of organizational actors, over time, which reveal structures.

Perhaps the clearest example of this problem is the embedded and utilitarian distinction developed earlier when considering technological and spatial factors. Embedded perspectives, since choices of technology and plant layout often involve conscious decisions by management, tend to be related to the planned side of the argument, while utilitarian approaches are clearly related to emergent views. Thus embedded elements provide a basic context for interaction, but utilitarian elements may determine more precisely which of many possible structures occur within this set of constraining factors. Thus the question becomes not which view is correct, but how the views can be synthesized.

One overriding observation can be made from the preceding discussions—there is no one best path to studying communication structure. Developing specific approaches, while increasing the depth at which particular problems can be explored, somewhat limits their usefulness across all structural problems. However, we must recognize that there may be no technique which can universally be applied to all structural problems with equal success. Each technique excels in the examination of some areas and is weak in the examination of others. Therefore, a total picture of communication structure can only arise through the use of all of the techniques. This creates problems for the current research environment for communication structure. The overwhelming bulk of the research is being done in network analysis. Clearly, network analysis has compelling strengths, but it also has very pronounced weaknesses, which are often overlooked. Just as a single research study can suffer from only one measure, so can the larger examination of a concept by just one approach.

Essentially, when it comes to communication structure we are in the same position as the proverbial blind men investigating the elephant. One, feeling the leg, proclaims the elephant to be like a tree; another, grabbing the tail, says no, it is like a rope; and so on. However, this analogy only partially captures our problem, since we as sighted persons can see the whole elephant. There is no direct analogy to this perspective when it comes to studying organizations, for, since no one can see the whole pattern, we are all blind men (Morgan, 1986).

COMMUNICATION STRUCTURE AND ORGANIZATIONAL COMMUNICATION THEORY

In focusing on organizational communication structure, we have been like the blind men who are using only one sense, touch. Other approaches to organizational communication bring considerably different senses, if still not sight, to the study of organizations. In many ways structural approaches are at the crossroads of these other approaches to organizational communication. Indeed, the roots of many particular structural approaches lie in these other theoretical perspectives (e.g., rules relating to culture partially determine structure, climate affects liaison emergence), but structural factors can determine things like how widespread a culture is.

Many organizational scholars in recent years have tried to specifically articulate what the overlaps between these approaches are (Albrecht, 1979; Jablin, 1980a, networks and climate; Falcione & Kaplan, 1984, climate and culture; Poole & McPhee, 1983, structure and climate). Their differences and similarities, however, may not be the real point. The dynamic interplay between them is. We strengthen our understanding of each of these approaches by understanding the differences between them; the strengths of one can inform us of the limitations of the others. Indeed, we only really understand the properties of things in assessing and comparing their relationships to other things.

But, more importantly, they can also enrich each other. This book has pointed to how these approaches relate in powerful ways to the overall conception of structure. This line of argument, and hopefully avenue for increased understanding of organizations, would not even have been possible 10 years ago, before the cultural approach to organizational communication was first systematically articulated. Thus, just as there are many approaches to organizational communication structure, structure is only one of the many available to investigate organizational communication.

References

Abelson, R. P. (1964). Mathematical models of the distribution of attitudes under controversy. In N. Frederiksen & H. Gulliksen (Eds.), *Contributions to mathematical psychology* (pp. 141–160). New York: Holt, Rinehart, and Winston.

Abelson, R. P. (1979). Social clusters and opinion clusters. In P. W. Holland & S. Leinhardt (Eds.), *Perspectives on social network research* (pp. 239–256). New York: Academic Press.

Adelman, M. B., Parks, M. R., & Albrecht, T. L. (1987). Beyond close relationships: Support in weak ties. In T. L. Albrecht & M. B. Adelman (Eds.), *Communicating social support* (pp. 126–147). Newbury Park, CA: Sage.

Aiello, J. R., & Thompson, D. E. (1980). Personal space, crowding, and spatial behavior in a cultural context. In I. Altman, A. Rapoport, & J. F. Wohlwill (Eds.), *Human behavior and environment: Advances in theory and research* (pp. 107–178). New York: Plenum.

Aiken, M., & Hage, J. (1971). The organic model and innovation. *Sociology, 5,* 63–82.

Alba, R. D. (1982). Taking stock of network analysis: A decade's results. In S. B. Bacharach (Ed.), *Research in the sociology of organizations* (pp. 39–74). Greenwich, CT: JAI Press.

Albrecht, T. L. (1979). The role of communication in perceptions of organizational climate. In D. Nimmo (Ed.), *Communication yearbook* (pp. 343–357). New Brunswick, NJ: Transaction Books.

Albrecht, T. L. (1982). Coping with occupational stress: Relational and individual strategies of nurses in acute health care settings. In M. Burgoon (Ed.), *Communication yearbook 6* (pp. 832–840). Beverly Hills, CA: Sage.

Albrecht, T. L., & Adelman, M. B. (1987a). Communicating social support: A theoretical perspective. In T. L. Albrecht & M. B. Adelman (Eds.), *Communicating social support* (pp. 18–39). Newbury Park, CA: Sage.

Albrecht, T. L., & Adelman, M. B. (1987b). Communication networks as structures of social support. In T. L. Albrecht & M. B. Adelman (Eds.), *Communicating social support* (pp. 40–63). Newbury Park, CA: Sage.

Albrecht, T. L., & Adelman, M. B. (1987c). Dillemas of supportive communication. In T. L. Albrecht & M. B. Adelman (Eds.), *Communicating social support* (pp. 240–254). Newbury Park, CA: Sage.

Albrecht, T. L., & Adelman, M. B. (1987d). Rethinking the relationship between communication and social support: An introduction. In T. L. Albrecht & M. B. Adelman (Eds.), *Communicating social support* (pp. 13–16). Newbury Park, CA: Sage.

Albrecht, T. L., & Hall, B. (1989, June). *Relational and content differences between elites and outsiders in innovation networks.* Paper presented to the Annual Meetings of the International Communication Association Convention, San Francisco.

Albrecht, T. L., Irey, K. V., & Mundy, A. K. (1982). Integration in communication networks as a mediator of stress: The case of a protective services agency. *Social Work, 27*, 225–236.

Albrecht, T. L., & Ropp, V. A. (1984). Communicating about innovation in networks of three U.S. organizations. *Journal of Communication, 34*, 78–91.

Aldrich, H. (1982). The origin and persistance of social networks. In P. V. Marsden & N. Lin (Eds.), *Social structure and network analysis* (pp. 281–293). Beverly Hills, CA: Sage.

Alexander, J. W., & Randolph, W. A. (1985). The fit between technology and structure as a predictor of performance in nursing subunits. *Academy of Management Journal, 28*, 844–859.

Allen, T. J. (1977). *Managing the flow of technology: Technology transfer and the dissemination of technological information within the R&D organization.* Cambridge, MA: MIT Press.

Allen, T. J., & Gerstberger, P.G. (1973). A field experiment to improve communications in a product engineering department: The non territorial office. *Human Factors, 15*, 487–498.

Amend, E. (1971). *Liaison communication roles of professionals in a research dissemination organization.* Unpublished doctoral dissertation, Michigan State University, East Lansing, MI.

Antonovsky, H. F., & Antonovsky, A. (1974). Commitment in an Israeli kibbutz. *Human Relations, 27*, 95–112.

Archea, J. (1973). Identifying direct links between behavior and its environment: Toward a predictive model. In T. O. Byerts (Ed.), *Environmental research and aging* (pp. 117–153). Washington, DC: Gerontological Society.

Archea, J. (1977). The place of architectural factors in behavioral theories of privacy. *Journal of Social Issues, 33*, 116–137.

Ashforth, B. E. (1985). Climate formation: Issues and extensions. *Academy of Management Review, 10*, 837–847.

Axley, S. R. (1984). Managerial and organizational communication in terms of the conduit metaphor. *Academy of Management Review, 9*, 428–437.

Bach, B. W., & Bullis, C. (1989). *An explication and test of relationship multiplexity as a predictor of organizational identification.* Paper presented to the Annual Convention of the International Communication Association, San Francisco.

Bacharach, S. B., & Aiken, M. (1977). Communication in administrative bureaucracies. *Academy of Management Journal, 20*, 365–377.

Bales, R. F. (1950). *Interaction process analysis.* Reading, MA: Addison-Wesley.

Bardwick, J. M. (1984). When ambition is no asset. *New Management, 1*, 22–28.

Barley, S. R. (1986). Technology as an occasion for structuring: Evidence from observations of CT scanners and the social order of radiology departments. *Administrative Science Quarterly, 31,* 78–108.

Barnes, J. A. (1972). *Social networks.* Reading, MA: Addison-Wesley.

Barnett, G. A. (1988). Communication and organizational culture. In G. M. Goldhaber & G. A. Barnett (Eds.), *Handbook of organizational communication* (pp. 101–130). Norwood, NJ: Ablex Publishing Corp.

Barnett, G. A., & Rice, R. E. (1985). Longitudinal non-Euclidean networks: Applying Galileo. *Social Networks, 7,* 287–322.

Barnlund, D.C., & Harland, C. (1963). Propinquity and prestige as determinants of communication networks. *Sociometry, 26,* 467–479.

Bateman, T. S., & Strasser, S. (1984). A longitudinal analysis of the antecedents of organizational commitment. *Academy of Management Journal, 27,* 540–549.

Baum, A., & Valens, S. (1977). *Architecture and social behavior: Psychological studies of social density.* Hillsdale, NJ: Erlbaum.

Becker, F. D. (1981). *Workspace: Creating environments in organizations.* New York: Praeger.

Becker, H. (1960). Notes on the concept of commitment. *American Journal of Sociology, 66,* 32–42.

Bennett, C. (1977). *Spaces for people: Human factors in design.* Englewood Cliffs, NJ: Prentice-Hall.

Bennis, W. G. (1965). Theory and method in applying behavioral science to planned organizational change. *Applied Behavioral Science, 1,* 337–360.

Berger, C. J., & Cummings, L. L. (1979). Organizational structure, attitudes, and behaviors. In B. M. Staw & L. L. Cummings (Eds.), *Research in organizational behavior* (Vol. 1, pp. 169–208). Greenwich, CT: Sage.

Berger, C. R., & Chaffee, S. H. (Eds.). (1987). *Handbook of communication science.* Newbury Park, CA: Sage.

Berlo, D. K. (1969). *Human communication: The basic proposition.* Unpublished paper, Department of Communication, Michigan State University, East Lansing, MI.

Bernard, H. R., & Killworth, P. D. (1977). Informant accuracy in social network data: II. *Human Communication Research, 4,* 3–18.

Bernard, H. R., Killworth, P. D., & Sailer, L. (1980). Informant accuracy in social network data IV: A comparison of clique-level structure in behavioral and cognitive network data. *Social Networks, 2,* 191–218.

Bernard, H. R., Killworth, P. D., & Sailer, L. (1982). Informant accuracy in social-network data V. An experimental attempt to predict actual communication from recall data. *Social Science Research, 11,* 30–66.

Beyer, J. M., & Trice, H. M. (1984, June). *The communication of power relations in organizations through cultural rites.* Paper presented to the International Communication Association, Honolulu, HI.

Blair, R., Roberts, K. H., & McKechnie, P. (1985). Vertical and network communication in organizations: The present and the future. In R. D. McPhee & P. K. Tompkins (Eds.), *Organizational communication: Traditional themes and new directions* (pp. 55–77). Beverly Hills, CA: Sage.

Blau, P. M. (1974a). Introduction. In P. M. Blau (Ed.), *On the nature of organizations* (pp. 1–20). New York: John Wiley.

Blau, P. M. (1974b). A formal theory of differentiation in organizations. In P. M. Blau (Ed.), *On the nature of organizations* (pp. 297–322). New York: John Wiley.

Blau, P. M. (1981). Introduction: Diverse views of social structure and their common denominator. In P. M. Blau & R. K. Merton (Eds.), *Continuities in structural inquiry* (pp. 1–23). Newbury Park, CA: Sage.

Blau, P. M. (1982). Structural sociology and network analysis: An overview. In P. V. Marsden & N. Lin (Eds.), *Social structure and network analysis* (pp. 273–279). Beverly Hills, CA: Sage.

Blau, G. J., & Boal, K. B. (1987). Conceptualizing how job involvement and organizational commitment affect turnover and absenteeism. *Academy of Management Review, 12,* 288–300.

Blau, P. M., & Schoenherr, R. (1971). *The structure of organizations.* New York: Basic Books.

Brass, D. J. (1981). Structural relationships, job characteristics, and worker satisfaction and performance. *Administrative Science Quarterly, 26,* 331–348.

Brass, D. J. (1985). Men's and women's networks: A study of interaction patterns and influence in an organization. *Academy of Management Journal, 28,* 327–343.

Brewer, J. (1971). Flow of communications, expert qualifications and organizational authority structures. *American Sociological Review, 36,* 475–484.

Brower, S. N. (1980). Territory in urban settings. In I. Altman, A. Rapoport, & J. F. Wohlwill (Eds.), *Human behavior and environment: Advances in theory and research* (pp. 179–207). New York: Plenum Press.

Brown, M. H., & McMillan, J. J. (1988, November). *Constructions and counter-constructions: Organizational power revisited.* Paper presented to the Annual Convention of the Speech Communication Association, New Orleans, LA.

Buchanan, B., III. (1974). Building organizational commitment: The socialization of managers in work organization. *Administrative Science Quarterly, 19,* 533–546.

Burt, R. S. (1980). Innovation as a structural interest: Rethinking the impact of network position on innovation adoption. *Social Networks, 2,* 327–355.

Burt, R. S. (1982). *Toward a structural theory of action: Network models of social structure, perception, and action.* New York: Academic Press.

Burt, R. S. (1983). A note on inference concerning network subgroups. In R. S. Burt & M. J. Minor (Eds.), *Applied network analysis: A methodological introduction* (pp. 283–301). Beverly Hills, CA: Sage.

Burt, R. S. (1987). Social contagion and innovation: Cohesion versus structural equivalence. *American Journal of Sociology, 92,* 1287–1335.

Burt, R. S., & Bittner, W. M. (1981). A note on inferences regarding network subgroups. *Social Networks, 3,* 71–88.

Buster, R. L., Eckert, M. B., Friedland, M. H., & Johnson, J. D. (1987). *Rites and rituals in a high-tech organization.* Paper presented to the Eastern Communication Association, Syracuse, NY

Buster, R. L., Friedland, M. H., Eckert, M. B., & Johnson, J. D. (1988, May). *The impact of communication rituals on role ambiguity and commitment in a high-tech organization.* Paper presented to the International Communication Association Annual Convention, New Orleans, LA.

Buttimer, A. (1980). Social space and the planning of residential areas. In A. Buttimer & D. Seamon (Eds.), *The human experience of space and place* (pp. 21–54). New York: St. Martin's Press.

Canter, D. (1983). The physical context of work. In D. J. Osborne & M. M. Gruneberg (Eds.), *The physical environment at work* (pp. 11–38). New York: John Wiley.

Canter, D. & Kenny, C. (1975). The spatial environment. In D. Canter & P. Stringer (Eds.), *Environmental interaction: Psychological approaches to our physical surroundings* (pp. 127–163). New York: International University Press.

Caplow, T. (1947). Rumors in war. *Social Forces, 25,* 298–302.

Carley, K. (1986). An approach for relating social structure to cognitive structure. *Journal of Mathematical Sociology, 12,* 137–189.

Carter, N. M. (1984). Computerization as a predominant technology: Its influence on the structure of Newspaper organizations. *Academy of Management Journal, 27,* 247–271.

Carter, N. M., & Cullen, J. B. (1983). *The computerization of newspaper organizations: The impact of technology on organizational structuring.* Lanham, MD: University Press of America.

Chao, K., & Gordon, W. I. (1979). Culture and communication in the modern Japanese corporate organization. In N. C. Jain (Ed.), *International and intercultural communication annual* (Vol. V, pp. 23–36). Phoenix: Jackson Graphic Services.

Chapanis, A. (1971). Prelude to 2001: Explorations in human communication. *American Psychologist, 26,* 940–961.

Cheng, J. L. C. (1983). Interdependence and coordination in organizations: A role-system analysis. *Academy of Management Journal, 26,* 156–162.

Cicourel, A. V. (1972). Basic and normative rules in the negotiation of status and role. In D. Sudnow (Ed.), *Studies in social interaction* (pp. 229–258). New York: Free Press.

Clayton, C. (1974). Communication and spatial structure. *Tijdschrift voor Economische en Sociale Geografie, 65,* 221–227.

Coch, L., & French, J. R. (1948). Overcoming resistance to change. *Human Relations, 1,* 512–532.

Collins, R. (1981). On the microfoundations of macrosociology. *American Journal of Sociology, 86,* 984–1014.

Connolly, T. (1977). Information processing and decision making in organizations. In B. M. Staw & G. R. Salancik (Eds.), *New directions in organizational behavior* (pp. 205–234). Chicago: St. Clair Press.

Conrad, C. (1983). Organizational power: Faces and symbolic forms. In L. L. Putnam & M. E. Pacanowsky (Eds.), *Communication and organizations: An interpretive approach* (pp. 173–194). Beverly Hills, CA: Sage.

Conrath, D. W. (1973). Communication environment and its relationship to organizational structure. *Management Science, 20,* 586–603.

Conrath, D. W., Buckingham, P., Dunn, E., & Swanson, J. N. (1975). An experimental evaluation of alternative communication systems as used for medical diagnosis. *Behavioral Science, 20,* 296–305.

Contractor, N. S., Monge, P. R., & Eisenberg, E. M. (1987, August). *Formal and emergent structures as predictors of agreement on organizational climate.* Paper presented to the National Academy of Management Meeting, New Orleans, LA.

Cook, K. S. (1982). Network structures from an exchange perspective. In P. V. Marsden & N. Lin (Eds.), *Social structure and network analysis* (pp. 177–199). Beverly Hills, CA: Sage.

Culnan, M. J., & Markus, M. L. (1987). Information technologies. In F. M. Jablin, L. L. Putnam, K. H. Roberts, & L. W. Porter (Eds.), *Handbook of organizational communication: An interdisciplinary perspective* (pp. 420–443). Beverly Hills, CA: Sage.

Cushman, D. P., King, S. S., & Smith, T., III. (1988). The rules perspective on organizational communication research. In G. M. Goldhaber & G. A. Barnett (Eds.), *Handbook of organizational communication* (pp. 55–94). Norwood, NJ: Ablex Publishing Corp.

Cushman, D. P., & Whiting, G. C. (1972). An approach to communication theory: Toward consensus on rules. *Journal of Communication, 22,* 217–238.

Czepiel, J. A. (1975). Patterns of interorganizational communications and the diffussion of a major technological innovation in a competitive industrial community. *Academy of Management Journal, 18,* 6–24.

Daft, R. L. (1978). A dual-core model of organizational innovation. *Academy of Management Journal, 21,* 193–210.

Daft, R. L. (1983). Learning the craft of organizational research. *Academy of Management Review, 8,* 539–546.

Daft, R. L., & Huber, G. P. (1987). How organizations learn: A communication framework. In N. D. Tomoso & S. B. Bacharach (Eds.), *Research in organizational behavior* (Vol. 5, pp. 1–36). Greenwich, CT: JAI Press.

Daft, R. L., & Lengel, R. H. (1986). Organizational information requirements. Media richness and structural design. *Management Science, 32,* 554–571.

Daft, R. L., & Macintosh, N. B. (1981). A tentative exploration into the amount and equivocality of information processing in organizational work units. *Administrative Science Quarterly, 26,* 207–224.

Dalton, D. R., Todor, W. D., Spendolini, M. J., Fielding, G. J., & Porter, L. W. (1980). Organization structure and performance: A critical review. *Academy of Management Review, 5,* 49–64.

Danes, J. E., Hunter, J. E., & Woelfel, J. (1978). Mass communication and belief change: A test of three mathematical models. *Human Communication Research, 4,* 243–252.

Daniels, T. D., & Spiker, B. K. (1983). Social exchange and the relationship between information adequacy and relational satisfaction. *Western Journal of Speech Communication, 47,* 118–137.

Danowski, J. A. (1980). Group attitude uniformity and connectivity of organizational communication networks for production, innovation, maintenance content. *Human Communication Research, 6,* 299–308.

Danowski, J. A. (1988). Organizational infographics and automated auditing: Using computers unobtrusively gather as well as analyze communication. In G. M. Goldhaber & G. A. Barnett (Eds.), *Handbook of organizational communication* (pp. 385–434). Norwood, NJ: Ablex Publishing Corp.

Danowski, J. A., & Edison-Swift, P. (1985). Crises effects on intraorganizational computer-based communication. *Communication Research, 12,* 251–270.

Dansereau, F., & Markham, S. E. (1987). Superior-subordinate communication: Multiple levels of analysis. In F. M. Jablin, L. L. Putnam, K. H. Roberts, & L. W. Porter (Eds.), *Handbook of organizational communication: An interdisciplinary perspective* (pp. 343–388). Newbury Park, CA: Sage.

Davis, K. (1973, July). The care and cultivation of the corporate grapevine. *Dun's Review, 108,* 44–47.

Davis, T. R. (1984). The influence of the physical environment in offices. *Academy of Management Review, 9,* 271–283.

Deal, T. E., & Kennedy, A. A. (1982). *Corporate cultures: The rites and rituals of corporate life.* Reading, MA: Addison-Wesley.

Deetz, S. A. (1982). Critical interpretive research in organizational communication. *Western Journal of Speech Communication, 46,* 131–149.

Dennis, H. S., Goldhaber, G. M., & Yates, M. P. (1978). Organizational communication theory and research: An overview of research methods. In D. Nimmo (Ed.), *Communication yearbook 2* (pp. 243–269). New Brunswick, NJ: Transaction Books.

Dewhirst, H. D. (1971). Influence of perceived information-sharing norms on communication channel utilization. *Academy of Management Journal, 14,* 205–315.

Dow, G. K. (1988). Configurational and coactivational views of organizational structure. *Academy of Management Review, 13,* 53–64.

Downs, A. (1967). *Inside bureaucracy.* Boston: Little, Brown.

Downs, C. W., Clampitt, P. G., & Pfeiffer, A. L. (1988). Communication and organizational outcomes. In G. M. Goldhaber & G. A. Barnett (Eds.), *Handbook of organizational communication* (pp. 171–212). Norwood, NJ: Ablex Publishing Corp.

Downs, C. W., & Hain, T. (1982). Productivity and communication. In M. Burgoon (Ed.), *Communication yearbook 5* (pp. 435–453). New Brunswick, NJ: Transaction Books.

Downs, C. W., & Larimer, M. W. (1974). The status of organizational communication in Speech Departments. *Speech Teacher, 23,* 325–329.

Drexler, J. A. (1977). Organizational climate: Its homogeneity within organizations. *Journal of Applied Psychology, 62,* 38–42.

Duncan, R., & Weiss, A. (1979). Organizational learning: Implications for organizational design. In S. B. Bacharach (Ed.), *Research in organizational behavior* (Vol. 1, pp. 75–123). Greenwich, CT: JAI Press.

Dunegan, K. J., Green, S. G., & Baker, N. R. (1987, August). *Coordination, critical resources, and R&D performance: A contextual profile.* Paper presented to the Academy of Management Annual Convention, New Orleans, LA.

Durlak, J. T. (1987). A typology of interactive media. In M. L. McLaughlin (Ed.), *Communication yearbook 10* (pp. 743–757). Beverly Hills, CA: Sage.

Dutton, W. H., Fulk, J., & Steinfield, C. (1982). Utilization of video conferencing. *Telecommunications Policy, 6,* 164–178.

Edstrom, A., & Galbraith, J. R. (1977). Transfer of managers as a coordination and control strategy in multinational organizations. *Administrative Science Quarterly, 22,* 248–263.

Edwards, J. A., & Monge, P. R. (1977). The validation of mathematical indices of communication structure. In B. D. Ruben (Ed.), *Communication yearbook I* (pp. 183–193). New Brunswick, NJ: Transaction Books.

Egelhoff, W. G. (1982). Strategy and structure in multinational corporations: An information processing approach. *Administrative Science Quarterly, 27,* 435–458.

Eggert, L. L., & Parks, M. R. (1987). Communication network involvement in adolescents' friendships and romantic relationships. In M. L. McLaughlin (Ed.), *Communication yearbook 10* (pp. 283–322). Beverly Hills, CA: Sage.

Eisenberg, E. M. (1984). Ambiguity as strategy in organizational communication. *Communication Monographs, 51,* 227–242.

Eisenberg, E. M. (1986). Meaning and interpretation in organizations. *Quarterly Journal of Speech, 72,* 88–113.

Eisenberg, E. M., Contractor, N. S., & Monge, P. R. (1988, May). *Semantic networks in an organization.* Paper presented to the Annual Meeting of the International Communication Association, New Orleans, LA.

Eisenberg, E. M., Farace, R. V., Monge, P. R., Bettinghaus, E. P., Kurchner-Hawkins, R., Miller, K. I., & Rothman, L. (1985). Communication linkages in interorganizational systems: Review and synthesis. In B. Dervin & M. Voigt (Eds.), *Progress in communication sciences* (Vol. 6, pp. 231–261). Norwood, NJ: Ablex Publishing Corp.

Eisenberg, E. M., Monge, P. R., & Miller, K. I. (1983). Involvement in communication networks as a predictor of organizational commitment. *Human Communication Research, 10,* 179–202.

Eisenberg, E. M., & Whetten, M. G. (1987). Reconsidering openness in organizational communication. *Academy of Management Review, 12,* 418–426.

Erickson, B. H. (1982). Networks, ideologies, and belief systems. In P. V. Marsden & N. Lin (Eds.), *Social structure and network analysis* (pp. 159–172). Beverly Hills, CA: Sage.

Etzioni, A. (1961). *A comparative analysis of complex organizations.* New York: The Free Press.

Euske, N. A., & Roberts, K. H. (1987). Evolving perspectives in organization theory: Communication implications. In F. M. Jablin, L. L. Putnam, K. H. Roberts, & L. W. Porter (Eds.), *Handbook of organizational communication: An interdisciplinary perspective* (pp. 41–69). Newbury Park, CA: Sage.

Evans, G. W. (1980). Environmental cognition. *Psychological Bulletin, 88,* 259–287.

Evans, M. C., & Wilson, M. (1949). Friendship choices of university women students. *Educational and Psychological Measurement, 9,* 307–312.

Fairhurst, G. T. (1985). Male-female communication on the job: Literature review and commentary. In M. L. McLaughlin (Ed.), *Communication yearbook 9*. Beverly Hills, CA: Sage.

Fairhurst, G. T., Rogers, L. E., & Sarr, R. A. (1987). Manager–subordinate control patterns and judgments about the relationship. In M. L. McLaughlin (Eds.), *Communication yearbook 10* (pp. 395–415). Beverly Hills, CA: Sage.

Fairhurst, G. T., & Snavely, B. K. (1983). A test of the social isolation of male tokens. *Academy of Management Journal, 26*, 353–361.

Falcione, R. L., & Kaplan, E. A. (1984). Organizational climate, communication, and culture. In R. N. Bostrom (Ed.), *Communication yearbook 8* (pp. 285–309). Beverly Hills: CA: Sage.

Falcione, R. L., Sussman, L., & Herden, R. P. (1987). Communication climate in organizations. In F. M. Jablin, L. L. Putnam, K. H. Roberts, & L. W. Porter (Eds.), *Handbook of organizational communication: An interdisciplinary perspective* (pp. 195–227). Newbury Park, CA: Sage.

Farace, R. V., & Johnson, J. D. (1974, May). *Comparative analysis of human communication networks in selected formal organizations*. Paper presented to the International Communication Association Annual Convention, New Orleans, LA.

Farace, R. V., & Mabee, T. (1980). Communication network analysis methods. In P. R. Monge & J. N. Cappella (Eds.), *Multivariate techniques in human communication research* (pp. 365–391). New York: Academic Press.

Farace, R. V., Monge, P. R., & Russell, H. (1977). *Communicating and organizing*. Reading, MA: Addison-Wesley.

Farace, R. V., Taylor, J. A., & Stewart, J. P. (1978). Criteria for evaluation of organizational communication effectiveness: Review and synthesis. In D. Nimmo (Ed.), *Communication yearbook 2* (pp. 271–292). New Brunswick, NJ: Transaction Books.

Farrell, D., & Peterson, J. C. (1984). Commitment, absenteeism, and turnover of new employees: A longitudinal study. *Human Relations, 37*, 681–692.

Feigenbaum, E., McCorduck, P., & Nii, H. P. (1988). *The rise of the expert company: How visionary companies are using artificial intelligence to achieve higher productivity and profits*. New York: Times Books.

Feldman, M. S., & March, J. G. (1981). Information in organizations as signal and symbol. *Administrative Science Quarterly, 26*, 171–186.

Fennell, M. L., Ross, C. O., & Warnecke, R. B. (1987). Organizational environment and network structure. In N. D. Tomoso & S. B. Bacharach (Eds.), *Research in the sociology of organizations* (Vol. 6). Greenwich, CT: JAI Press.

Festinger, L., Schacter, S., & Back, K. (1950). *Social pressures in informal groups: A study of a housing project*. New York: Harper.

Fidler, L. A., & Johnson, J. D. (1984). Communication and innovation implementation. *Academy of Management Review, 9*, 704–711.

Ford, J. D., & Slocum, J. W., Jr. (1977). Size, technology, environment and the structure of organizations. *Academy of Management Review, 2*, 561–575.

Form, W. H. (1972). Technology and social behavior of workers in four countries. A sociotechnical perspective. *American Sociological Review, 37*, 727–738.

Foster, B. L. (1979). Formal network studies and the anthropological perspective. *Social Networks, 1*, 241–255.

French, J. R. P. (1956). A formal theory of social power. *Psychological Review, 63*, 181–194.

Friedkin, N. (1980). A test of structural features of Granovetter's strength of weak ties theory. *Social Networks, 2*, 411–422.

Friedkin, N. E. (1982). Information flow through strong and weak ties in intraorganizational social networks. *Social Networks, 3*, 273–285.

Friedkin, N. E. (1984). Structural equivalence and cohesion explanations of social homogeniety. *Sociological Methods and Research, 3*, 235–261.

Friemuth, V. S. (1987). The diffusion of supportive information. In T. L. Albrecht & M. B. Adelman (Eds.), *Communicating social support* (pp. 212–237). Newbury Park, CA: Sage.

Frost, P. J. (1987). Power, politics, and influence. In F. M. Jablin, L. L. Putnam, K. H. Roberts, & L. W. Porter (Eds.), *Handbook of organizational communication: An interdisciplinary perspective* (pp. 503–548). Newbury Park: CA: Sage.

Fry, L. W., & Slocum, J. W., Jr. (1984). Technology, structure, and workgroup effectiveness: A test of a contingency model. *Academy of Managment Journal, 27*, 221–246.

Fry, L. W., & Smith, D. A. (1987). Congruence, contingency, and theory building. *Academy of Management Review, 12*, 117–132.

Fulk, J., Steinfield, C. W., Schmitz, J., & Power, J. G. (1987). A social information processing model of media use in organizations. *Communication Research, 14*, 529–552.

Galbraith, J. R. (1973). *Designing complex organizations.* Reading, MA: Addison-Wesley.

Galbraith, J. R. (1974). Organization design: An information processing view. *Interfaces, 4*, 28–36.

Galbraith, J. R. (1982). Designing the innovating organization. *Organizational Dynamics, 10*, 5–25.

Giddens, A. (1985). Time, space and regionalisation. In D. Gregory & J. Urry (Eds.), *Social relations and spatial structures* (pp. 265–295). Hong Kong: MacMillan.

Gioia, D. A., & Poole, P. P. (1984). Scripts in organizational behavior. *Academy of Management Review, 9*, 449–459.

Goldberg, S. C. (1954). Three situational determinants of conformity to social norms. *Journal of Abnormal and Social Psychology, 49*, 325–329.

Goldhaber, G. M., Yates, M. P., Porter, T. D., & Lesniak, R. (1978). Organizational communication: 1978. *Human Communication Research, 5*, 76–96.

Goldhar, J. D., Bragaw, L. K., & Schwartz, J. J. (1976). Information flows, management styles, and technological innovation. *IEEE Transactions on Engineering Management, 23*, 51–62.

Granovetter, M. S. (1973). The strength of weak ties. *American Journal of Sociology, 78*, 1360–1380.

Granovetter, M. (1979). The theory-gap in social network analysis. In P. W.

Holland & S. Leinhardt (Eds.), *Perspectives on social network research* (pp. 501–518). New York: Academic Press.

Granovetter, M. (1982). The strength of weak ties: A network theory revisited. In P. V. Marsden & N. Lin (Eds.), *Social structure in network analysis* (pp. 105–130). Beverly Hills: CA: Sage.

Gregory, D. (1978). Social change and spatial structures. In T. Carlstein, D. Parkes, & N. Thrift (Eds.), *Making sense of time* (pp. 38–46). New York: John Wiley.

Gregory, D. (1985). Suspended animation: The stasis of diffusion theory. In D. Gregory & J. Urry (Eds.), *Social relations and spatial structures* (pp. 296–336). Hong Kong: MacMillan.

Gregory, D., & Urry, J. (1985). Introduction. In D. Gregory & J. Urry (Eds.), *Social relations and spatial structures* (pp. 1–8). Hong Kong: MacMillan.

Guetzkow, H. (1965). Communication in organizations. In J. G. March (Ed.), *Handbook of organizations* (534–573). Chicago: Rand-McNally.

Guetskow, H., & Simon, H. A. (1955). The impact of certain communication nets upon organization and performance in task-oriented groups. *Management Science, 1,* 233–250.

Gullahorn, J. T. (1952). Distance and friendship as factors in the gross interaction matrix. *Sociometry, 15,* 123–134.

Hackman, J. R. (1982). Preface. In J. E. McGrath, J. Martin, & R. A. Kulka (Eds.), *Judgment calls in research* (pp. 7–9). Beverly Hills: CA: Sage.

Hackman, J. (1983). Group influences on individuals. In M. Dunette (Ed.), *Handbook of industrial and organizational psychology* (pp. 1455–1525). New York: John Wiley.

Hagarstrand, T. (1953). *Innovation diffusion as a spatial process.* Chicago: University of Chicago Press.

Hagarstrand, T. (1965). Aspects of the spatial structure of social communication and the diffusion of information. *Regional Science Association, Papers, XVI,* 27–42.

Hagarstrand, T. (1982). Diorama, path and project. *Tijdschrift voor Econische en Sociale Geografie, 73,* 323–339.

Hage, J. (1974). *Communication and organizational control: Cybernetics in health and welfare settings.* New York: John Wiley.

Hage, J., & Aiken, M. (1970). *Social change in complex organizations.* New York: Random House.

Hage, J., Aiken, M., & Marrett, C. B. (1971). Organization structure and communications. *American Sociological Review, 36,* 860–871.

Hare, A. P. (1960). The dimensions of social interaction. *Behavioral Science, 5,* 211–215.

Harriman, B. (1974, Sept.–Oct.). Up and down the communication ladder. *Harvard Business Review, 52,* 143–151.

Harris, S. G., & Sutton, R. I. (1986). Functions of parting ceremonies in dying organizations. *Academy of Management Journal, 29,* 5–30.

Harrison, P. R. (1974). A technique for analyzing the distance between organisms in observational studies. *Journal of General Psychology, 91,* 269–271.

Hartman, R. L., & Johnson, J. D. (1990). Formal and informal group communication structures: An examination of their relationship to role ambiguity. *Social Networks, 12,* 1–24.

Hartman, R. L., & Johnson, J. D. (1989). Social contagion and multiplexity: Communication networks as predictors of commitment and role ambiguity. *Human Communication Research, 15,* 523–548.

Hatch, M. J. (1987). Physical barriers, task characteristics, and interaction activity in research and development firms. *Administrative Science Quarterly, 32,* 387–399.

Heimstra, G. (1982). Teleconferencing, concern for face, and organizational culture. In M. Burgoon (Ed.), *Communication yearbook 6* (pp. 874–904). Beverly Hills, CA: Sage.

Heimstra, G. (1983). You say you want a revolution? "Information technology" in organizations. In R. N. Bostrom (Ed.), *Communication yearbook 7* (pp. 802–827). Beverly Hills, CA: Sage.

Hellweg, S. A. (1987). Organizational grapevines. In B. Dervin & M. J. Voight (Eds.), *Progress in communication sciences* (Vol. VIII, pp. 213–230). Norwood, NJ: Ablex Publishing Corp.

Hewes, D. E., & Planalp, S. (1987). The individual's place in communication science. In C. R. Berger & S. H. Chaffee (Eds.), *Handbook of communication science* (pp. 146–183). Newbury Park, CA: Sage.

Hiltz, S., & Kerr, E. (1980). *On-line scientific communities.* Norwood, NJ: Ablex Publishing Corp.

Hirokawa, R. Y., & Miyahara, R. K. (1986, May). *A comparison of influence strategies utilized by managers in American and Japanese organizations.* Paper presented to the Annual Meetings of the International Communication Association, Chicago.

Hoffman, E., & Roman, P.M. (1984). The effect of organizational emphases upon the diffusion of information about innovations. *Journal of Management, 10,* 277–291.

Hofstede, G. (1980). *Culture's consequences: International differences in work-related values.* Beverly Hills: CA: Sage.

Hofstede, G. (1984). The cultural relativity of the quality of life construct. *Academy of Management Review, 3,* 389–398.

Holland, W. E., Stead, B. S., & Leibrock, R. C. (1976). Information channel/source selection as a correlate of technical uncertainty in a research and development organization. *IEEE Transactions on Engineering Management, 23*(4), 163–167.

Hrebiniak, L., & Alluto, J. (1972). Personal and role-related factors in the development of organizational commitment. *Administrative Science Quarterly, 17,* 555–572.

Huber, G. P., & McDaniel, R. R., Jr. (1986). Exploiting information technologies to design more effective organizations. In M. Jarke (Ed.), *Managers, micros and mainframes* (pp. 221–236). New York: Wiley.

Indik, B. P. (1965). Organization size and member participation: Some empirical tests of alternative explanations. *Human Relations, 18,* 339–350.

Infante, D. A., & Gorden, W. I. (1987). Superior and subordinate communicator profiles: Implications for independent-mindedness and upward effectiveness. *Central States Speech Journal, 38*, 73–80.

Ittelson, W. H., Rivlin, L. G., & Proshansky, H. M. (1970). The use of behavioral maps in environmental psychology. In H. M. Proshansky, W. H. Ittelson, & L. G. Rivlin (Eds.), *Environmental psychology: Man and his physical setting* (pp. 658–668). New York: Holt, Rinehart, & Winston.

Jablin, F. M. (1978). Message response and "openness" in superior-subordinate communication. In B. D. Ruben (Ed.), *Communication yearbook 2* (pp. 293–309). New Brunswick, NJ: Transaction Books.

Jablin, F. M. (1979). Superior-subordinate communication: The state of the art. *Psychological Bulletin, 86*, 1201–1222.

Jablin, F. M. (1980a). Organizational communication theory and research: An overview of communication climate and network research. In D. Nimmo (Ed.), *Communication yearbook 4* (pp. 327–347). New Brunswick, NJ: Transaction Books.

Jablin, F. M. (1980b). Superior's upward influence, satisfaction and openness in superior-subordinate communication: A reexamination of the "Pelz effect." *Human Communication Research, 6*, 210–220.

Jablin, F. M. (1980c). Subordinates's sex and superior-subordinate status differentiations as moderators of the Pelz effect. In D. Nimmo (Ed.), *Communication yearbook 4* (pp. 349–366). New Brunswick, NJ: Transaction Books.

Jablin, F. M. (1981). An exploratory study of subordinates perceptions of supervisory politics. *Communication Quarterly, 29*, 269–275.

Jablin, F. M. (1982). Formal structural characteristics of organizations and superior-subordinate communication. *Human Communication Research, 8*, 338–347.

Jablin, F. M. (1984). Assimilating new members into organizations. In R. N. Bostrom (Ed.), *Communication yearbook 8* (pp. 594–626). Beverly Hills: CA: Sage.

Jablin, F. M. (1985). Task/work relationships: A life-span perspective. In G. R. Miller & M. L. Knapp (Eds.), *Handbook of interpersonal communication* (pp. 615–654). Beverly Hills, CA: Sage.

Jablin, F. M. (1987). Formal organization structure. In F. M. Jablin, L. L. Putnam, K. H. Roberts, & L. W. Porter (Eds.), *Handbook of organizational communication: An interdisciplinary perspective* (pp. 389–419). Newbury Park, CA: Sage.

Jablin, F. M., & Krone, K. J. (1987). Organizational assimilation. In C. R. Berger & S. H. Chaffee (Eds.), *Handbook of communication science* (pp. 711–746). Newbury Park, CA: Sage.

Jablin, F. M., Putnam, L. L., Roberts, K. H., & Porter, L. W. (Eds.). (1987). *Handbook of organizational communication: An interdisciplinary persepctive.* Newbury Park, CA: Sage.

Jacobson, E. W., & Seashore, S. E. (1951). Communication practices in complex organizations. *Journal of Social Issues, 7*, 28–40.

James, L. R., & Jones, A. P. (1976). Organizational structure: A review of structural dimensions and their conceptual relationships with individual attitudes and behavior. *Organizational Behavior and Human Performance, 16*, 74–113.

Johnson, B. M., & Rice, R. E. (1987). *Managing organizational innovation: The evolution of word processing to office information systems.* New York: Columbia University Press.

Johnson, J. D. (1980, April). *Conceptual approaches to the study of small group interaction.* Paper presented to the annual meeting of the Central States Speech Association, Chicago. (ERIC Document Reproduction Service No. ED 220 899)

Johnson, J. D. (1982). Modeling social interaction: Tests in three situations, *Central States Speech Journal, 33,* 281–298.

Johnson, J. D. (1984). A model of social interaction: Phase III, Tests in varying media situations. *Communication Monographs, 51,* 168–184.

Johnson, J. D. (1985). A model of social interaction: Phase II, tests in radio and television situations. *Central States Speech Journal, 36,* 62–71.

Johnson, J. D. (1986). A comparison of communication gradients and of network analysis: Two alternative approaches for analyzing communication structure. In H. G. Guental & M. J. Kavanaugh (Eds.), *Proceedings of the Eastern Academy of Management* (pp. 244–249). Albany: Eastern Academy of Management.

Johnson, J. D. (1987a). Effects of communicative work dependency, communicative response satisfaction, and physical structure on communication frequency: Phase II. In N. J. Beutell & D. J. Lenn (Eds.), *Proceedings of the Eastern Academy of Management* (pp. 164–167). Albany: Eastern Academy of Management.

Johnson, J. D. (1987b). *Effects of spatial elements of physical structure on organizational communication.* Paper presented to the Speech Communication Association Annual Convention, Boston, MA.

Johnson, J. D. (1987c). *Technological and spatial factors related to organizational communication structure.* Unpublished paper, Department of Communication, SUNY/Buffalo.

Johnson, J. D. (1987d). Multivariate communication networks. *Central States Speech Journal, 38,* 210–222.

Johnson, J. D. (1987e). UCINET: A software tool for network analysis. *Communication Education, 36,* 92–94.

Johnson, J. D. (1988a). On the use of communcation gradients. In G. M. Goldhaber & G. Barnett (Eds.), *Handbook of organizational communication* (pp. 361–383), Norwood, NJ: Ablex Publishing Corp.

Johnson, J. D. (1988b). Software review of STRUCTURE. *Communication Education, 37,* 172–174.

Johnson, J. D. (1989, June). *Technological and spatial factors related to communication structure.* Paper presented at the International Communication Association Annual Convention, San Francisco, CA.

Johnson, J. D. (1990). Effects of communicative factors on participation in innovations. *Journal of Business Communication, 27,* 7–23.

Johnson, J. D., & Smith, D. A. (1985). Effects of work dependency, response satisfaction, and proximity on communication frequency. *Western Journal of Speech Communication, 49*, 217–231.

Jones, A. P., & James, L. R. (1979). Psychological climate: Dimensions and relationships of individual and aggregated work environment perceptions. *Organizational Behavior and Human Performance, 23*, 201–250.

Joyce, W. F., & Slocum, J. W. (1984). Collective climate: Agreement as a basis for defining aggregate climates in organizations. *Academy of Management Journal, 27*, 721–742.

Kanter, R. M. (1977). *Men and women of the corporation.* New York: Basic Books.

Kanter, R. M. (1983). *The change masters: Innovation and entrepreneurship in the American corporation.* New York: Simon & Schuster.

Kanter, R. M. (1988). Three tiers for innovation research. *Communication Research, 15*, 509–523.

Katz, D., & Kahn, R. L. (1966). *The social psychology of organizations.* New York: John Wiley.

Katz, D., & Kahn, R. L. (1978). *The social psychology of organizations.* New York: John Wiley.

Katz, E. (1957). The two step flow of communication: An up-to-date report of a hypothesis. *Public Opinion Quarterly, 20*, 61–78.

Katz, E. (1961). The social itenerary of technical change: Two studies on the diffussion of innovation. *Human Organization, 20*, 70–82.

Katz, R., & Tushman, M. (1979). Communication patterns, project performance, and task characteristics: An empirical evaluation and integration in an R & D setting. *Organizational Behavior and Human Performance, 23*, 139–162.

Keller, R. T. (1989, August). *A cross-national study of communication networks and technological innovation in research and development organizations.* Paper presented to the National Meetings of the Academy of Management, Washington, DC.

Kelman, H. C. (1961). Processes of opinion change. *Public Opinion Quarterly, 25*, 57–78.

Keyton, J. (1987, May). *Meta-analysis of experimental studies using teleconferencing and mediated modes of communication.* Paper presented to the International Communication Association Annual Convention, Montreal, Canada.

Killworth, P. D., & Bernard, H. R. (1976). Informant accuracy in social network data. *Human Organization, 35*, 269–286.

Killworth, P. D., & Bernard, H. R. (1979). Informant accuracy in social network data III: A comparison of triadic structure in behavioral and cognitive data. *Social Networks, 2*, 19–46.

Kim, L. (1980). Organizational innovation and structure. *Journal of Business Research, 2*, 225–245.

Kimberly, J. R., & Evanisko, M. J. (1981). Organization innovation: The influence of individual, organizational, and contextual factors on hospital adoption of technological and administrative innovations. *Academy of Management Journal, 24*, 689–713.

Kirmeyer, S. L., & Lin, T. R. (1987). Social support: Its relationship to observed communication with peers and superiors. *Academy of Management Journal, 30,* 138–150.

Klauss, R., & Bass, B. M. (1982). *Interpersonal communication in organizations.* New York: Academic Press.

Kling, R. (1980). Social analyses of computing: Theoretical perspectives in recent empirical research. *Computing Surveys, 12,* 61–110.

Klovdahl, A. S. (1981). A note on images of networks. *Social Networks, 3,* 197–214.

Knoke, D., & Kuklinski, J. H. (1982). *Network analysis.* Beverly Hills, CA: Sage.

Komsky, S. H. (1989, June). *Electronic mail and democratization of organizational communication.* Paper presented to the Annual Meeting of the International Communication Association, San Francisco, CA.

Korzenney, F. (1978). A theory of electronic propinquity: Mediated communication in organizations. *Communication Research, 5,* 3–24.

Krackhardt, D. (1989, August). *Graph theoretical dimensions of informal organizations.* Paper presented to the National Meetings of the Academy of Management, Washington, DC.

Krackhardt, D., & Porter, L. W. (1985). When friends leave: A structural analysis of the relationship between turnover and stayer's attitudes. *Administrative Science Quarterly, 30,* 242–261.

Laumann, E. O., Marsden, P. V., & Prensky, D. (1983). The boundary specification problem in network analysis. In R. S. Burt & M. J. Minor (Eds.), *Applied network analysis* (pp. 18–34). Beverly Hills, CA: Sage.

Lawrence, P. R., & Lorsch, J. W. (1967). *Organization and environment: Managing differentiation and integration.* Boston: Harvard Business School.

Leavitt, H. J. (1951). Some effects of certain communication patterns on group performance. *Journal of Abnormal and Social Psychology, 46,* 38–50.

Lee, A. M. (1970). *Systems analysis frameworks.* London: McMillan.

Lee, Y., & Larwood, L. (1983). The socialization of expatriate managers in multinational firms. *Academy of Management Journal, 26,* 657–665.

Leifer, R., & Triscari, T., Jr. (1987, August). *Organizational design and computer based information systems design: Basic conformations.* Paper presented to the National Academy of Management Annual Meeting, New Orleans, LA.

Leiter, M. P. (1988). Burnout as a function of communication patterns: A study of a multidisciplinary mental health team. *Group & Organization Studies, 13,* 111–128.

Lengel, R. H., & Daft, R. L. (1988). The selection of communication media as an executive skill. *Academy of Management Executive, 2,* 225–232.

Levi-Strauss, C. (1963). *Structural anthropology.* New York: Basic Books.

Lewis, M. L., Cummings, W. W., & Long, L. W. (1982). Communication activity as a predictor of the fit between worker motivation and worker productivity. In M. Burgoon (Ed.), *Communication yearbook 5* (pp. 473–501). Beverly Hills, CA: Sage.

Lewis, P. V. (1975). The status of "Organizational Communication" in colleges of business. *Journal of Business Communication, 12,* 25–28.

Liebson, D. E. (1981). How Corning designed a 'talking' building to spur productivity. *Management Review, 70,* 8–13.

Likert, R. (1967). *The human organization: Its management and value.* Hightstown, NJ: McGraw-Hill.

Lincoln, J. R. (1982). Intra-(and inter-) organizational networks. In S. B. Bacharach (Ed.), *Research in the sociology of organizations* (pp. 1–38). Greenwich, CT: JAI Press.

Lincoln, J. R., & McBride, K. (1985). Resources, homophily, and dependence: Organizational attributes and asymmetric ties in human service networks. *Social Science Research, 14,* 1–30

Lincoln, J. R., & Miller, J. (1979). Work and friendship ties in organizations: A comparative analysis of relational networks. *Administrative Science Quarterly, 24,* 181–199.

Lodahl, T. M. (1964). Patterns of job attitudes in two assembly technologies. *Administrative Science Quarterly, 8,* 482–519.

Longenecker, C. O., Gioia, D. A., & Sims, H. P., Jr. (1987). Behind the mask: The politics of employee appraisal. *Academy of Management Executive, 1,* 183–194.

Lord, R. G., & Kernan, M. C. (1987). Scripts as determinants of purposeful behavior in organizations. *Academy of Management Review, 12,* 265–277.

Lowrance, W. W. (1980). The nature of risk. In R. C. Schwing & W. A. Albers (Eds.), *Societal risk assessment: How safe is safe enough?* (pp. 5–14). New York: Plenum.

Lucas, R. (1987). Political-cultural analysis of organizations. *Academy of Management Review, 12,* 144–156.

MacDonald, D. (1976). Communication roles and communication networks in a formal organization. *Human Communication Research, 2,* 365–375.

March, J. G., & Simon, H. A. (1958). *Organizations.* New York: John Wiley.

Markus, M. L. (1988, August). *Information richness theory, managers, and electronic mail.* Paper presented to the Annual Meetings of the Academy of Management, Anaheim, CA.

Martin, R. D. (1974). Friendship choices and residence hall proximity among freshman and upper year students. *Psychological Reports, 34,* 118.

Massey, D. (1985). New directions in space. In D. Gregory & J. Urry (Eds.), *Social relations and spatial structures* (pp. 9–19). Hong Kong: MacMillan.

McCain, B. E., O'Reilly, C., & Pfeffer, J. (1983). The effects of departmental demography on turnover: The case of a university. *Academy of Management Journal, 26,* 626–641.

McCann, J., & Galbraith, J. R. (1981). Interdepartmental relations. In P. C. Nystrom & W. H. Starbuck (Eds.), *Handbook of organizational design* (pp. 60–84). Oxford: Oxford University Press.

McCarrey, M. W., Peterson, L., Edwards, S., & von Kulmiz, P. (1974). Landscape office attitudes: Reflections of perceived degree of control over transactions with the environment. *Journal of Applied Psychology, 59,* 401–403.

McCarthy, D., & Saegert, S. (1978). Residential density, social overload, and social withdrawal. *Human Ecology, 6,* 253–271.

McGaffey, T. N., & Christy, R. (1979). Information processing capability as a predictor of enterpreneurial effectiveness. *Academy of Management Journal, 18,* 857–863.

McLaughlin, M. L., & Cheatam, T. R. (1977). Effects of communication isolation on job satisfaction on bank tellers. A research note. *Human Communication Research, 3*, 171–175.

McNeil, K., & Thompson, J. D. (1971). The regeneration of social organizations. *American Sociological Review, 36*, 624–637.

McPhee, R. D. (1985). Formal structure and organizational communication. In R. D. McPhee & P. K. Tompkins (Eds.), *Organizational communication: Traditional themes and new directions*. Beverly Hills, CA: Sage.

McPhee, R. D. (1988). Vertical communication chains: Toward an integrated approach. *Management Communication Quarterly, 1*, 455–493.

Merton, R. K. (1948). Social psychology of housing. In W. Dennis (Ed.), *Current trends in social psychology* (pp. 163–217). Pittsburgh: University of Pittsburgh Press.

Meyer, A. D. (1984). Mingling decision making metaphors. *Academy of Mangement Review, 9*, 6–17.

Meyer, J. W., & Rowan, B. (1977). Institutionalized organizations: Formal structure as myth and ceremony. *American Journal of Sociology, 83*, 340–363.

Milardo, R. M. (1983). Social networks and pair relationships: A review of substantive and measurement issues. *Sociology and Social Research, 68*, 1–18.

Miller, K. I., Zook, E. G., & Mack, L. J. (1987, May). *Communication artifacts and organizational culture: An investigation of internal company newsletters.* Paper presented to the Annual Convention of the International Communication Association, Montreal, Canada.

Miller, P., & O'Leary, T. (1989). Hierarchies and American ideals. *Academy of Management Review, 14*, 250–265.

Minor, M. J. (1983). New directions in multiplexity analysis. In R. S. Burt & M. J. Minor (Eds.), *Applied network analysis: A methodological introduction* (pp. 223–244). Beverly Hills, CA: Sage.

Mitchell, J. C. (1969). The concept and use of social networks. In J. C. Mitchell (Ed.), *Social networks in urban situations: Analyses of personal relationships in Central African towns* (pp. 1–50). Manchester, England: Manchester University Press.

Moch, M. K. (1980). Job involvement, internal motivation, and employees' integration into networks of work relationships. *Organizational Behavior and Human Performance, 25*, 15–31.

Moch, M., Feather, J. N., & Fitzgibbons, D. (1983). Conceptualizing and measuring the relational structure in organizations. In S. E. Seashore, E. E. Lawler III, P. H. Mirvis, & C. Cammann (Eds.), *Assessing organizational change: A guide to methods, measures, and practices* (pp. 203–228). New York: John Wiley.

Moch, M. K., & Morse, E. V. (1977). Size, centralization and organizational adoption of innovations. *American Sociological Review, 42*, 716–725.

Mohr, L. B. (1971). Organizational technology and organizational structure. *Administrative Science Quarterly, 16*, 444–459.

Monge, P. R. (1987). The network level of analysis. In C. R. Berger & S. H.

Chaffee (Eds.), *Handbook of communication science*. Newbury Park, CA: Sage.

Monge, P. R., & Contractor, N. S. (1987). Communication networks: Measurement techniques. In C. H. Tardy (Ed.), *A handbook for the study of human communication* (pp. 107–138). Norwood, NJ: Ablex Publishing Corp.

Monge, P. R., Edwards, J. A., & Kirste, K. K. (1978). The determinants of communication and communication structure in large oranizations: A review of research. In B. D. Rubin (Ed.), *Communication yearbook 2* (pp. 311–331). New Brunswick, NJ: Transaction Books.

Monge, P. R., & Eisenberg, E. M. (1987). Emergent communication networks. In F. M. Jablin, L. L. Putnam, K. H. Roberts, & L. W. Porter (Eds.), *Handbook of organizational communication: An interdisciplinary perspective* (pp. 304–342). Newbury Park, CA: Sage.

Monge, P. R., Farace, R. V., Eisenberg, E. M., Miller, K. I., & White, L. L. (1984). The process of studying process in organizational communication. *Journal of Communication, 34*, 22–43.

Monge, P. R., & Kirste, K. K. (1980). Measuring proximity in human organizations. *Social Psychology Quarterly, 43*, 110–115.

Monkhouse, F. J., & Wilkonson, H. R. (1971). *Maps and diagrams: Their compilation and construction*. London: Methuen.

Morey, N. C., & Luthans, F. (1985). Refining the displacement of culture and the use of scenes and themes in organizational studies. *Academy of Management Review, 10*, 219–229.

Morgan, D. (1979). *Merchants of grain*. New York: Penguin.

Morgan, G. (1986). *Images of organization*. Beverly Hills, CA: Sage.

Morris, J. H. (1988, May). *Grounding media richness theory: An interpretive/critical viewpoint*. Paper presented to the Annual Meetings of the International Communication Association, New Orleans.

Morris, J. H., & Steers, R. M. (1980). Structural influences on organizational commitment. *Journal of Vocational Behavior, 17*, 50–57.

Morton, J. A. (1971). *Organizing for innovation*. New York: McGraw-Hill.

Mowday, R. T., Porter, L. M., & Steers, R. M. (1982). *Employee-organizational linkages: The psychology of commitment, absenteeism, and turnover*. New York: Academic Press.

Mowday, R. T., Steers, R. M., & Porter, L. M. (1979). The measurement of organizational commitment. *Journal of Vocational Behavior, 14*, 224–247.

Mullins, N. C. (1968). The distribution of social and cultural properties in informal communication networks among biological scientists. *Administrative Science Quarterly, 33*, 786–794.

Mumby, D. K. (1987). The political function of narrative in organizations. *Communication Monographs, 54*, 113–127.

Nahemow, L., & Lawton, M. P. (1975). Similarity and propinquity in friendship formation. *Journal of Personality and Social Psychology, 32*, 205–213.

Norton, R. W., & Pettigrew, L. S. (1979). Attentiveness as a style of communication: A structural analysis. *Communication Monographs, 46*, 13–26.

Oldham, G. R., & Brass, D. J. (1979). Employee reaction to an open office: A naturally occurring quasi-experiment. *Administrative Science Quarterly, 24*, 267–284.

Oldham, G. R., & Hackman, J. R. (1981). Relationships between organizational structure and employee reactions: Comparing alternative frameworks. *Administrative Science Quarterly, 26*, 66–83.

O'Neill, B. (1984). Structures for nonhierarchical organizations. *Behavioral Science, 29*, 61–77.

Ouchi, W. G. (1981). *Theory Z.* New York: Avon.

Pacanowsky, M. E. (1989). Communication in the empowering organization. In J. A. Anderson (Ed.), *Communication yearbook 11* (pp. 356–379). Newbury Park, CA: Sage.

Pacanowsky, M. E., & O'Donnell-Trujillo, N. (1982). Communication and organizational cultures. *Western Journal of Speech Communication, 46*, 115–130.

Pacanowsky, M. E., & O'Donnell-Trujillo, N. (1983). Organizational communication as cultural performance. *Communication Monographs, 50*, 126–147.

Pace, R. W., & Ross, R. F. (1983). The basic course in Organizational Communication. *Communication Education, 32*, 402–412.

Page, N., & Wiseman, R. L. (1988, November). *Supervisory behavior and job satisfaction: An examination of management practices in the United States, Mexico, and Spain.* Paper presented at the Annual Meeting of the Speech Communication Association, New Orleans, LA.

Papa, M. J. (1989, June). *Communication network patterns and employee performance with new technology.* Paper presented to the Annual Meeting of the International Communication Association, San Francisco, CA.

Parks, M. R., & Adelman, M. B. (1983). Communication networks and the development of romantic relationships: An expansion of uncertainty reduction theory. *Human Communication Research, 10*, 55–79.

Parks, M. R., Stan, C. M., & Eggert, L. L. (1983). Romantic involvement and social network involvement. *Social Psychology Quarterly, 46*, 116–131.

Parsons, T. (1969). Theory and polity. In T. Parsons (Ed.), *Politics and social structure.* New York: Free Press.

Patchen, T. (1970). *Participation, achievement, and involvement on the job.* Englewood Cliffs, NJ: Prentice-Hall.

Payne, R. L., & Mansfield, R. (1973). Relationships of perceptions of organizational climate to organizational structure, context, and hierarchical position. *Administrative Science Quarterly, 18*, 515–526.

Pearce, W. B., & Conklin, R. (1979). A model of hierarchical meanings on coherent conversation and a study of "indirect responses." *Communication Monographs, 46*, 75–87.

Pelz, D. C. (1952). Influence: A key to effective leadership in the first-line supervisor. *Personnel, 29*, 209–217.

Penley, L. E. (1977). Organizational communication: Its relationships to the structure of work groups. In R. C. Huseman, C. M. Logue, & D. L. Freshley (Eds.), *Readings in interpersonal and organizational communication* (pp. 112–130). Boston: Holbrook Press.

Perlmutter, H. V. (1965). *Toward a theory and practice of social architecture: The building of indispensible institutions.* London: Travistock.

Perrow, C. B. (1970). *Organizational analysis: A sociological view.* Belmont, CA: Brooks/Cole.

Perrow, C. (1972). *Complex organizations: A critical essay.* Glenview, IL: Scott, Foresman.

Peters, T. J., & Waterman, R. H. (1982). *In search of excellence: Lessons from America's best-run companies.* New York: Harper & Row.

Pfeffer, J. (1978). *Organizational design.* Arlington Heights, IL: AHM Publishing.

Pfeffer, J. (1982). *Organizations and organization theory.* Boston: Pitman.

Pfeffer, J., & Leblebici, H. (1977). Information technology and organizational structure. *Pacific Sociological Review, 20,* 241–259.

Picot, A., Klingenberg, H., & Kranzle, H. P. (1982). Office technology: A report on attitudes and channels selection from field studies in Germany. In M. Burgoon (Ed.), *Communication yearbook 6* (pp. 674–693). Beverly Hills, CA: Sage.

Pile, J. (1978). *Open office planning.* New York: Whitney Library of Design.

Planty, E., & Machaver, W. (1952). Upward communications: A project in executive development. *Personnel, 28,* 304–318.

Pondy, L. R., & Mitroff, I. I. (1979). Beyond open system models of orgaization. In S. M. Bacharach (Ed.), *Research in organizational behavior* (Vol. 1, pp. 3–39). Greenwich, CT: JAI Press.

Pool, I. D. (1973). Communication systems. In I. D. Pool & W. Schramm (Eds.), *Handbook of communication.* Chicago: Rand McNally.

Poole, M. S., & McPhee, R. D. (1983). A structurational analysis of organizational climate. In L. L. Putnam & M. E. Pacanowsky (Eds.), *Communication and organizations: An interpretive approach* (pp. 195–220). Beverly Hills, CA: Sage.

Porter, L. W., Allen, R. W., & Angle, H. L. (1981). The politics of upward influence in organizations. In S. M. Bacharach (Ed.), *Research in organizational behavior* (pp. 109–149). Greenwich, CT: JAI Press.

Porter, L., & Lawler, E. E. (1965). Properties of organizational structure in relation to job attitudes and job behavior. *Psychological Bulletin, 64,* 23–51.

Porter, L. W., Lawler, E. E., III, & Hackman, J. R. (1975). *Behavior in organizations.* New York: McGraw-Hill.

Presthus, R. (1962). *The organizational society.* New York: Random House.

Putnam, L. L., & Pacanowsky, M. E. (Eds.). (1983). *Communication and organizations: An interpretive approach.* Beverly Hills, CA: Sage.

Randall, D. M. (1987). Commitment and the organization: The organization man revisited. *Academy of Management Review, 12,* 460–471.

Randolph, W. A. (1978). Organizational technology and the media and purpose dimension of organization communications. *Journal of Business Research, 6,* 237–259.

Randolph, W. A., & Finch, F. E. (1977). The relationship between organization technology and the direction and frequency dimensions of task communications. *Human Relations, 30,* 1131–1145.

Ranson, S., Hinings, B., & Greenwood, R. (1980). The structuring of organizational structures. *Administrative Science Quarterly, 25,* 1–17.

Rapoport, A. (1982). *The meaning of the built environment: A nonverbal communication approach.* Beverly Hills, CA: Sage.

Ray, E. B. (1983). Job burnout from a communication perspective. In R. N. Bostrom (Ed.), *Communication yearbook 7* (pp. 738–755). Beverly Hills, CA: Sage.

Ray, E. B. (1987). Supportive relationships and occupational stress in the workplace. In T. L. Albrecht & M. B. Adelman (Eds.), *Communicating social support* (pp. 172–191). Newbury Park, CA: Sage.

Read, W. H. (1962). Upward communication in industrial hierarchies. *Human Relations, 15,* 3–15.

Redding, W. C. (1979). Organizational communication theory and ideology: An overview. In D. Nimmo (Ed.), *Communication yearbook 3* (pp. 309–341). New Brunswick, NJ: Transaction Books.

Reichers, A. E. (1985). A review and reconceptualization of organizational commitment. *Academy of Management Review, 10,* 465–476.

Reif, W. E. (1968). *Computer technology and management organization.* Iowa City: University of Iowa.

Reynolds, E. V., & Johnson, J. D. (1982). Liaison emergence: Relating theoretical perspectives. *Academy of Management Review, 7,* 551–559.

Rice, L. E., & Mitchell, T. R. (1973). Structural determinants of individual behavior in organizations. *Administrative Science Quarterly, 18,* 56–70.

Rice, R. E. (1979, May). *Investigations into validity and reliability of NEGOPY, a computer program for communication network analysis.* Paper presented to the International Communication Association Annual Convention, Philadelphia, PA.

Rice, R. E. (1982). Communication networking in computer-conferencing systems: A longitudinal study of group roles and system structure. In M. Burgoon (Ed.), *Communication yearbook 6* (pp. 925–944), Beverly Hills, CA: Sage.

Rice, R. E., & Love, G. (1987). Electronic emotion: Socioemotional content in a computer-mediated communication network. *Communication Research, 14,* 85–108.

Rice, R. E., Grant, A., Schmitz, J., & Torobin, J. (1988). *Organizational information processing, critical mass and social influence: A network approach to predicting the adoption and outcomes of electronic messaging.* Unpublished paper, University of Southern California, Los Angeles, CA.

Rice, R. E., & Manross, G. G. (1987). The case of the intelligent telephone: The relationship of job category to the adoption of an organizational communication technology. In M. L. McLaughlin (Ed.), *Communication yearbook 10* (pp. 727–742). Beverly Hills, CA: Sage.

Rice, R. E., & Richards, W. D. (1985). An overview of network analysis methods and programs. In B. Dervin & M. J. Voigt (Eds.), *Progress in communication sciences* (Vol. 6, pp. 105–165). Norwood, NJ: Ablex Publishing Corp.

Rice, R. E., & Shook, D. (1986, May). *Access to and usage of integrated office systems. Implications for organizational communication.* Paper presented to Annual Meetings of the International Communication Association, Montreal, Canada.

Richards, W. D. (1985). Data, models, and assumptions in network analysis. In R. D. McPhee & P. K. Tompkins (Eds.), *Organizational communication:*

Traditional themes and new directions (pp. 109–128). Beverly Hills, CA: Sage.

Richards, W. D., & Rice, R. E. (1981). NEGOPY network analysis program. *Social Networks, 3,* 215–223.

Riley, P. (1983). A structurationist account of political culture. *Administrative Science Quarterly, 28,* 414–437.

Roberts, K. H., & O'Reilly, C. A., III. (1979). Some correlations of communication roles in organizations. *Academy of Management Journal, 4,* 283–293.

Rogers, D. P. (1979). The content of Organizational Communication texts. *Journal of Business Communication, 16,* 57–64.

Rogers, E. M. (1983). *Diffusion of innovations.* New York: Free Press.

Rogers, E. M. (1987, November). *Performance, problems, and promise of the interpretive approach in communication research.* Paper presented to the annual convention of the Speech Communication Association, Boston, MA.

Rogers, E. M., & Adhikayra, R. (1979). Diffusion of innovations: An up-to-date review and commentary. In D. Nimmo (Ed.), *Communication yearbook 3* (pp. 67–81). New Brunswick, NJ: Transaction Books.

Rogers, E. M., & Agarwala-Rogers, R. (1976). *Communication in organizations.* New York: Free Press.

Rogers, E. M., & Kincaid, D. L. (1981). *Communication networks: Toward a new paradigm for research.* New York: The Free Press.

Rogers, E. M., & Shoemaker, F. F. (1971). *Communication of innovations.* New York: Free Press.

Romney, A. K., & Faust, K. (1982). Predicting the structure of a communication network from recalled data. *Social Networks, 4,* 285–304.

Ruchinskas, J. E. (1983, May). *Predictors of media utility: Influence on manager's perceptions of business communications systems.* Paper presented to the Annual Meetings of the International Communication Association, Dallas, TX.

Saarinen, T. F., & Sell, J. L. (1980). Environmental perception. *Progress in Human Geography, 4,* 535–548.

Saarinen, T. F., & Sell, J. L. (1981). Environmental perception. *Progress in Human Geography, 5,* 525–547.

Sack, R. (1980). Conceptions of geographic space. *Progress in Human Geography, 4,* 313–345.

Salancik, G. R. (1977). Commitment and control of organizational behavior and belief. In B. M. Staw & G. R. Salancik (Eds.), *New directions in organizational behavior* (pp. 1–54). Chicago: St. Clair Press.

Salancik, G. R., & Pfeffer, J. (1977). An examination of need-satisfaction models of job attitudes. *Administrative Science Quarterly, 22,* 427–453.

Salancik, G. R., & Pfeffer, J. (1978). A social information processing approach to job attitudes and task design. *Administrative Science Quarterly, 23,* 224–253.

Salichtchev, K. A. (1983). Cartographic communication: A theoretical survey. In D. R. F. Taylor (Ed.), *Graphic communication and design in contemporary cartography* (Vol. II, pp. 11–35). New York: John Wiley.

SAS Institute. (1981). *SAS/GRAPH user's guide*. Cary, NC: SAS Institute.

SAS Institute. (1982). *SAS user's guide: Basics*. Cary, NC: SAS Institute.

Schall, M. S. (1983). A communication-rules approach to organizational culture. *Administrative Science Quarterly, 28*, 557–581.

Schein, E. H. (1965). *Organizational psychology*. Englewood Cliffs, NJ: Prentice-Hall.

Schilit, W. K., & Locke, E. A. (1982). A study of upward influence in organizations. *Administrative Science Quarterly, 27*, 304–316.

Schmid, C. F., & Schmid, S. E. (1979). *Handbook on graphic presentation* (2nd ed.). New York: John Wiley.

Schmidt, D. E., & Keating, J. P. (1979). Human crowding and personal control: An integration of the research. *Psychological Bulletin, 86*, 680–700.

Schmitz, J. (1988). *Electronic communication: A longitudinal view*. Paper presented to the Annual Convention of the Academy of Management, Anaheim, CA.

Schrader, C. B., Lincoln, J. R., & Hoffman, A. (1986). *The network structures of organizations: Effects of task contingencies and distributional form*. Paper presented to the Sunbelt VI Social Network Conference, Santa Barbara, CA.

Schramm, W. S., & Roberts, D. F. (1971). *The process and effects of mass communication*. Urbana, IL: Univeristy of Illinois Press.

Schreiman, D. B., & Johnson, J. D. (1975). *A model of cognitive complexity and network role*. Paper presented at the International Communication Association, Chicago, IL.

Schroder, J. M., Driver, J. J., & Streufert, S. (1967). *Human information processing*. New York: Holt, Rinehart and Winston.

Schwartz, D. F., & Jacobsen, E. (1977). Organizational communication network analysis: The liaison communication role. *Organizational Behavior and Human Performance, 18*, 158–174.

Seamon, D. (1980). Body-subject, time-space routines, and place ballets. In A. Buttimer & D. Seamon (Eds.), *The human experience of space and place* (pp. 148–165). New York: St. Martins Press.

Sept, R. (1989). *Bureaucracy, communication, and information system design*. Paper presented to the Annual Meetings of the International Communication Association, San Francisco, CA.

Shaw, M. E. (1971). *Group dynamics: The psychology of small group behavior*. New York: McGraw-Hill.

Sheldon, M. E. (1971). Investments and involvement as mechanisms producing commitment to the organization. *Administrative Science Quarterly, 16*, 142–150.

Shimanoff, S. B. (1980). *Communication rules: Theory and research*. Beverly Hills, CA: Sage.

Short, J., Williams, E., & Christie, B. (1976). *The social psychology of telecommunications*. New York: John Wiley.

Simmel, G. (1902). The number of members as determining the sociological form of the group: I. *American Journal of Sociology, 8*, 1–46.

Simon, H. A. (1960). 'The executive as decision maker' and 'Organizational design: man–machine systems for decision making'. *The new science of management decision making* (pp. 1–8). New York: Harper & Row.

Simpson, R. L. (1952). Vertical and horizontal communication in formal organizations. *Administrative Science Quarterly,* 188–196.

Sitkin, S. B., Sutcliffe, K. M., & Barrios-Choplin, J. R. (1989, August). *Determinants of communication media choice in organizations.* Paper presented to the Annual Meeting of the National Academy of Management, Washington, DC.

Smelser, N. J. (1963). *The sociology of economic life.* Englewood Cliffs, NJ: Prentice-Hall.

Smirchich, L., & Calas, M. B. (1987). Organizational culture: A critical assessment. In F. M. Jablin, L. L. Putnam, K. H. Roberts, & L. W. Porter (Eds.), *Handbook of organizational communication: An interdisciplinary perspective* (pp. 228–263). Newbury Park, CA: Sage.

Smith, C. J. (1980). Social networks as metaphors, models and methods. *Progress in Human Geography, 4,* 500–524.

Sommer, R. (1967). Small group ecology. *Psychological Bulletin, 67,* 145–152.

Spiker, B. K., & Daniels, T. D. (1981). Information adequacy and communication relationships: An empirical examination of 18 organizations. *Western Journal of Speech Communication, 45,* 342–354.

Steele, F. (1973). *Physical setting and organizational development.* Boston: Addison-Wesley.

Steers, R. M. (1977). Antecedents and outcomes of organizational commitment. *Administrative Science Quarterly, 22,* 46–56.

Steinfield, C. W. (1985). Dimensions of electronic mail use in an organizational setting. In J. Pearce & R. Robinson (Eds.), *Proceedings of the Academy of Management* (pp 239–243). Mississippi State University, Academy of Management.

Steinfield, C. W., Jin, B., & Ku, L. L. (1987). *A preliminary test of a social information processing model of media use in organizations.* Paper presented to the annual meeting of the International Communication Association, Montreal, Canada.

Steinfield, C. W., & Fulk, J. (1986). *Information processing in organizations and media choice.* Paper presented to the International Communication Association Annual Convention, Chicago, IL.

Stevenson, W. B., Pearce, J. L., & Porter, L. W. (1985). The concept of "coalition" in organization theory and research. *Academy of Management Review, 10,* 256–268.

Stohl, C., & Kakarigi, D. (1985, November). *The NEGOPY network analysis program: A critical appraisal.* Paper presented to the Speech Communication Association Annual Convention, Denver, CO.

Stohl, C., & Redding, W. C. (1987). Message and message exchange processes. In F. M. Jablin, L. L. Putnam, K. H. Roberts, & L. W. Porter (Eds.), *Handbook of organizational communication: An interdisciplinary perspective* (pp. 451–502). Newbury Park, CA: Sage.

Stott, J. P. (1977). Review of surface modeling. In Institution of Civil Engineers (Eds.), *Surface modeling by computer.* London: Institution of Civil Engineers.

Strassman, W. P. (1959). *Risk and technological innovation.* Ithaca, NY: Cornell University Press.

Sundstrom, E., Burt, R. E., & Kamp, D. (1980). Privacy at work: Architectural correlates to job satisfaction and job performance. *Academy of Management Journal, 23,* 110–117.

Sykes, R. E. (1983). Initial interaction between strangers and acquaintances: A multivariate analysis of factors affecting choice of communication partners. *Human Communication Research, 10,* 27–53.

Sypher, B. D., & Zorn, T. E. (1986). Communication-related abilities and upward mobility. *Human Communication Research, 12,* 420–431.

Szilagyi, A. D., & Holland, W. E. (1980). Changes in social density: Relationships with functional interaction and perceptions of job characteristics, role stress, and work satisfaction. *Journal of Applied Psychology, 65,* 28–33.

Taylor, D. R. F. (1983). Graphic communication and design in contemporary cartography: An introduction. In D. R. F. Taylor (Eds.), *Graphic communication and design in contemporary cartography* (Vol. II, pp. 1–10). New York: John Wiley.

Taylor, M. (1968). Towards a mathematical theory of influence and attitude change. *Human Relations, 98,* 121–139.

Thompson, J. D. (1967). *Organizations in action.* New York: McGraw-Hill.

Tichy, N. M. (1981). Networks in organizations. In P. Nystrom & W. Starbuck (Eds.), *Handbook of organizational design* (Vol. 2, pp. 225–249). New York: Oxford University Press.

Tichy, N. M., Tushman, M. L., & Fombrun, C. (1979). Social network analysis for organizations. *Academy of Management Review, 4,* 507–519.

Ting-Toomey, S. (1985). Toward a theory of conflict and culture. In W. B. Gudykunst, L. P. Stewart, & S. Ting-Toomey (Eds.), *International and intercultural communication annual* (pp. 71–86). Beverly Hills, CA: Sage.

Trevino, L. K., Lengel, R. H., Bodensteiner, W., & Gerloff, E. (1988). *Managerial media choice: The interactive influence of cognitive style and message equivocality.* Paper presented to the Annual Meetings of the Academy of Management, Anaheim, CA.

Trevino, L. K., Lengel, R., & Daft, R. L. (1987). Media symbolism, media richness, and media choice in organizations: A symbolic interactionist perspective. *Communication Research, 14,* 553–574.

Triandis, H. C., & Albert, R. D. (1987). Cross-cultural perspectives. In F. M. Jablin, L. L. Putnam, K. H. Roberts, & L. W. Porter (Eds.), *Handbook of organizational communication: An interdisciplinary perspective* (pp. 264–295). Newbury Park, CA: Sage.

Trice, H. M., & Beyer, J. M. (1984). Studying organizational cultures through rites and ceremonials. *Academy of Management Review, 9,* 653–669.

Tsui, A. S., & O'Reilly, C. A., III. (1989). Beyond simple demographic effects: The importance of relational demography in superior-subordinate dyads. *Academy of Management Journal, 32,* 402–423.

Tukey, J. W. (1980). Methodological comments focused on opportunities. In J. N. Cappella & P. R. Monge (Eds.), *Multivariate techniques in human communication research* (pp. 489–528). New York: Academic Press.

Tushman, M. (1977). Communication across organizational boundaries: Special boundary roles in the innovation process. *Administrative Science Quarterly, 22,* 587–605.

Tushman, M. (1978). Technical communication in R & D laboratories. The impact of project work characteristics. *Academy of Management Journal, 21,* 624–645.

Tutzhauer, F. (1989). *A statistic for comparing behavioral and cognitive networks.* Paper presented to the International Communication Association Annual Convention, San Francisco, CA.

Urry, J. (1985). Social relations, space and time. In D. Gregory & J. Urry (Eds.), *Social relations and spatial structures* (pp. 20–48). Hong Kong: MacMillan.

Van de Ven, A. H., Delbecq, A. L., & Koenig, R. (1976). Determinants of coordination modes within organizations. *Administrative Science Quarterly, 41,* 322–338.

Victor, B., & Blackburn, R. S. (1987). Interdependence: An alternative conceptualization. *Academy of Management Review, 12,* 486–498.

Viega, J. F. (1988). Face your problem subordinates now! *Academy of Management Executive, 2,* 145–154.

Wager, L. W. (1962). Channels of interpersonal and mass communication in the organizational setting: Studying the diffusion of information about a unique organizational change. *Sociological Inquiry, 31,* 88–107.

Walker, G. (1985). Network position and cognition in a computer software firm. *Administrative Science Quarterly, 30,* 103–130.

Weick, K. E. (1969). *The social psychology of organizing.* Reading, MA: Addison-Wesley.

Weick, K. E. (1979). Cognitive processes in organizations. In S. B. Bacharach (Ed.), *Research in organizational behavior* (Vol. 1., pp. 41–74). Greenwich, CT: JAI Press.

Weick, K. E. (1983). Organizational communication: Toward a research agenda. In L. L. Putnam & M. E. Pacanowsky (Eds.), *Communication and organizations: An interpretive approach* (pp. 13–29). Beverly Hills, CA: Sage.

Weick, K. E. (1987). Theorizing about organizational communication. In F. M. Jablin, L. L. Putnam, K. H. Roberts, & L. W. Porter (Eds.), *Handbook of organizational communication: An interdisciplinary perspective* (pp. 97–122). Newbury Park, CA: Sage.

Weick, K. E., & Bougon, M. G. (1986). Organizations as cognitive maps. In H. P. Sims & D. A. Gioia (Eds.), *The thinking organization* (pp. 102–135). San Francisco: Jossey-Bass.

Weimann, G. (1983). The strength of weak conversational ties in the flow of information and influence. *Social Networks, 5,* 245–267.

Weinshall, W. D. (1966). The communicogram: A method for describing the pattern, frequency, and accuracy of organization and communication. In J. R. Lawrence (Ed.), *Operational research and the social sciences* (pp. 619–633). London: Travistock.

Wendlinger, R. M. (1973). Improving upward communication. *Journal of Business,* *46,* 17–23.

Whisler, T. L. (1970). *Information technology and organizational change.* Belmont, CA: Wadsworth.

White, H. C., Boorman, S. A., & Breiger, R. L. (1976). Social structures from multiple networks. I. Blockmodels of roles and positions. *American Journal of Sociology, 81,* 730–780.

Whyte, W. F. (1949). The social structure of the restaurant. *American Journal of Sociology, 54,* 302–310.

Wigand, R. T. (1977). Some recent developments in organizational communication: Network analysis—a systematic representation of communication relationships. *Communications, 3,* 181–200.

Wigand, R. T. (1988). Communication network analysis: History and overview. In G. M. Goldhaber & G. A. Barnett (Eds.), *Handbook of organizational communication* (pp. 319–360). Norwood, NJ: Ablex Publishing Corp.

Wilkins, A. L., & Ouchi, W. G. (1983). Efficient cultures: Exploring the relationship between culture and organizational performance. *Administrative Science Quarterly, 28,* 468–481.

Withey, M., Daft, R. L., & Cooper, W. H. (1983). Measures of Perrow's work unit technology. An empirical assessment and new scale. *Academy of Management Journal, 26,* 45–63.

Woelful, J., Cody, M. J., Gillham, J., & Holmes, R. A. (1980). Basic premises of multidimensional attitude change theory: An experimental analysis. *Human Communication Research, 6,* 153–167.

Womack, S. M. (1984). *Toward a clarification of boundary spanning.* Paper presented to the Speech Communication Association Annual Convention, Denver, CO.

Woodward, J. (1965). *Industrial organization.* London: Oxford University Press.

Zajonc, R. B., & Wolfe, D. M. (1966). Cognitive consequences of a person's position in a formal organization. *Human Relations, 19,* 139–150.

Zalesny, M. D., & Farace, R. V. (1987). Traditional versus open offices: A comparison of sociotechnical, social relations, and symbolic meaning perspectives. *Academy of Management Journal, 30,* 240–259.

Zaltman, G., & Duncan, R. (1977). *Strategies for planned change.* New York: Wiley.

Zaltman, G., Duncan, R., & Holbek, J. (1973). *Innovations and organizations.* New York: Wiley.

Zenger, T. R., & Lawrence, B. S. (1989). Organizational demography: The differential effects of age and tenure distributions on technical communication. *Academy of Management Journal, 32,* 353–376.

Zimbardo, P. G. (1960). Involvement and communication discrepancy as determinants of opinion conformity. *Journal of Abnormal and Social Psychology, 60,* 86–94.

Author Index

Subject Index

A

Access, 97–98
Antecedents, 11–12
  and the approaches, 178–180, Chapters
    6, 7, 8
Asymmetry, 37
Attitudes and networks, 142–144

B

Boundary spanning, 147–148

C

Centralization, 23, 112–113
Channels, 108–111, 161–163
Chart, organizational, 18–21
Coactivational vs configurational,
    29–30
Cognition, 183–186
Cognitive complexity, 50, 183
Cohesion, 129–130
Commitment, 12, 144–147
  and the approaches, 181
Communication circuits, 22
Communication gradients, 11, Chapter 4
  and individual outcomes, 139–140
  and organizational outcomes, 172–173
  and network analysis, 176
  and space, 102
  and technology, 117–119
Communigrams, 45
Complexity, 23
Configurations, 8–9
  and human environment, 135–136
  and technology, 113–114
  compared across dimensions, 175–176
  in communication gradients, 59–60
  in cultural approaches, 79–87

in formal approaches, 18–25
in network analysis, 44–53
Congruence, 170
Context, 8
  and human environment, 130–132
  and space, 100–101
  and technology, 104–106
  compared across dimensions, 186–187
  in communication gradients, 69–71
  in cultural approaches, 87–88
  in formal approaches, 27–28
  in network analysis, 27–28
Coordination, 18–21
Criticality, 52
Cultural approaches, 11, Chapter 5
  and boundary spanning, 147–148
  and commitment, 181
  and individual outcomes, 153–158
  and innovations, 165–166
  and organizational outcomes, 171–173
  and space, 102
  and technology, 105–106, 120

D

Definition of structure, 5–11
Demography, 124–127
Differentiation, 17–18, 168–171
  and entities, 25
Dysfunctions, 4–5

E

Embedded elements, 114–116
Entities
  and cultural approaches, 76
  and definition of structure, 7–8
  and formal approaches, 18–19; 24–27
  and network analysis, 44

226